Marcel Danesi
Signs of Crime

CW01455039

Marcel Danesi

Signs of Crime

———

Introducing Forensic Semiotics

DE GRUYTER
MOUTON

ISBN 978-1-61451-552-4
e-ISBN 978-1-61451-316-2

Library of Congress Cataloging-in-Publication Data
A CIP catalog record for this book has been applied for at the Library of Congress.

Bibliographic information published by the Deutsche Nationalbibliothek
The Deutsche Nationalbibliothek lists this publication in the Deutsche Nationalbibliografie;
detailed bibliographic data are available in the Internet at http://dnb.dnb.de.

© 2014 Walter de Gruyter, Inc., Boston/Berlin
Typesetting: RoyalStandard, Hong Kong
Printing and binding: Hubert & Co. GmbH & Co. KG, Göttingen
♾ Printed on acid-free paper
Printed in Germany

www.degruyter.com

FSC
www.fsc.org

MIX
Papier aus verantwor-
tungsvollen Quellen
FSC® C016439

Acknowledgments

I would like to thank the following research assistants at the University of Toronto for helping me gather the relevant information for this book and for providing me with their own insights and astute observations: Stacy Costa, Lydia Bojeczko, Sophia Chadwick, Stephanie Turenko, Mariana Bockarova, Lorraine Bryers, Patrick Kelly, Christopher Mastropietro, and Siobhan Maclean. I also wish to express my gratitude to the Principal of Victoria College, Angela Esterhammer, for giving me the opportunity to develop an undergraduate course in forensic semiotics that I teach at the college and Maureen Peng, the Academic Administrator, for allowing me to set up a research center at the college (Research in Forensic Semiotics) and for all her support and encouragement in my endeavors.

Table of contents

Acknowledgments —— v
List of Figures and Tables —— ix
Introduction —— 1

1   Forensics and Semiotics —— 4
1.1   Forensic Science —— 5
1.2   Branches —— 11
1.3   Semiotics —— 14
1.4   Forensic Semiotics —— 25

2   Signs of Deception —— 30
2.1   Lie Detection —— 31
2.2   The Face, the Eyes, and the Head —— 39
2.3   Body Language —— 43
2.4   First-Order Forensic Semiotics —— 49

3   Signs of Identity —— 52
3.1   Prints —— 53
3.2   Other Types of Evidence —— 60
3.3   Analyzing the Evidence —— 64
3.4   Inferring the Criminal's Identity —— 68

4   The Language of Crime —— 72
4.1   Forensic Linguistics —— 73
4.2   Handwriting, Content, and Style —— 78
4.3   Criminal Speech —— 89
4.4   Metaphor Analysis —— 93

5   The Criminal Mind —— 98
5.1   Forensic Psychology —— 99
5.2   Criminal Profiling —— 104
5.3   Inside the Criminal Mind —— 105
5.4   The Serial Killer —— 110

6   Symbols and Rituals of Crime —— 119
6.1   Crime Scene Investigations —— 120
6.2   Symbolism —— 123
6.3   Ritual —— 129
6.4   Thinking Like Sherlock Holmes —— 135

7   Criminality and Its Representations —— 138
7.1   Fictional and Real Crime —— **139**
7.2   Crime on the Screen —— **144**
7.3   The Simulacrum Effect —— **148**
7.4   Objectives of Second-Order Forensic Semiotics —— **151**

Conclusion —— 153
Glossary —— 155
References —— 165
Index —— 171

List of Figures and Tables

Figure 1.   Parts of a fingerprint
Figure 2.   The DNA
Figure 3.   Blood spatter analysis
Figure 4.   Elements of the semeion
Figure 5.   Saussure's binary model of the sign
Figure 6.   Peircean model of the sign
Figure 7.   The polygraph
Figure 8.   Basic emotions
Figure 9.   Fingerprint patterns
Figure 10.   CODIS
Figure 11.   Voiceprint
Figure 12.   Son of Sam note
Figure 13.   Son of Sam letter
Figure 14.   Zodiac letter
Figure 15.   A cryptic message from the Zodiac
Figure 16.   JonBenet Ramsey ransom note
Figure 17.   Another Son of Sam letter

Table 1.   The components of the Autonomic Nervous System
Table 2.   Eye contact patterns
Table 3.   Personality typology
Table 4.   Metaphor Analysis

Introduction

Almost all crime is due to the repressed desire for aesthetic expression.

Evelyn Waugh (1903–1966)

Crime fascinates us at the same time that it terrifies us. There are more television programs, movies, novels, magazines, and websites dealing with crime and criminals than there are dealing with most other subjects. We seem to be obsessed, as a culture (perhaps as a world culture), with this phenomenon, both in its real and fictional forms. Actually, the systematic study of real crime, called *forensic science*, has a lot in common with portrayals of crime in fiction and the media. It is no coincidence that the detective story genre and modern forensic science emerged at about the same point in time in the latter part of the nineteenth century, both mirroring each other in every way.

Studying the link between real and fictional crime is an area that has received little systematic attention from mainstream forensic scientists. To do so, therefore, a new discipline is required. It can be called *forensic semiotics*. This book will introduce this discipline, illustrating how and why it belongs alongside other branches of forensic science. It is based, in part, on my experiences of working with youth gangs in Toronto and with using my knowledge of semiotics to decode their symbols and rituals. From these experiences, it became obvious to me that many teenagers were motivated to join criminal groups because of the emotional power of the symbols, which allowed them to construct a new identity and to gain a sense of belonging to something meaningful. I also discovered that many of the teens were influenced by the movies and other media, being attracted to a criminal lifestyle by images of toughness and sexual attractiveness that Hollywood outlaws espouse and convey to audiences. Clearly, I thought, all this has definite implications for the study of crime. I also came to believe that the basic concepts and techniques that semioticians use to study all kinds of human phenomena, from body language to the meanings of secret codes, may have concrete applications to the process of investigating actual crimes. Semiotics can, for example, help investigators understand how the "signs of crime" left by perpetrators at crime scenes are interconnected with the culture in which the crime has been committed and its system of beliefs. This perspective can reveal, perhaps, why the crime has significance to a perpetrator. It might also help investigators interpret clues more pointedly. In effect, I believe that forensic semiotics has many more applications to the study of crime in all its facets than may have previously been envisaged.

This book will look at some of these applications. It contains seven chapters, each one describing a particular putative subfield of forensic semiotic analysis, which when integrated, will delineate an overall framework for establishing the new discipline. Sequentially, the chapters deal with:

1. the history of both forensic science and semiotics, with a discussion of the place of forensic semiotics in the study of crime;
2. facial expressions and body language and how semiotic theory can complement the work of forensic science in developing techniques for identifying deception;
3. evidence analysis and how semiotics can aid in identifying perpetrators;
4. criminal communication, including the notes left by serial killers, and how semiotics can aid in the decipherment of their meanings;
5. the criminal mind and the factors that shape it;
6. crime scenes and how semiotics can be used profitably in decoding the clues left by perpetrators;
7. the relation between real crime, representations of crime, and the media.

Crime is not easy to define. In the medieval world, rather than calling some serious offense a crime, the concept of sin was used instead. In Christian theology, a sin is defined as a moral failing that seriously interfered with living a spiritual life. The seven deadly sins were anger, covetousness, envy, gluttony, lust, pride, and sloth. These were a common subject in the sermons, plays, and art of the Middle Ages. The most important theological discussion of the sins appears in the *Summa Theologica*, written in the late 1200s by the great theologian Saint Thomas Aquinas. As the role of religion in everyday life started declining by the Renaissance, the sins started being redefined as crimes, both legally and socially. But what constitutes a crime defies definition, being subject to social trends and processes. In Western countries, witchcraft is no longer considered to be a crime, even though many women were accused, convicted, and punished for it in the past. On the other hand, today air pollution is considered to be a crime – an act that received little or no attention from the legal sphere before the 1800s. Medieval theology would explain sin as a manifestation of the devil's influence on us; criminologists would explain crime as a manifestation of mental malfunction caused by factors such as upbringing.

The relation between sin and crime was explored brilliantly by the movie *Se7en* (1995), which is about the hunt for a serial killer who justifies his crimes as warnings to a world that is foolishly ignoring the reality of the seven deadly sins, replacing them with unwise psychological theories of crime. A similar subtext is found in the 1990 movie *Mr. Frost*, which is about a horrific serial killer who presents himself as the devil, engaging in a philosophical dialogue with a psychiatrist who, by the end, starts to believe that he may be indeed who he claims to be. Like these movies, one of the goals of forensic semiotics will be to look at the historical meanings we assign to crime and how these determine our understanding of crimes and criminals.

With some exceptions, the examples used in this book will be based on North American criminal cases. These are the ones that I know best. However, many of them have received international attention and are thus well known throughout the world. In addition to forensic scientists and semioticians, this book might be of interest to criminologists, psychologists, linguists, anthropologists, sociologists, lawyers, police organizations and other individuals and groups involved in the study or investigation of crime. It may also be used as a textbook in forensic science or applied semiotics courses. To this end, I have attached a glossary of technical terms. Hopefully, by studying the relation between signs, meaning, culture, and crimes semioticians can help solve the overall "mystery of crime" in the human species.

Chapter 1
Forensics and Semiotics

Crime is a fact of the human species, a fact of that species alone, but it is above all the secret aspect, impenetrable and hidden. Crime hides, and by far the most terrifying things are those which elude us.

Georges Bataille (1897–1962)

In an insightful collection of studies, titled *Dupin, Holmes, Peirce: The Sign of Three* (1983) and edited by semioticians Umberto Eco and Thomas A. Sebeok, the birth of modern-day semiotics is connected, both implicitly and explicitly, to the mystery stories of Edgar Allan Poe. Literary historians consider Poe's three stories *The Murders in the Rue Morgue* (1841), *The Gold Bug* (1843), and *The Purloined Letter* (1844) as the first true examples of the modern fictional detective story, itself a derivative of the Gothic novels of the nineteenth century. Poe introduced the figure of the detective hero to the world – a hero who solves crimes with a brilliant display of reasoning. His name is C. Auguste Dupin. One of the founders of modern semiotics, the American pragmatist philosopher and scientist Charles S. Peirce, became intrigued by the thinking style manifested by Dupin, who makes hunches by interpreting the signs left behind by the criminal. Peirce called this style *abduction*, in contrast to the well-known logical forms of reasoning known as deduction and induction. Actually, Dupin uses all three modes of logic at various stages of his investigations. He applies deductive reasoning initially to classifying the signs in a systematic way; he then employs inductive reasoning to draw a general picture of the situation; and finally he uses abduction to interpret that picture, which ultimately reveals the true story behind the crime.

Dupin is a semiotician – someone who reads signs and then reasons backwards to figure out what they mean. He does this by putting himself into the criminal's mind in order to understand the criminal's motivation. Sherlock Holmes, the successor to Dupin, created by Sir Arthur Conan Doyle, uses the exact same type of reasoning skills. In the first story, *A Study in Scarlet* (1867), Holmes's assistant, Doctor Watson, compares Holmes to Dupin, thus paying tribute to the founder of the detective story. Dupin makes appearances in other tales of mystery and crime, such as in Michael Harrison's *Ellery Queen's Mystery Magazine* of the 1960s, testifying to the appeal of Poe's invention – a genre of fiction that constitutes a metaphor of who we are and why we do what we do. Our fascination with crime mysteries is the same as our fascination with life's mysteries. The former is a small-scale version of the latter.

With the rise in popularity of the detective story in the late nineteenth century came a rise in the scientific interest in crime and criminals. Needless to say, philosophical interest in crime is ancient, but the purely scientific investigation of crime, now known as *forensic science* (or simply *forensics*), really started at about the same time as Poe's fictional foray into the mind of the criminal. There is a definite connection between the two, with fiction influencing science in this case, providing insights into how crime detection might unfold in the real world. As crime writer Raymond Chandler wrote in 1962: "The private detective of fiction is a fantastic creation who acts and speaks like a real man. He can be completely realistic in every sense but one, that one sense being that in life as we know it such a man would not be a private detective." Influenced by Poe's writings, Peirce equated the study of signs to the study of the clues found at crime scenes. Semiotics and forensics have clearly a lot in common, even though in the history of both rarely have they ever been connected conceptually. The purpose of this opening chapter is to lay the foundations for making such a connection, looking at the history of both disciplines and discussing some of their basic methods and techniques.

1.1 Forensic Science

The word *forensic* derives from Latin *forensis* "public forum," alluding to the fact that, in Rome, an accuser would present and argue a case against suspects in a public forum, with the latter defending themselves in the same place. The one with the most convincing argument would typically win the case. From this comes the practice of legal argumentation in a court of law, where cases are presented and argued by lawyers and adjudicated by arbitrators or juries. Today, the term *forensics* refers to the science of crime or, more accurately, to the application of scientific methods to the investigation of crimes and to the analysis of criminal behavior.

Forensics is often equated with *criminology*. Although the two share much common ground, the former is more concerned with the techniques of solving actual crimes and identifying perpetrators, analyzing the evidence and then presenting a case to the legal system. Criminologists concentrate more on identifying the causes of crime, including the role of upbringing, personality, brain structure, social factors, and so on. Many consider the book written by an Italian economist named Cesare Beccaria in 1764, *On Crimes and Punishments*, as the foundational text of criminology. In it, Beccaria laid down the principles of penology that are still in use today, suggesting that a valid justice system should conform to the ideas of rationalist philosophy and enlightenment science.

1.1.1 Origins

In the ancient world, criminal investigations and trial proceedings relied mainly on confessions and witness testimony and, as we saw, on presenting a logical argument in public. The concept of deciphering evidence was practically unknown. One of the first written testaments of the use of scientific reasoning to solve a crime comes from thirteenth century China. It relates to the case of someone who was murdered with a sickle. This fact was used by an unknown investigator to solve the crime. The investigator demanded that all those who were in the victim's circle of acquaintances bring their sickles to a specified location, aware that common flies were attracted by the smell of blood. His method was a simple yet ingenious one. He exposed the sickle of each acquaintance to flies in the open air. Eventually, he found that flies gathered on a particular sickle. Confronted with this evidence, the murderer confessed. Other accounts from the same period in China give advice on how to differentiate between drowning and strangulation in criminal cases. In the former, the victim will show water in the lungs; in the latter, the victim will show broken neck cartilage. These seem to be the first accounts indicating the use of scientific knowledge and logical reasoning to determine how a victim died and, thus, who the perpetrator of the crime might be.

A systematic approach to crimes emerged at about the same time in twelfth-century England when the Office of the Coroner was established to keep records of all criminal matters. The early coroners investigated all deaths thought to be the result of homicide or suicide. Some of their incipient techniques would be considered to be unreliable or spurious today, but they did lay the groundwork for the development of a science of crime to come centuries later. The British colonists brought the coroner system to America. In 1877 Massachusetts adopted a statewide system headed by a physician – today called the medical examiner. Soon after other states approved similar systems. At about the same time new crime-solving techniques, such as fingerprinting, were emerging in Europe and America. Already in 1829, the Metropolitan Police Act established the world-famous Scotland Yard detective department in Great Britain, which investigated crimes in London and, occasionally, other parts of the British Empire. This was the first major step in modern crime detection. In the United States, large cities patterned their police efforts after the successful British model. Hans Gross, an Austrian judge, probably proposed the word *criminalistics* in his book *Criminal Investigation* (1893) to suggest that a science of crime investigation, based on the analysis of evidence, was starting to materialize. By the late 1800s, the study of criminals themselves also surfaced. Cesare Lombroso, an Italian physician, was the most important figure in this movement. He examined the psychical appearances of known criminals, classifying common traits of facial expression, cranium size, eye structure, and so on, coming to the conclusion that certain physical traits differentiated criminals from the general population. These could thus be used in the identification of real and potential perpetrators. Although his ideas are now largely rejected, or certainly disputed, his approach laid the basis for the modern science of criminal profiling, which operates under the principle that criminals act and behave in similar ways.

In the subsequent twentieth century, forensics and criminology initiated a partnership that is still intact today, with forensic scientists focusing on the development of investigative methods and technologies and criminologists focusing instead on theories of criminality. The American criminologist Edwin H. Sutherland developed the notion of *differential association*, which claimed that criminal behavior is acquired through association with criminals or people with unfavorable attitudes toward society. Other theories followed, putting the spotlight on the role of specific social systems, or types of upbringing, on the crystallization of criminal lifestyles. Unlike Lombroso, the early criminologists argued that society produces crime, not nature, and thus that crime can be eliminated only by changing society. Some of these ideas are still being debated today as heatedly as they were over a century ago.

1.1.2 Evidence

Most cities and police forces have a crime-solving unit, sometimes called a Crime Scene Investigation (CSI) unit, where forensic scientists gather, classify and interpret evidence connected with crimes. For example, glass splinters found at the scene of a crime may be matched with splinters found on a suspect's clothing; or gun bullets collected at the scene might be matched to the gun possessed by a suspect. The pattern of bloodstains or blood spatter near a body may indicate how a murder was committed. Other types of evidence collected by CSI specialists includes fibers, fingerprints, footprints, hair, soil, and anything else that can potentially provide insights into how a crime was committed and, possibly, who committed it. A forensic scientist calls these *clues*; a semiotician would call them *signs*. This distinction is a useful one, as will be argued in this book, because a sign (unlike a clue) can be connected more extensively to a broader context of meaning and it is this context that might ultimately help solve a crime, as Dupin and Holmes certainly knew. Whatever they are called, the clues (or signs) of crime constitute *evidence* (from Latin *evidens* "obvious to the eye"), or information that can be used to prove or disprove a fact in question.

There are three main steps involved typically in handling crime-scene evidence:

1. collecting the evidence at the crime scene with the use of special equipment and devices;
2. analyzing the evidence in a crime laboratory or sending it off for special analysis to other experts, such as anthropologists, linguists, and medical specialists;
3. presenting the evidence to the police and eventually at a trial.

The evidence collected at a crime scene is called *trace evidence*. The equipment used to gather such evidence includes a plastic container called a vacuum trap, which fits on the end of a vacuum cleaner hose. This gathers fibers, hairs, sand, wood splinters, glass, paint, and the like and allows for their identification and preservation. Larger forms of evidence, such as bullets and firearms, are collected by hand and then tested in laboratories for brand make, as well as for determining the angle of fire. Digital photographic equipment is used to photograph specific kinds of evidence, such as fingerprints. Frequently, video recordings of the scene with audio commentary are also made. In the case of a murder, the body is taken to the medical examiner's office and an autopsy is performed to determine the cause of death.

The use of scientific techniques to analyze evidence or relevant information started in the nineteenth century. Alphonse Bertillon, a French statistician, developed a method of identifying persons according to their body measurements. Called the Bertillon system, it was first used by the police in Paris in 1879 and shortly thereafter adopted throughout the world, evolving eventually into the modern-day "mugshot." The idea was to measure parts of the body of every known criminal and then to make a record of the height, the length of arms and legs, and the length and width of the skull. These measurements, eleven in all, do not change greatly in a person's life cycle and so can be used to match evidence at a crime scene against these physical records of suspects with a criminal background.

Fingerprinting has mostly replaced the Bertillon system because it is more accurate. In fact, it is one of the most important types of evidence collected at a crime scene. First, a forensic expert dusts (or brushes) a surface with a special powder. The powder sticks to the oils left on a surface by one or more fingers. The print is photographed and then lifted from the surface with a clear adhesive tape. The impression left on the tape is then transferred to a piece of special paper, which forms a permanent record of the print. A special computer is then used in a crime laboratory to compare the fingerprints collected at a scene with those contained in a central file. Each human being has a unique fingerprint. So, if the computer comes up with a match, the possessor of the fingerprint found at the scene can be determined and subsequently interrogated.

Fingerprints are either visible or latent (hidden). Most are made by fingers soiled with blood, dirt, or other substances; latent prints are made by the perspiration and oils that accumulate naturally on the fingers. Fingerprints are classified according to specific shapes and patterns, and the number of ridges between certain points within the patterns. There are four main types: (1) loops, whereby the ridges begin on one side, curving back sharply, and ending on the same side; (2) arches, whereby the ridges extend from one side of the finger to the other, rising in the center; (3) ridges in a whorl pattern, which have a circular form; and (4) accidental, which have no specific form. Many fingerprint patterns combine loops, whorls, and arches:

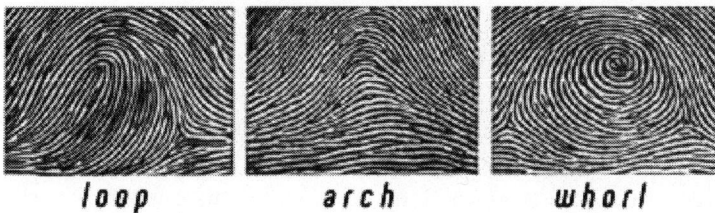

loop   arch   whorl

Figure 1: Parts of a fingerprint

Sir William J. Herschel, a British colonial administrator in India during the late 1800s, was probably the first person to devise a workable method of fingerprint classification. Historians credit British scientist Sir Francis Galton with developing Herschel's method into a modern system of fingerprint identification in the 1880s. Galton showed that no two people could have exactly the same fingerprint patterns. By the late 1910s, fingerprinting had replaced the Bertillon system (mentioned above) almost entirely. In the United States, the Federal Bureau of Investigation (FBI) established a fingerprint file in 1924. Today, newer systems using computers are used to classify and compare fingerprints.

Another key type of evidence found at a crime scene is the DNA (deoxyribonucleic acid) collected from blood, hairs, and other human substances. The DNA is the genetic material found in the nucleus of every living cell in threadlike structures called chromosomes that directs the formation, growth, and reproduction of cells and organisms. Short sections, called genes, determine heredity. A molecule of DNA consists of two chains, which are strands of chemical compounds called nucleotides. These are arranged like a twisted ladder, in a double helix (spiral). The nucleotides in one DNA strand correspond to the nucleotides in the other DNA strand, forming pairs in a predictable pattern:

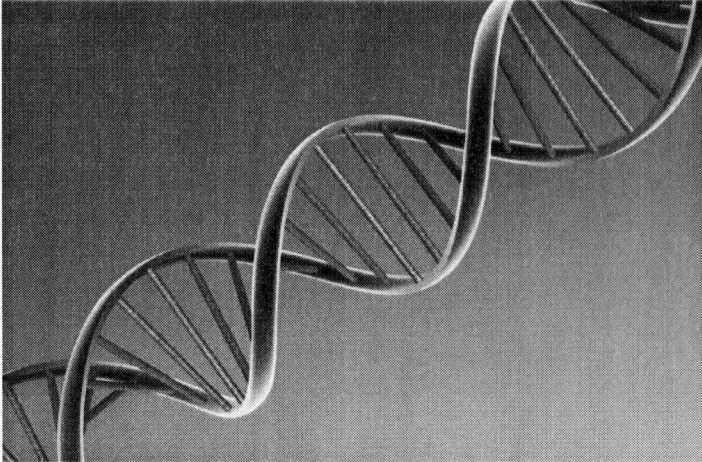

Figure 2: The DNA

DNA was first used as evidence in the United States in 1986 in Pennsylvania. Since then, it has become widely accepted by the courts in both criminal and civil cases, having become a powerful form of evidence in criminal investigations, based on the fact that it is extremely unlikely that any two unrelated individuals possess identical DNA. Investigators may compare DNA found at the crime scene with DNA from a suspected criminal. On the basis of this comparison, a specific suspect can be included or excluded as a possible source of the DNA found at the scene of the crime. Investigators can analyze the DNA found in the cells of almost any body fluid or tissue, including bone, blood, semen, hair, or teeth. In traditional DNA analysis, known as *Restriction Fragment Length Polymorphism* (RFLP) analysis, a restriction enzyme is used to cut the DNA into fragments for comparison. RFLP analysis has been virtually replaced by a more sensitive and effective method called the *Polymerase Chain Reaction* (PCR) technique, which involves the use of the enzyme polymerase to create numerous copies of specific sections of a DNA molecule. These may then be used for comparison to determine whether an individual contributed to an evidence sample or not.

Law enforcement agencies have developed DNA profile databases. One such database, called the National DNA Indexing System (NDIS), is maintained by police agencies throughout the United States, and is now part of a national database of DNA profiles called the Combined DNA Index System (CODIS). CODIS allows crime laboratories to compare the DNA profiles of convicted offenders with samples from crime scenes. It has been used to help solve numerous crimes.

However, attorneys sometimes attack certain kinds of DNA evidence because of the ever-present danger of evidence contamination.

The medical examiner is the central figure in the forensic investigation of crimes involving a victim. The medical examiner visits the crime scene, conducts an autopsy in cases of death, examines the crime evidence and laboratory reports, scrutinizes the victim's medical history, and puts all this information together in a report to the legal authorities. Medical examiners are usually physicians who have specialized in forensic pathology, the study of structural and functional changes in the body as a result of injury or trauma.

1.2 Branches

Fingerprint, DNA, and trace evidence analysis are the basic techniques of forensic science. Often, however, the insights of other sciences may be required to shed light on a case. Today, these make up different branches of forensic science. Some of these are:

- *computational forensics*, which deals with the development of algorithms and software to assist criminal investigations;
- *digital forensics*, which involves the use of computer science techniques in order to recover data from digital media connected with a crime or a suspect;
- *forensic anthropology*, which comprises the use of concepts and techniques from physical and archeological anthropology to recover, identify, and analyze skeletal human remains and to determine the time and even manner of death;
- *forensic botany*, which uses botanical science in order to analyze plant specimens found at a crime scene and what they might reveal about the crime;
- *forensic chemistry*, which applies chemical methods to the identification of the chemical composition of materials and substances found at a crime scene;
- *document analysis*, which consists in dating and analyzing documents in order to determine whether or not they are forged or copied, as well as what their contents indicate about a criminal event or a suspect;
- *handwriting analysis*, which is the study of patterns in the handwriting of notes in order to glean from them who the writer is or what his or her emotional state might be;
- *forensic linguistics*, which uses linguistic science to help investigators determine the significance of notes and other verbal materials left at a crime scene, as well as to decode other verbal phenomena that can be connected with crime and criminality;

- *forensic entomology*, which deals with the examination of insects in, on and around human remains so as to assist investigators in determining the time or location of death, or if the body was moved after death;
- *forensic geology*, which examines trace evidence such as soils, minerals and petroleum in order to see what they indicate about a crime;
- *forensic odontology*, which uses dental science to examine bite marks on corpses as well as tooth imprints in order to identify either victims or suspects;
- *forensic podiatry*, which is the science of footprint patterns so that investigators can establish the identity of people at crime scenes;
- *blood spatter analysis*, which is the scientific examination of blood spatter patterns found at a crime scene, allowing investigators to reconstruct how a murder may have occurred;
- *forensic psychology*, which is the psychological study of criminal behavior;
- *forensic toxicology*, which studies the presence of drugs in a victim in order to determine the cause of death;
- *forensic pathology*, which studies the cause of death by examination of a corpse by means of an autopsy.

1.2.1 Examples

To grasp how a specific branch can contribute to crime analysis, let us look at a few examples. Consider the expertise that a forensic entomologist would bring to a case. Already in thirteenth century China we saw that an investigator used knowledge of how flies behave to solve a crime. In the same century, investigators used knowledge of the stages of development and sizes of insect larvae on a body to establish the time of death. This type of evidence is important because body fluids and soft tissues soon dissipate from a corpse. Entomological analysis can also indicate if a body was moved from the insect's natural habitat. Some flies prefer to lay eggs indoors or outdoors, at night or in daylight. So, this kind of pattern can inform the investigator as to the place and time of the death. The concentration of insects on a part of the body may also show where wounds are located.

Forensic anthropology, forensic pathology, and blood spatter analysis have many important and sometimes overlapping functions. A post-mortem examination of human bones is used by forensic anthropologists to help determine the identity of a corpse and thus, perhaps, help establish the time and cause of death. Such examination is also used to help identify the age, sex, height, and race of a victim, as well has his or her injuries. In contrast, the pathologist carries out autopsies to examine bodies that have not decomposed. Autopsies allow medical experts to examine the internal and external parts of the deceased. If murder seems evident, the pathologist may visit the crime scene to assess the position of the victim. Blood spatter analysis is useful for indicating the direction of travel or impact angle of a traumatic event on the corpse. A blood spatter specialist can thus help identify how the murder may have taken place. The direction of travel can be easily inferred by the way in which a blood spot hits a surface as a splotch and then becomes more narrow or threadlike. By measuring the length and width of the splotch and its thinning out pattern the "direction of travel" can be determined.

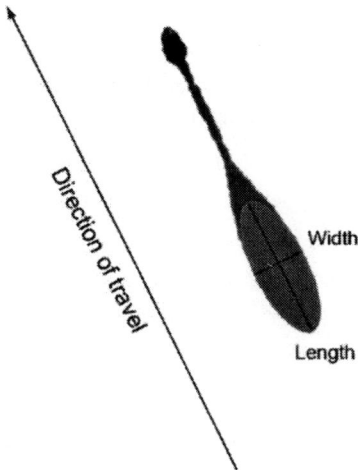

Figure 3: Blood spatter analysis

As these few examples show, forensic science is a powerful detection science because, in addition to its own methods and techniques, it utilizes the tools of other disciplines in a complementary fashion. It is a *de facto* interdisciplinary science.

1.2.2 Criminology

As mentioned, criminology and forensic science overlap somewhat, with the latter focusing more on developing techniques for detecting and solving crimes and the former with studying the causes of crime. Criminologists conduct research on the psychological and social factors that may cause crime, focusing on such things as the environmental conditions associated with crimes and on the connection between crime and biological factors such as brain structure and chemical imbalances. Among the social factors that criminologists investigate are the influence of criminals or people who have little regard for the law on young people (known as *social learning theory*) and the effects of poverty, upbringing, and urban overcrowding on individuals (known as *social disorganization theory*).

Criminologists also study systems of *penology*, the science of the punishment and treatment of criminals. During the early part of the twentieth century, criminologists started to stress rehabilitation – the treatment of offenders with the objective of reinstating them to useful lives. Research in the 1970s showed that rehabilitation had little successful outcomes leading to different penological theories today, such as ensuring that prison life is constructive and humane. One of the objectives of forensic semiotics is to investigate the underlying motivations for crime from the perspective of how it unfolds in specific life contexts.

1.3 Semiotics

The types of analyses that forensic scientists conduct, such as DNA profiling and fingerprinting, are fundamentally interpretive techniques. And this is where semiotics might come into the picture. This is not a casual or superficial observation. As Charles Peirce realized in reading the mystery stories of Edgar Allan Poe, detective work is sign-interpretation work. A fingerprint, fundamentally, is a natural sign connected with a unique individual. A blood spatter pattern is a complex sign, called a *text*, that allows for the hypothetical reconstruction of real events through an interpretation of its structure. All clues at a crime scene are *de facto* signs standing for referents that must be inferred hermeneutically (interpretively and contextually). To use a simple example, forensic investigators might interpret nail polish as a sign of female participation in a crime scene, but they may also see it is a sign that contains information that can potentially help them locate its manufacturer and subsequently identify the retail stores that may have sold it. This might then help them locate the wearer of the nail polish through store receipts, video recordings, and the like. It is the interpretive process itself on which semiotics can shed considerable light.

What is semiotics? It is the science of interpretation. Since the middle part of the twentieth century, semiotics has grown into a broad field of interdisciplinary inquiry. It has been applied to the study of body language, the mass media, advertising, comics, verbal language, artifacts, movies, gesture, facial expression, clothing, architecture, cuisine, rituals – in a phrase, to anything that human beings produce and use to communicate and represent something in some meaningful way. But this seemingly eclectic pastiche of applications is hardly random or haphazard. It has a specific purpose – to flesh out recurrent patterns in human meaning production and their *raison d'être*.

1.3.1 Historical Sketch

The term *semeiotics* (now spelled without the "e" as *semiotics*) comes from Greek *sêmeiotikos* "observant of signs." It was coined by Hippocrates, the founder of Western medicine, to designate the study of the warning signs produced by the human body, known today as symptoms. Hippocrates argued that medical practice was basic *semiotiké* (sign analysis), since the particular physical form that a *semeion*, body sign, takes, constitutes a vital clue for finding its source within the body. To use an analogy with forensics, the semeion is trace evidence of a disease, malady, or ailment. This notion was entrenched permanently into medical practice shortly thereafter by the physician Galen of Pergamum who saw it as the epistemological basis for the conduct of medical science (Sebeok 2001). The physician's primary task, to this day, is to unravel what a body sign stands for. For example, a dark bruise, a rash, or a sore throat might stand respectively for a broken finger, a skin allergy, or a cold respectively (the potential referents):

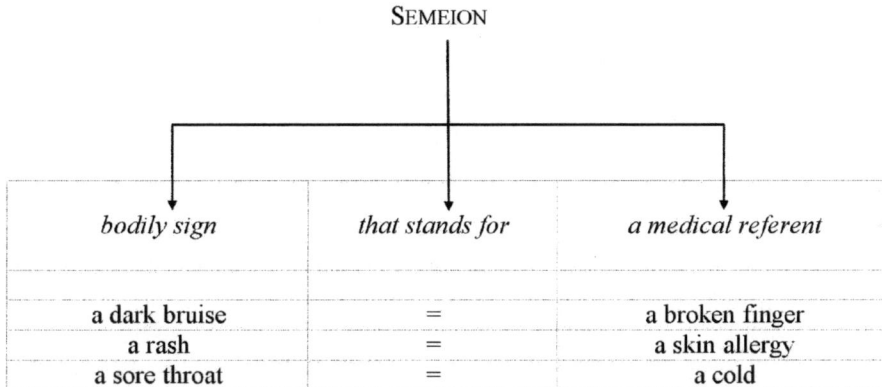

SEMEION

bodily sign	that stands for	a medical referent
a dark bruise	=	a broken finger
a rash	=	a skin allergy
a sore throat	=	a cold

Figure 4: Elements of the semeion

The concept of the *semeion* as "something physical" standing for "something else" (a disease) was expanded in antiquity to include human-made, or conventional, signs (such as words) that stood for psychological or emotional states. Among the first to differentiate between bodily (or natural) and conventional signs was the Greek philosopher Plato, who realized that conventional forms such as words reveal a propensity to unravel the meanings of things by referring to them in general abstract ways. It would be impracticable to name everything in concrete ways because we would then have to create as many words as there are things. Aristotle, who was Plato's pupil, argued on the contrary that words start out as practical strategies for naming singular objects, not abstract properties. It is only after we discover that certain objects have similar properties that we start classifying them into abstract categories. For instance, we refer to certain plants with words such as *rose, tulip, daisy,* and so on. But we learn through our own vocabulary that these form a general category. We name that category with the word *flower.*

The question arose at some point in the ancient world as to whether or not there was any connection between the natural signs studied by physicians and the conventional ones studied by philosophers. This was first discussed by the Stoics, members of a Greek school of philosophy that emerged around 308 BCE. They argued that conventional signs functioned in a similar fashion to natural ones, connecting human thoughts and emotions to the real world by simply referring to it. It was the early Christian church father, St. Augustine, who argued for a fundamental difference between the two in his masterwork *De doctrina christiana* ("On Christian Doctrine"). He saw natural signs *(signa naturalia)* as products of nature, thus lacking intentionality. Bodily symptoms, the rustling of leaves, the colors of plants, the signals that animals emit, and so on, have no intent behind them. They just are this way. We humans are the ones who interpret them in our own particular way, not nature. To do so, we use conventional signs *(signa data).* These are products of our intentions and needs. They help use encode reality and store it in our brains. St. Augustine also considered miracles to be signs, sent from God and, thus, sacred. These can only be understood on faith, although such understanding is partly based on our specific interpretations of them.

Interest in linking human understanding with sign-production waned, unexplainably, after the death of St. Augustine. The interest was rekindled in the eleventh century after the translation of the works of Plato, Aristotle, and other key Greek philosophers into Latin and even into some of the emerging European languages. The outcome was the movement known as *Scholasticism*, spearheaded by Christian theologians and teachers who sought to solve abiding philosophical problems, such as the provability of the existence of God. The Scholastics believed that signs are the mental tools we use to encode practical, scientific, and sacred truths. We give names to these truths because we come to understand them better through the names. This view of signs is known as *realism*.

But within Scholasticism there was a splinter group – called the *nominalists* – who argued that "truth" was a matter of subjective opinion and that our signs captured, at best, only our variable versions of it. So, we can never know the reality behind a word since all it reveals is a particular choice, not a reference to something immanent that calls out for understanding. John Duns Scotus and William of Ockham, two fervent nominalists, stressed that in the end signs ended up referring to other signs, rather than to actual things or categories. The great Scholastic theologian St. Thomas Aquinas countered that signs did indeed refer to real things, even if these things were simple selections. About the same time, the English philosopher and scientist Roger Bacon put forth one of the first comprehensive taxonomies of signs, claiming that, without a firm understanding of the nature of the signs themselves, discussing what truth is or is not would end up being a trivial matter of subjective or solipsistic opinion. The debate between realists and nominalists is still ongoing, even though it has taken different designations. It will likely never be resolved, since we need to use signs in the debate itself.

A neglected, but important figure, in this debate was John Poinsot who, in his 1632 *Treatise on Signs* (Deely 2001), defined the sign as would a cognitive scientist today – as an intermediary form between thoughts and things. Poinsot suggested that we invent signs so that we can refer to those things in the world that have significance for us. So, like the nominalists, he understood that signs offer up a slice or particular version of reality – but, like the realists, he also understood that it was still reality. With Poinsot, semiotics was beginning to emerge as a kind of cognitive science of the mind leading, a half century later, to English philosopher John Locke's proposal of incorporating the formal study of signs into philosophy in his *Essay Concerning Human Understanding* (1690). However, Locke saw semiotics not as a study of cognition, but as an aid to philosophical inquiry, furnishing a kind of "metalanguage" – a language that scholars could use to discuss philosophical notions, yet remain conceptually distinct from them.

The idea of fashioning an autonomous discipline of sign study had to wait until the late nineteenth century, when the Swiss linguist Ferdinand de Saussure put this very idea forward in his *Cours de linguistique générale* (1916), a textbook compiled after his death by two of his students at the University of Geneva. Saussure used the term *sémiologie* (English *semiology*) – which he had used in personal correspondence as far back as 1894 – to designate the new discipline. As the following citation from the *Cours* shows, Saussure suggested that the main goal of semiology (should it ever come into being) was to understand the social function of signs (Saussure 1916: 15–16):

> It is possible to conceive of a science which studies the role of signs as part of social life. It would form part of social psychology, and hence of general psychology. We shall call it *semiology* (from the Greek *semeion*, "sign"). It would investigate the nature of signs and the laws governing them. Since it does not yet exist, one cannot say for certain that it will exist. But it has a right to exist, a place ready for it in advance. Linguistics is only one branch of this general science. The laws which semiology will discover will be laws applicable in linguistics, and linguistics will thus be assigned to a clearly defined place in the field of human knowledge.

Saussure went on to suggest that of all human sign systems language was "the most complex and universal" (1916: 58), and that this was so because "There are no pre-existing ideas, and nothing is distinct before the appearance of language" (1916: 112).

Saussure may have been unaware that the first appearance of the French word *sémiologie* occurred in the *Dictionnaire de Trévoux* (1752) with a medical meaning, harking back to Hippocratic method. The *Imperial Dictionary* of England (1883) also contained an entry for *semeiology* with the definition "doctrine of signs." Today, Hippocrates's and Locke's term *(semeiotics)*, spelled *semiotics*, is the preferred one, ever since it was adopted by the International Association of Semiotic Studies in 1969. Actually, it was Charles Peirce (1931) who put Locke's term into wide circulation with his many studies of signs (Peirce 1931–1958). Although his writing style is dense and his ideas not easily apparent, Peirce's basic model of the sign has become a central one. Perhaps his greatest insight was that our sensory and emotional experiences of the world influence why and how we make and use signs. As we have seen, he called these abductions. The term *significs*, coined by Victoria Lady Welby in 1896, is also used in the technical semiotic literature to refer to the study of how experiential processes influence sign production and comprehension (Petrilli 2009). It is no coincidence that Peirce's and Welby's ideas are rather similar, given that they corresponded frequently with each other.

Following on the coattails of Saussure and Peirce, a number of key people developed semiotics into the sophisticated discipline that it has become today. Only a few can be mentioned in passing here. The American philosopher and semiotician Charles Morris (1938, 1946) divided semiotic analysis into three domains: the study of sign assemblages, which he called *syntactics*; the analysis of the relations that exist between signs and their meanings, which he called *semantics*; and the investigation of the relations that are formed between signs and their users, which he termed *pragmatics*. This tripartite division is still used today, both in semiotics and linguistics. The Russian-born American semiotician Roman Jakobson (1978) is best known for his model of communication, which suggests that sign exchanges among interlocutors are hardly ever neutral, but involve subjectivity and goal-attainment of some kind. The French semiotician Roland Barthes (1957) illustrated the power of using semiotics for decoding the hidden meanings in popular culture spectacles and texts such as wrestling matches and Hollywood blockbuster movies. The French semiotician Algirdas J. Greimas (1987) developed the branch of semiotics known as *narratology*, which studies how human beings in different cultures invent similar kinds of stories with virtually the same stock of sign structures. The Hungarian-born American semiotician Thomas A. Sebeok was influential in expanding the semiotic paradigm to include the study of animal signaling systems, which he termed *zoo-semiotics*, and the study of sign systems in all living things, which has come to be called *biosemiotics*. He also recycled the term *semiosis*, introduced by Peirce, to designate the ability to produce and comprehend signs in a species-specific way. The interweaving and blending of ideas, findings, and discourses from different disciplinary domains was, Sebeok claimed, the distinguishing feature of biosemiotics. Finally, Italian semiotician Umberto Eco (1976) has contributed significantly to understanding how we interpret signs and texts.

Names such as Jacques Derrida, Claude Lévi-Strauss, Maurice Merleau-Ponty, Gilles Deleuze, Paul Ricoeur, John Deely, Floyd Merrell, Yuri Lotman, Louis Hjelmslev, Julia Kristeva, Jacques Lacan, Michel Foucault, Emile Bénveniste, Susan Langer, among others, are key ones in the modern historiography of the discipline. Their influence on semiotic theory and practice has hardly been negligible.

1.3.2 Basic Notions

How does one go about studying something as elusive as "meaning" since it cannot be accessed separately from the signs that are constructed to capture and preserve it? To do so practically, semiotics has developed a theoretical apparatus that focuses on the structure, function, and uses of signs, rather than on what meaning is in an abstract sense. In short, semiotics studies *semiosis* – the production and comprehension of signs. It is often equated with communication science. Although the two fields share much of the same theoretical and methodological territory, the latter focuses more on the technical study of how messages are transmitted (vocally, electronically) and on the mathematical and psychological laws governing the transmission, reception, and processing of information. Semiotics, on the other hand, pays more attention to *what* information is and on *how* we interpret it.

To avoid the ambivalence of the English term *meaning*, the terms *reference, sense,* and *definition* are often used in semiotics (and in other fields as well). *Reference* is the process of pointing out or identifying something, whatever it may be (an object, a feeling, an idea, an imaginary construct); *sense* is what that something elicits cognitively, emotionally, historically, and socially; and *definition* is a statement about what that something means. Words may refer to the same (or similar) things, known as *referents*, but they have different *senses*. For example, the "long-eared, short-tailed, burrowing mammal of the family Leporidae" is called either *rabbit* or *hare* in English. Both *refer* essentially to the same type of mammal. But there is a difference of *sense* between the two – the word *hare* is used if it is larger, has longer ears and legs, and does not burrow; *rabbit* refers instead to a smaller mammal, with shorter ears and legs. The word *rabbit* also evokes a social sense, namely that of "pet," whereas a *hare* is unlikely to do the same. This distinction was discussed at length by the German philosopher Gottlob Frege (1879). Frege pointed out that the "fourth smallest planet and the second planet from the Sun" is named both *Venus* and the *Morning Star*. These refer to the same thing, but imply different senses – *Venus* designates the planet in a straightforward referential way (nevertheless with latent allusions to the goddess of love and beauty of Roman mythology), while *Morning Star* brings out the fact that the planet is visible in the east just before sunrise. The difference was explored further by philosopher Willard O. Quine (1953). Suppose a linguist overhears the word *Gavagai* from the mouth of a native informant when a rabbit is sighted scurrying through the bushes. The linguist, Quine suggests, cannot determine if the word means "rabbit," "undetached rabbit parts," or "rabbit stage" because, as discovered from previous interactions with the informants, these are all the senses that the word evokes. The meaning, therefore, will remain indeterminate unless it can be inferred from the context in which *Gavagai* occurs. From Quine's analysis awareness of the importance of context spread throughout semiotics, philosophy, and the human and social sciences.

Definition, as mentioned, is a statement about what something means by using other words and other signs (for example, pictures). As useful as it is, the act of defining something leads inevitably to circularity. Take the dictionary definition of *cat* as "a small carnivorous mammal domesticated since early times as a catcher of rats and mice and as a pet and existing in several distinctive breeds and varieties" (Danesi 2007). A problem that immediately surfaces from this definition is the use of *mammal* to define *cat* – one word has been used to replace another. What is the meaning of *mammal*? A *mammal*, the dictionary states in another location, is "any of various warm-blooded vertebrate animals of the class Mammalia." But this too is hardly a viable way out of an emerging circle of references. What is an *animal*? The dictionary defines *animal* as an *organism*, which it defines, in turn, as an individual form of *life*, which it then defines as the property that distinguishes living *organisms*. Alas, at that point the dictionary has gone into a referential loop, since it has employed an already-used concept, *organism*, to define *life*. This looping pattern surfaces in all domains of human knowledge, not just in the area of definitions. It suggests that signs can never be understood in the absolute, only in relation to other signs. But the looping structure is still knowledge-making, revealing the connective propensities of the human brain. We cannot go into the nature of connectivity and its neural correlates (Fauconnier and Turner 2002, Alexander 2011, Danesi 2007). Suffice it to say that it is within the looping structures themselves that meaning resides, even though it cannot be flushed out directly.

In semiotics proper, the terms *denotation* and *connotation* are preferred to reference and sense. Consider, again, the word *cat*. The word elicits an image of a "creature with four legs, whiskers, retractile claws." This is its *denotative* meaning, which is intended to point out what distinguishes a *cat* from some other mammal so that we can determine if something real or imaginary under consideration is an exemplar of a "cat." Similarly, the word *square* refers to a figure characterized by the distinctive features "four equal straight lines" and "meeting at right angles." It is irrelevant if the lines are thick, dotted, 2 meters long, 80 feet long, or colored differently. If the figure has "four equal straight lines meeting at right angles," it qualifies as a square.

All other images associated with the words *cat* and *square* are connotative – that is, they extend their meanings. Some connotative senses of *square* can be seen in expressions such as the following: *She's so square* ("old fashioned"); *He has a square disposition* ("forthright," "honorable"); *Put it squarely on the table* ("evenly," "precisely"). An old-fashioned person, an honorable individual, and the action of laying something down evenly imply the denotation of "square" in an extensive way. The concept of "square" is an ancient one and, thus, probably known by everyone (hence "old-fashioned"); it is also a figure with every part equal (hence "forthright"); and it certainly is an even-sided figure (hence "evenly"). Connotation encompasses all kinds of senses, including emotional ones. Essentially it is a record of meanings that a sign has accrued over time. This can be called the sign's "historical repertoire of meanings." It is the operative sense-making and sense-extracting mode in the production and decipherment of all kinds of texts, even technical ones. As current work on figurative processes in the brain has shown, scientific theories and models involve connotative (or metaphorical) reasoning, even though they end up being interpreted denotatively over time (Black 1962, Lakoff and Núñez 2000). Connotation is not an option, as some traditional theories of meaning continue to sustain to this day; it is something we can easily extract from a sign if we have access to its historical repertoire of meanings.

The distinction between denotation and connotation is, by and large, analogous to Frege's distinction between reference and sense. These terms are used interchangeably in the relevant semiotic literature, as are the terms *intension* (= denotation) and *extension* (= connotation), proposed by the logician Rudolf Carnap (1937). While there are subtle differences among these terms, it is beyond the present purpose to compare them. Suffice it to say that in current semiotic practice they are used in a virtually synonymous manner.

Denotation is fairly stable across cultures in cases where the same referent is used and encoded in sign form. Connotation is what varies. A *cat* is defined as an animal across the world, no matter what linguistic name it assumes and how it is classified vis-à-vis other animals. Variation in its meaning occurs at the connotative level. In our culture, a *cat* is considered to be a domestic companion, among other things; in others it is viewed as a sacred animal; and in others still it is considered to be a source of food (cat meat). Thus, while the sign refers to virtually the same animal in different cultures denotatively (no matter what name is used), its connotation varies considerably, constituting a source of supplementary and culture-specific semiosis.

Ultimately, signs allow people to recognize certain patterns in the world over and over again, thus acting as directive guides for taking action in the world. Signs are thus closely tied to social needs and aspirations – a fact emphasized by many semioticians, especially the Russian theorist Mikhail Bakhtin (1981). Bakhtin even went so far as to claim that signs gain meaning only as they are exchanged by people in social dialogue or discourse, maintaining that all human meaning is constructed socially. Some caution must however be exercised in adopting such theories of meaning. The fact is that there is a constant interaction between nature and culture, or between the *biosphere* and the *semiosphere*, in the production of signs, as the biologist Jakob von Uexküll (1909) and the Estonian cultural semiotician Yuri Lotman (1991) argued. It is more accurate to say that sign-formation and sign-interpretation are partly the result of adaptation to the biosphere and partly of exposure to the semiosphere – the universe of meanings in which humans are reared.

1.3.3 Semiosis

As mentioned, the basic question that motivates semiotic inquiry is: How does semiosis occur? Today, answers to this question are guided by two fundamental models – the one associated with Saussure and the one with Peirce.

Saussure put forward a "binary" model of the sign – a structure with two components, one physical and one conceptual. He termed the physical part of the sign, such as the sounds that make up the word *cat*, the *signifier*, and the concept or mental image that the sign elicits, the *signified* (literally "that which is signified by the sign"). Saussure claimed, moreover, that there is no foreseeable perceptual motivation or reason for creating the word *cat* other than the social need to do so. Any other signifier would have done the job just as effectively. This is why his model of the sign is also called "arbitrary." While this is disputed by semioticians today, the relevant notion in Saussure's model that the two parts imply each other – that is, they are bidirectional – is still valid. Cognitively this means that when we use or hear a word such as *tree* an image of the referent appears concomitantly in our brains, even if a real tree is not present. If the referent is present, then what materializes in the brain is the word for the referent – the distinctive sound sequence *tree*.

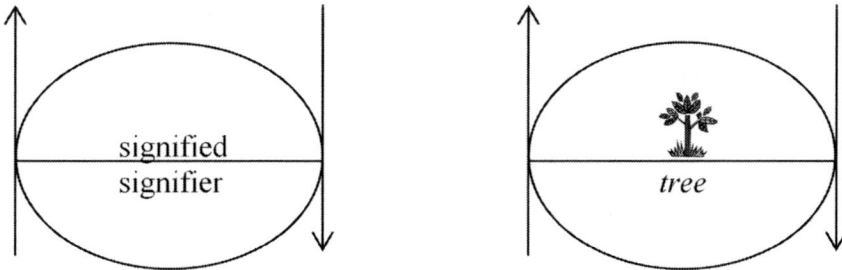

Figure 5: Saussure's binary model of the sign

Peirce's model is called "triadic" because it posits three main components in sign constitution, rather than the Saussurean two – the actual physical sign, the thing to which it refers, and the interpretation that it elicits. Peirce called the sign a *representamen* ("something that does the representing"), the concept that it stands for the *object* ("something cast outside for observation"), and the meaning that we get from it the *interpretant*. The latter constitutes a "derived" sign itself, because it entails the further production of interpretation. So, when we interpret something as a "cat" we ignite a further process of semiosis – *cat* suggesting *pet*, suggesting the role of *animals* in human life, and so on theoretically ad infinitum:

Representamen

Semiosis

Object   Interpretant

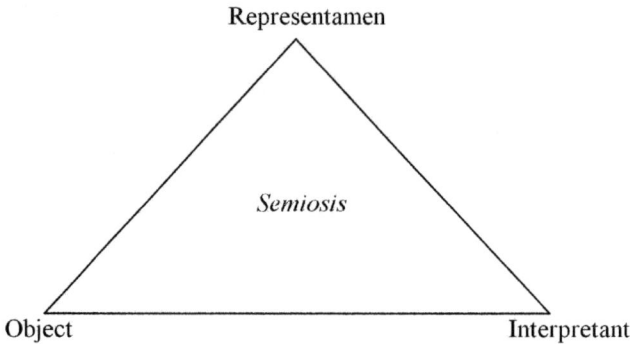

Figure 6: Peircean model of the sign

Peirce also developed a comprehensive typology of signs – a typology that has yet to be eclipsed. He identified 66 types in total. The main ones are the *icon*, the *index*, and the *symbol*, which have become part of every semiotician's repertoire of notions.

Unlike Saussure, Peirce viewed semiosis as originating in the perception of some property in an object. He termed the act of sign creation or sign interpretation a *firstness* event, or the tendency to create or interpret signs as simulations of reality. He called this process *iconicity*. Since iconic signs are fashioned in specific contexts, their manifestations are not universal, even though they spring from the same human perceptual (abductive) apparatus. Peirce used the term *hypoicon* to acknowledge this context-constraining dimension of firstness. Nevertheless, because it is a sensory-based representamen the referent can be figured out even by those who are not part of the contextual situation, if they are told how a sign simulates, resembles, or substitutes it. Thus, if someone who does not speak English is told that the expression *cock-a-doodle-do* stands for the sound a rooster is perceived to make, then that person would have no difficulty connecting the sign to the referent. A *secondness* tendency in semiosis consists in relating objects in some way or in indicating the locus of their existence. He called this tendency *indexicality.* The pointing finger is a basic example of a secondness sign, known as an *index.* When we point to something, we are in fact relating it to our location as pointers. If it is close by we refer to it as *near* or *here.* If not, we refer to it as *far* or *there.* Finally, Pierce claimed that there exists a *thirdness* dimension in semiosis, which consists in learning and using signs in conventional ways. He called such signs *symbols.* The cross figure used to stand for Christianity is a perfect example of a symbol. Although it represents the figure of a cross on which Christ was crucified, it is interpreted historically and conventionally as a sign standing for the religion that was founded after Christ's death.

It is accurate to say that semioticians today use a combination of Saussurean and Peircean concepts and techniques at various stages of analysis and for diverse purposes. Semiotics also frequently aims to access and utilize ideas and findings from related or cognate disciplines in order to understand some aspect of semiosis better. This interdisciplinary mode of inquiry is a two-way street, since many ideas developed within semiotics are now found scattered in these disciplines. It was actually Saussure who originated the interdisciplinary orientation of semiotics by claiming that semiology should be considered a part of psychology and linguistics a part of semiology, thus delineating an early interlacing web of connections among the human sciences.

1.3.4 Semiotics as a Science

Like psychology and linguistics, semiotics is a human science. Although it is true that meaning cannot be studied with the same objectivity as, say, physical matter is by chemists, semiotics is a science in the traditional sense of the word for five fundamental reasons, as Umberto Eco (1976: 74) has cogently argued:
1. It is an autonomous discipline.
2. It has a set of standardized theoretical tools that allow semioticians to seek answers to specific kinds of questions.
3. It has the capacity to generate hypotheses about semiosis, by analyzing the products of semiosis.
4. It affords the possibility of making predictions, such as how societies and cultures will evolve through semiosis.
5. Its findings can lead to a modification of the actual state of the objective world.

Any claim to "objectivity" is to be tempered with caution and wariness. This is not unique to semiotics, however. It is a characteristic of all the sciences, ever since Werner Heisenberg, the German physicist and Nobel laureate, put forward his now famous *indeterminacy principle* during the first part of the twentieth century, which debunked the notion of an objective reality independent of culture and of the scientist's personal participation in the understanding of reality (see Heisenberg 2007).

1.4 Forensic Semiotics

As Sebeok and Umiker-Sebeok, two leading semioticians, argued in 1980, Peircean semiotics is identical to detective science, dubbing Peirce a "consulting detective" and Sherlock Holmes a "consulting semiotician." Despite Holmes's common exhortation in the Conan Doyle stories that he never guesses, Sebeok and Umiker-Sebeok demonstrate how his logic and guesswork exemplifies perfectly what Peircean abduction is all about: "Testing a hypothesis as to the identity of a person through the collection of clues from that individual's physical appearance, speech patterns, and the like, always involves a certain amount of guessing, for which reason Peirce calls it abductory induction" (Sebeok and Umiker-Sebeok 1980: 63). As the two scholars suggest, semiotics and crime detection are two sides of the same cognitive (inference-based) coin. In such comments and observations it is logical to locate the need for *forensic semiotics*. Indeed, the correlation between detective fiction and modern-day forensics is undeniable.

In his novel, *The Name of the Rose* (1983), semiotician Umberto Eco shows masterfully how crime detection and semiotic analysis are indistinguishable ontologically. The plot takes place in a cloistered medieval monastery where monks are being murdered by a serial killer living amongst them. The hero who investigates the crimes is a learned Franciscan monk named William of Baskerville – a name that is transparently allusive to the Sherlock Holmes classic detective tale *The Hound of the Baskervilles* (1902) and its dark and ominous setting. The monk solves the crimes in the same manner and style of Holmes, interpreting the signs left by the killer at each crime scene by a radiant display of abductive reasoning – putting the clues together in such a way as to tell the story of the crime and to expose the mind of the killer.

The term *forensic semiotics* is not new. It has been used sporadically to indicate various things, such as its use by William Buckland (2007) to refer to writing patterns that can be used to identify authorship (length of sentence, vocabulary patterns, word frequencies, and so on). To the best of my knowledge, the use of the term *forensic semiotics* to refer to the inclusion of semiotics as a branch of criminology and forensics has never been proposed previously.

So, what can semiotics bring to the study of crime detection and of the more general question of what crime is? Suffice it to say at this initial junction that the epistemological apparatus of semiotics, which is built on the interpretation of signs, can only help understand such critical forensic concepts as evidence, deception, and the like from its particular angle. Clues are signs. They require interpretation and, as banal as this may sound, semiotics can help in this regard because it is the science of interpretation. Moreover, crime itself is a form of behavior that manifests itself through signs, as criminal profilers certainly know, as will be discussed in subsequent chapters. The more forensic scientists and criminologists know how signs work in the criminal mind, the more will we be able to understand crime and the more will we be able to do something about it.

1.4.1 First-Order and Second-Order Forensic Semiotics

There are two basic ways in which semiotics can be used in forensics. The first one can be called *first-order forensic semiotics* (FS[1]). The aim of FS[1] is to provide specific insights on the evidence collected by forensic scientists in order to help them decode it from a complementary perspective. It can also help interrogators and investigators understand how facial expressions, gesture, language, and so on can be used to recognize deception and to identify perpetrators.

The second basic way in which semiotics can be used in the study of crime is to help gauge the connection among crime, fictional depictions of it, and cultural definitions and perceptions of crime. There is a synergy among these three. The study of this synergy comes under *second-order forensic semiotics* (FS[2]). An obvious example of this synergy is in the partnership that the media and the police have established, with both investigating a crime in tandem. There are many real crime magazines, websites, and television programs that bring an investigation to the general public, at the same time that forensic scientists and police investigators examine the same crime. Often, the police will ask the media to intervene in publicizing evidence in the hope of attracting witnesses to the crime.

As Ronald Thomas (1999) has perceptively written, the provenance of a specific crime-solving technique or technology (such as the lie detector, the mug shot, fingerprinting, photographic analysis, and more) can be traced first to fictional detective stories. Vice versa, the latter showcase forensic science to the general public, albeit in a glorified and simplistic way. The comic strip *Dick Tracy* featured a detective using forensic techniques. In the *Perry Mason* stories by Erle Stanley Gardner the main character, a lawyer named Perry Mason, used forensic techniques to argue his cases in court. One of the earliest TV programs that directly used forensics was *Quincy, M.E.* (1976–1983). Shortly thereafter the number of *Crime Scene Investigation* (CSI) programs proliferated with names such as *CSI Miami, Dexter, Cold Case, Bones, Law & Order, Body of Proof,* and many others. There are now as many non-fiction TV programs and series dealing with crime and CSI as there are fictional ones, including a special channel called *Identification Discovery.* FS[2] constitutes a means of studying this fascination at the same time that it allows us to better understand the effects it might have on real crime. As such, FS[2] is more precisely a branch of criminology than it is of forensic science.

FS[2] has actually started receiving broad attention from criminologists, although it is not named as such. There is now even a major journal, *Crime, Media, Culture* that publishes research on the relationship between crime, criminal justice, media, and cultural trends. One of the interesting phenomena that criminologists study is called the *crime multiplier effect*, which refers to the impacts of real criminal events on social perceptions and mores through media exposure. The case of the O. J. Simpson chase scene in 1994 and subsequent trial is a case-in-point. Given that Simpson was a media icon the whole event became a spectacle that shaped people's opinions about his guilt or innocence in the double murder of his ex-wife Nicole Simpson and her friend Ronald Goldman. And given the racial subtext of the case, the trial turned into a racial justice trial. It showed, as Cotterill (2002) has argued, that media-showcased trials are theatrical events that influence their outcomes.

The O. J. Simpson case also brought out a basic distinction in the legal definition of crime – the difference between criminal and civil law. Simpson was tried and exonerated for the murders. So, the families of the two victims filed a civil suit against him for causing the deaths. The jury in that case found Simpson *liable* (not *guilty*) for the deaths. Simpson could not be put in prison, because it was a civil, not criminal, trial. Rather, he was ordered to pay over thirty million dollars to the two families. Civil trials such as this one are reminiscent of tribal councils and other forms of retributive justice, including the trials involving religious authorities whereby *crimes* are more likely to be perceived as *sins* – acts of an immoral nature.

The earliest laws were established by custom and passed on orally from one generation to the next. The invention of writing enabled people to assemble codes of law. The first such code was by a Babylonian king named Ur-Nammu about 2100 BCE. Another Babylonian king named Hammurabi put together a code in the 1700s BCE that is the prototype of modern law systems. It consisted mainly of a list of rules to settle specific types of matters such as the unfaithfulness of a wife, the theft of a farm animal, and the faulty work of a house builder. From about 1000 to 400 BCE, the Israelites amalgamated their religious and social laws into a code that reflected the teachings of Moses, stressing moral principles based on the Ten Commandments. The ancient Greeks and Romans believed that human beings had the power to make laws and to change them as the need arises, not just the divinities. The distinction between divine and human law became the rule ever since in western society. By the 800s, Europeans had developed a political and social system known as feudalism. A lord enforced the law in his feudal territory and granted protection to the people who served in his armies and who lived and worked on his land. With the demise of feudalism came the rise of a "common law" system that spread throughout Europe and subsequently imported to America. The system actually originated in England in the twelfth century and was based on court decisions, on the ethical notions implicit in those decisions, and on customs and usages rather than just on codified laws. This system has been modified over the years, but is still the basis for legal systems in the West.

But legal systems and cultural systems do not always coincide. Despite principles such as equality in the law and in culture, someone like Simpson is still seen as different from ordinary citizens. Criminals are, in fact, perceived and represented as "the others." They are our modern-day "sinners," marginalized for their evil deeds. It is in this area that FS^2 can help criminology study these perceptions and representations.

Chapter 2
Signs of Deception

Whenever, therefore, people are deceived and form opinions wide of the truth, it is clear that the error has slid into their minds through the medium of certain resemblances to that truth.

Socrates (469–399 BC)

Human beings communicate over two-thirds of their ideas and feelings through the body, rather than through vocal language, utilizing up to 700,000 bodily signs, including 1,000 different postures, 5,000 hand gestures, and over 250,000 facial expressions (Morris et al. 1979). Across the world, such nonverbal forms of communication are perceived as meaningful, not just decorative accompanying features of spoken or written language. Some societies even have dual forms of language – vocal and gestural – for special reasons. The Plains people of North America, for example, use a common gestural language so that tribes with different vocal languages can communicate with each other. It is so elaborate that a detailed conversation is possible using the gestures alone (Mallery 1972).

In forensic science, knowledge of the characteristics of nonverbal signage is particularly important during the interrogation of suspects, since it can help determine whether they are lying or not. It is in this area that first-order semiotics (FS[1]) can come into play, not only to provide general theoretical information on how nonverbal signage and communication unfold, but also to suggest specific techniques for detecting lies during investigations. Lying is a deceptive use of signs. Umberto Eco (1976: 7) once defined semiotics as the discipline which, in principle, should study "everything that can be used in order to lie." As Polish semiotician Jerzy Pelc (1992: 249) also puts it:

> Those who lie, always use signs. There is no lying without the use of signs. Lying is a semiotic activity, with a sender and a receiver. It is thus an activity taking place in society.

In criminal interrogations, it is anticipated that criminals will lie. Observing the criminal's body language, facial expressions, and eye contact patterns, therefore, has become a standard practice among investigators, because when people lie, an asymmetry between the words used and the bodily reflexes associated with them typically manifests itself. This is what Eco (1976: 58) calls a sign function produced by lying: "Every time there is possibility of lying there is a sign function; which is to signify (and then to communicate) something to which no real state of things corresponds. The possibility of lying is the proprium of semiosis." The forensic semiotician can best study these sign functions by exploring three basic questions: (1) What does a certain nonverbal sign function (a gesture, a facial expression, and so on) imply? (2) What bodily reflexes does it bring about? (3) Which nonverbal signs correlate with verbal ones during deception?

2.1 Lie Detection

People lie all the time, often to avoid negative outcomes or to gain some advantage. Moreover, people typically tend to ignore the signs of lying when speaking with others. As psychologist Ken Ashwell (2012: 211) observes:

> Often lies go undetected because we do not attempt to detect them, a phenomenon dubbed the "ostrich effect" by psychologist Aldert Vrij. It may reflect the emotional cost of recognizing and dealing with lies – in other words, people do not always want to hear the truth. Claims that lying can be detected by EEG or functional MRI scanning have been disputed and the field remains a contentious part of neuroscience.

Finding systematic ways to detect lying has, actually, fascinated us for a long time. In 1730, the British novelist Daniel Defoe wrote an essay in which he recommended taking the pulse of a suspected criminal in order to determine if he or she was lying. Then, in 1878, the Italian physiologist Antonio Mosso invented a machine called a *plethysmograph* that could record and measure the emotional reactions by subjects who were asked various questions. In this way, Mosso was able to correlate these reactions to cardiovascular and respiratory patterns. The machine recorded changes in blood pressure and pulse rate that Mosso explained as the effects of lying. In 1892, Sir James MacKenzie, a medical doctor, developed the *clinical polygraph* to detect pulses in his patients. Eventually this led to the invention of the modern *polygraph* device. Since then, there has been an abundant use of this machine by police forces and forensic investigators. Although contentious, the validity of the polygraph rests on the widely-documented fact in psychology and semiotics that the body undergoes predictable changes when lying occurs. Lie detection is an area, therefore, to which FS[1] can contribute directly, given that the changes that the body undergoes are specific kinds of signs. For the sake of convenience, these can be called "lie-signs" or L-signs, for short. They can be defined as the unwitting telltale signs produced spontaneously by the body during deception.

2.1.1 Autonomic Nervous System

The Autonomic Nervous System (ANS) produces, or at least mediates, most of the physiological changes that occur when people experience emotions. It is the source of L-signs, since it regulates the involuntary reactions emanating from the vertebrate nervous system. Recording these reactions is the goal of lie detection technologies. The ANS consists of nerves that connect the heart, blood vessels, smooth muscles and glands. It consists of two components: the *sympathetic division*, which mobilizes bodily resources, and the *parasympathetic division*, which conserves them:

Table 1: The components of the Autonomic Nervous System

Parasympathetic (Conserves):	Sympathetic (Mobilizes):
the pupils constrict	the pupils dilate
salivation is stimulated	salivation is inhibited
the bronchial passages are constricted	the bronchial passages are dilated
respiration decreases	respiration increases
the heart rate decreases	the heart rate increases
digestion is stimulated	digestion is inhibited
the bladder contracts	the bladder relaxes

The ANS is directive of many common behaviors. One of these is called *Fight or Flight Response*, whereby a person faced with peril may react by fighting or fleeing. The specific response, and its degree, is regulated by the release of adrenal hormones that are sent through the body. The conflictual or perilous situation does not have to be extreme; it could be as simple as a confrontation between two people or the simple fear of something or someone (for example, airplane flying or interacting with an authority figure).

When deception is involved, the ANS is the source of L-signs, such as sweating, pupil dilation, goose bumps, among others. Interpreting these correctly is of obvious importance for the purposes of criminal investigations. Devices such as the polygraph monitor key arousal indicators, such as changes in heart rate, blood pressure, respiration rate and galvanic skin response (a change in the electrical conductivity of the skin that occurs when sweat glands activity is increased). But these indicators may or may not be L-signs. To the semiotician, only by matching them to the situation, the context, and other variables that characterize human interaction can they be construed as constituting signs of deception. Only in this way is the probability of making an accurate conclusion about the truth or falsity of some statement achievable.

2.1.2 The Polygraph

The polygraph device used today was designed originally by William Moulton Marston in 1917. He built it to measure the changes in blood pressure that characterize deception. Marston was also the creator of the comic book character *Wonder Woman* who captured evildoers with a rope, forcing them to tell the truth. The polygraph was developed further in 1921 by John A. Larson, an American psychologist, and was quickly adopted by police forces throughout North America. The device was further improved in 1945 by American criminologist John Edward Reid. In 1966, the American Polygraph Association was established. Its mission is to supervise the use of polygraphs and to establish qualifications for the examiners.

The polygraph records the ANS-based physical changes that occur in subjects as they react to questions. The measurements are accurate, but what they tell us is open to question. For this reason, polygraph results are not acceptable in most courts of law. The best-known example of the polygraph's unreliability in some instances is that of Gary Ridgway, the "Green River Killer," who murdered prostitutes in and around the Green River in Washington State. In 1983, he was brought in several times for questioning by the police, but he denied everything convincingly and passed two polygraph tests (McNab 2010: 56).

The polygraph is useful mainly as an investigative tool before a case is sent to trial. The questions are the key to polygraph testing. Some are related directly to the crime; others are unrelated or only slightly so, but are included as "control questions" that improve the accuracy of the test, because they establish a response pattern for truth-telling that can be compared to the response pattern that might reveal lying. Each question is designed to elicit a *yes* or *no* answer. If a person lies, the graph will typically show a change in one or more of the indicators being recorded. A polygraph, as mentioned, monitors changes in blood pressure, pulse, respiration, the electrical conductivity of the skin, and muscular movements. These are transmitted through a small panel unit into synchronized readings on moving graph paper. The parallel graphs are then correlated and interpreted to determine whether the subject is lying:

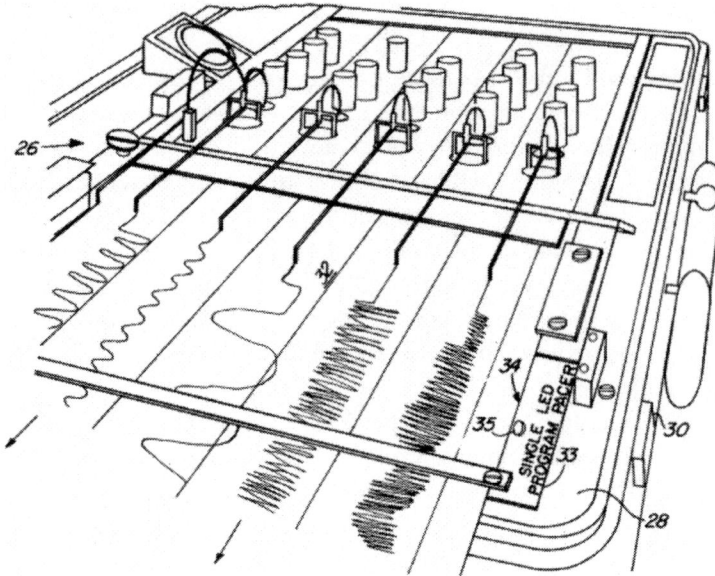

Figure 7: The polygraph

As discussed several times, the semiotician would not consider the results of polygraph tests as accurate in any absolute way. They are only suggestive. The likelihood that the changes recorded by the polygraph are truly L-signs increases only when other kinds of tests and lie-detection strategies point in the same direction. This can be called the Principle of Synchronization and defined as the principle whereby the probability of detecting a lie increases in proportion to the similitude of outcomes that results from using various lie-detection techniques in combination.

2.1.3 Other Lie-Detection Devices and Techniques

In 1972, the American inventor Allen Bell developed a device called a *psychological stress evaluator*, which detects slight tremblings in the voice. This too is now used to determine if a person is telling the truth or not. The device is accurate, but what it tells us is open to interpretation. However, if used together with a polygraph, and with other lie-detection techniques, then its usefulness increases.

Another lie-detection technique is the *Facial Action Coding System*, developed by psychologist Paul Ekman (2003) and his research associates. FACS is also controversial because the measurements it has produced have turned out to be highly variable, making it unlikely that one can confidently use it with all suspects. The main reason is that people of different cultures or with dissimilar social backgrounds show substantial differences in their facial expressions. Without knowing the impact of cultural factors, it is risky to interpret certain expressions as L-signs. Nevertheless, various police forces use FACS in combination with polygraph and other tests to help assess if testimony or verbally reported evidence is believable or not, at least in an initial hypothetical fashion.

Used by the great fictional detectives Dupin and Holmes, the strategy of interrogation itself is still the most effective technique for fleshing out truth from falsehood. In contemporary police interrogations, the following three types of questioning techniques are used in a sequential manner:

1. The irrelevant question phase consists of questions meant to establish a baseline at the beginning of a session: *What is your full name? Where do you live?* This is sometimes called the Control Question Test (CQT) phase because the response patterns it produces allows interrogators to control subsequent responses of the suspect and evaluate them contrastively.
2. The relevant question phase consists of questions that aim to link the suspect to the criminal event, encouraging the subject to lie if he or she is indeed guilty: *You where there, weren't you? You knew the victim, didn't you?*
3. The comparison phase consists of questions about the crime that can be compared with the responses in (1) and (2): *Why did you use a rope to strangle her? Why did you use a butcher knife?*

Video and audio recordings of the interrogations can subsequently be analyzed systematically for further lie-detection analysis. Liars consistently take longer to start answering questions than truth-tellers, except when they have time to plan their answers, whereby they actually start their responses more quickly. Liars also talk less and their speech is agitated (DePaulo et al. 1996). They tend to repeat words and phrases more than others and use fewer hand gestures to deliver their responses.

James Pennebaker (2011), an American social psychologist, has developed a method known as the *Linguistic Inquiry and Word Count* (LIWC) that purportedly allows interrogators to sift out lies during interrogations by observing specific grammatical and lexical cues in the conversation repartee. Pennebaker found that deception frequently entails the unconscious use of distinct types of markers, such as, for example, the use of fewer first-person pronouns (*I, we*), allowing the liars to distance themselves from their statements, and the use of fewer exclusionary words (*but, except, or*), allowing them to differentiate between what they did and did not do. Again, this technique does not seem to take into account cultural background influences. Some languages do not have the obligatory use of pronouns (as is the case in Italian). Native speakers of these languages, when being interrogated in a different language (such as English), will likely not use such markers in the same way as do native speakers, due to linguistic and cultural interference. So, the LIWC, like the FACS, the polygraph and other lie-detection techniques, produces results that require semiotic-based interpretation and, only in line with the Principle of Synchronization, can they have any foreseeable effective usage in criminal investigations.

Some techniques, however, may transcend the influence of cultural background factors. A lie will activate the blood flow in both brain hemispheres; telling the truth, on the other hand, activates flow in one hemisphere only. This fact has led to the development of another lie-detection device known as a *cognitive polygraph*, a brain-scanning apparatus that is being used more and more by interrogators and forensic scientists because it produces results that are free of subjective control. Even really good liars cannot stop the scan from detecting a lie-based flow pattern.

Other devices and techniques used today include:
- *Voice Analysis*, which uses recording equipment and computers that detect minute fluctuations in voice patterns that characterize lying;
- *Functional Magnetic Resonance Imaging* (fMRI), which shows which portions of the brain are using more oxygen during a specific task; fMRI can potentially catch the lie at the source, but the neural systems that relate to lying are currently poorly understood – a 2007 episode of the television program *Mythbusters* showed, in fact, that it is unreliable with some people;
- *Brain fingerprinting*, which uses electroencephalography to detect changes in brain processes thought to occur while lying.

Voice Analysis is based on the fact that the physical properties of speech sounds are connected to emotional systems in the brain. Thus, such features as tone of voice and rate of speech may be signs of lying. Functional Magnetic Resonance Imaging (fMRI) does not require any physical contact with the brain. It produces images similar to X rays that show which parts of the brain are active while a person carries out a specific mental or physical task. An electroencephalogram is an instrument that measures and records the electrical voltages produced by neurons (nerve cells) in the brain. A recording of this electrical activity is also called an electroencephalogram. Both electroencephalograph and electroencephalogram are abbreviated EEG.

2.1.4 Markedness Theory

Lying leaves its signs on or through the body because it activates the ANS and neural systems in specific ways. When someone is telling a lie, the pupils tend to dilate, an eyebrow may lift, and the corner of the mouth may twitch. The human body is not designed for lying; so when humans lie, their bodies react in a tell-tale fashion, producing recognizable L-signs. Using basic semiotic theory, it can be said, furthermore, that L-signs are *marked* forms. In order to understand what this means, it is instructive to go over the theory of markedness in a schematic way here.

A founding principle of semiotics is called *opposition theory* (Andrews 1990, Andrews and Tobin 1996, Battistella 1990, 1996), which claims that we grasp the meanings of signs not in isolation, but in relation to other forms. Saussure (1916) called this principle *différence*. When we hear the word *cat* we recognize it as a distinct meaning-bearing sign because it is differentiated in our minds from other words in various ways. For example, at the level of sound, we perceive *cat* as standing in contrast to a quasi-identical word such as *rat*, recognizing the relevant *différence* through a differential sound cue in the initial position of the two words: *cat*-versus-*rat* = /k/-versus-/r/. At the level of conceptualization, we perceive *cat* as standing in contrast to *rat* through denotative differences that can be shown as a *feline*-versus-*rodent* opposition (among others). In other words, we come to understand the meaning of *cat* in relation to other signs at different levels. In the late 1920s, a group of linguists met regularly in Prague, Czech Republic, to discuss and develop this theory. Known as the Prague Linguistic Circle, they established it as the primary approach to the study of sign systems.

The essence of the theory is that there exists a small set of binary concepts, such as *yes*-versus-*no* and *right*-versus-*left* that are encoded by the sign systems of cultures across the world. The two parts of such binary oppositions are called *poles*. Other kinds of concepts fall between the two poles, implying "gradience" in conceptualization. For instance, in the *white*-versus-*black* polar opposition, color concepts such as *yellow, red*, and *blue* are gradient ones since they fall between these two poles. This resonates with the research on color terms – words for the polar concepts (expressed in English with the terms *white* and *black* or *light* and *dark*) have been found in all languages; gradient ones (*yellow, green, pink*, and so on), on the other hand, show great variation across the world's languages. In like manner, between the polar concepts of *day* and *night*, which are encoded in different linguistic ways across the world, concepts such as *twilight, dawn, noon, afternoon*, and so on, show culture-specific gradience. Polar concepts form binary oppositions; gradient concepts may or may not (depending on use). In English, it is difficult to put, say, *yellow* into a binary opposition with another color, and if this is done it is a selection carried out for a specific purpose. Moreover, as psychologist Charles K. Ogden (1932) pointed out early on in the development of the theory, some oppositions, such as *town-*versus-*country*, are binary in some cultures, but not universal. These details and complexities need not occupy us here. Suffice it to say that opposition theory is a basic tool in semiotics.

Like Saussure, the Prague School theorists first applied opposition theory to the study of sound systems, identifying various types and tokens of oppositional structure within them. In an opposition, such as the one between /p/ and /b/ (for example, *pin-*versus-*bin*), one of the two is considered to be more basic, and the other connected to it in some way. In this case, the /p/ is assigned basic status, called *unmarked*, and the /b/ is assigned a *marked* status for several reasons – it is less frequent in initial position; it has a feature (it is produced with the vocal cords vibrating) that makes it more noticeable; and so on. What-ever the reason, the idea is that in an opposition one pole is perceived as being basic (*unmarked*) and the other as derivative or related to it in some way (*marked*). The marked one always stands out. For instance, in a simple alarm bell system, based on a *silent-*versus-*on* opposition, we assume the system to be in a *silent* mode most of the time. When the alarm bell goes *on* we instantly understand that something is wrong. *Silence* is the unmarked (or expected) mode in this binary system; *on* is the marked or unexpected (but more informa-tion-bearing) mode.

Many polar concepts seem to be formed on the basis of an overriding "meta-opposition," as it can be called: *presence-*versus-*absence*. In the *day-*versus-*night* opposition, for example, *night* is more likely to be conceived as being "absence of daylight," while *day* would not normally be conceived as being "absence of night." Not all oppositions show such clear-cut markedness, however. They may be equipollent, as in the *give-*versus-*accept* opposition, since either pole in it could be assigned unmarked status, depending on the situation or on the viewpoint of those using the opposition. In benevolent societies *giving* is the expected mode of interaction; but in the case of those suffering poverty, *accept-ing* is the unmarked form because of conditions.

Now, the claim to be made here is that markedness theory has specific implications for lie-detection in forensic investigations. Simply put, the *lie-*versus-*truth* opposition is a universal meta-opposition with lying as the marked pole (= absence of truth). L-signs are, in effect, marked signs. Research would certainly have to be conducted to determine which bodily signs are marked for lying and which are not through basic semiotic analysis in combination with psychology and neuroscience.

2.1.5 Kinesics

The general study of bodily signs is called *kinesics*. It was first developed by the American anthropologist Ray L. Birdwhistell (1952), who analyzed slow-motion films of people interacting during conversations noting that specific bodily actions and reactions surfaced typically in them. He adopted notions from linguistics to characterize the patterns, believing that they were similar in function to the grammatical and lexical signs of language. For this reason, the system of nonverbal signs studied in this way came to be called (and continues to be called) "body language." Kinesic signs can be innate (involuntary), learned (voluntary), or a mixture of the two. Blinking, throat clearing, and facial flushing are innate (involuntary) signs, as are facial expressions of happiness, surprise, anger, disgust, and other basic emotions. Laughing, crying, and shrugging the shoulders are examples of mixed signs. They may originate as instinctive actions, but cultural rules shape their structure, timing, and uses. Winking, raising a thumb, or saluting with the hands are learned (voluntary) signs. Logically, their meanings vary from culture to culture.

The various areas of kinesic analysis (such as eye contact, gesture, posture, and so on) will be discussed below. At this point, suffice it to say that knowledge of kinesics can be useful in several ways in criminal investigations: (1) it will provide a more accurate descriptive vocabulary for characterizing and thus understanding the L-signs that manifest themselves during deception; (2) it can offer a subsidiary way of assessing the truth or falsity of statements through a specialized approach to bodily analysis; (3) it can point out which L-signs are culturally marked and which are not, thus allowing investigators to consider the marked ones in their assessments of the truthfulness of people's statements.

2.2 The Face, the Eyes, and the Head

Studies have consistently documented that lies leave unconscious traces on facial expression. Meyer (2010) and Heussen, Binkofski, and Jolij (2011), for instance, have confirmed that pupil dilation does indeed surface in deception, although the degree will vary considerably from culture to culture and according to the nature of the interrogation process. This means that, by and large, lies can be tracked, measured, and recorded in the structure of facial expressions as part of assessing the content of interrogations. Needless to say, those who are skilled at artifice can suppress some facial expressions, but many cannot be stopped. It would be nearly impossible to trick one's brain into camouflaging all the facial expressions that might give away one's true thoughts.

2.2.1 Facial Expression

Interest in facial expression as a vehicle of emotional communication started with Charles Darwin's book *Expression of the Emotions in Man and Animals*, which was published in 1872. Prior to Darwin, the expressions of the face were considered by philosophers, artists, and scientists to be signs for discerning personality and intelligence – not emotional or cognitive phenomena. Darwin broke from this tradition, putting emphasis instead on how facial movements revealed intentions and internal thought processes. Darwin's perspective led, a century later, to the scientific study of facial expressions. A schematic timeline of such study is the following one:

- *1960s:* Anthropologist Margaret Mead's (1964) study of isolated tribal communities suggested that facial expressions are, by and large, culture-specific.
- *1960s:* At about the same time, psychologist Silvan Tomkins and his research associates (Tomkins and Izard 1965) argued that some expressions are cross-cultural.
- *1970s–1980s:* Psychologist Gordon H. Bower (1980) linked emotional states to memory, suggesting indirectly that facial expressions may be shaped by environmental forces.
- *1970s-present time* Paul Ekman started systematic scientific work on facial expressions leading to the development and adoption of his FACS system in criminal investigations.

Ekman started his research project already in the 1960s, establishing the Human Interaction Laboratory in the Department of Psychiatry at the University of California at San Francisco in 1963. He was joined by Wallace V. Friesen in 1965 and Maureen O'Sullivan in 1974. Over the years, Ekman and his team have identified certain facial expressions as universal and others as culture-specific (Ekman 1976, 1980, 1982, 1985, 2003, Ekman and Friesen 1975). In other words, facial expression is a mixed sign system. Of special value to forensic science is Ekman's breakdown of facial expressions into units of eyebrow position, eye shape, mouth shape, nostril size, and so on, by describing their geometrical configurations. In various combinations these determine the meaning of a particular expression (see also Peck 1987). From this, a standard set of units (which he called *microexpressions*) can be catalogued and studied for consistency and variation across cultures. One of the findings has confirmed that the basic emotions (disgust, fear, anger, contempt, sadness, surprise, happiness) activate the same microexpression patterns across the world. The following is taken from Ryan et al. (2010). In the photo the last figure shows how microexpression analysis uses geometry to map the face:

Figure 8: Basic emotions (Source: Ryan, Andrew et al., *Automated Facial Expression Recognition System*: http://humansensing.cs.cmu.edu/papers/Automated.pdf)

Classificatory schemas of microexpressions provide a useful template for assessing how a subject is reacting to certain questions. They also allow investigators to flesh out culture-specific microexpressions from universal ones. This type of knowledge will certainly help in determining the truth or falsity of statements in combination with other lie-detection techniques.

2.2.2 Eye Contact

Eye contact constitutes a mixed sign system – that is, it is both natural (involuntary) and conventionally-based (voluntary). Like other species, humans perceive a direct stare as a threat or challenge and, like dogs and primates, will break eye contact as a signal of surrender. This is a universal pattern. However, many other types of eye contact patterns are shaped by culture, not nature. Knowing which is which is critical during criminal interrogations because the background or upbringing of the person being interrogated will affect how eye contact unfolds. Again, this is an area of research that FS[1] can explore, developing a typology of eye contact L-signs that would be divided into instinctive-versus-cultural categories. Below are some of the things already known about these categories:

Table 2: Eye contact patterns

Instinctive	Cultural
Staring is interpreted as a challenge; making eyes at someone is normally interpreted as flirtation	The length of time involved in eye contact conveys what kinds of relationships people have with each other in contextualized ways.
When the pupils dilate during excited states, they tend to elicit a sexual response in an observer or else reveal lying.	Making eye contact early or late during a verbal exchange indicates the kind of relationship one wishes to have with the interlocutor.
Narrow eyelids communicate pensiveness across cultures.	Southern Europeans will tend to look more into each other's eyes during conversation than will North Americans.
Making the eyebrows come nearer together communicates thoughtfulness universally; when they are made to rise they convey surprise.	In some cultures males do not look into female eyes unless they are married to them or else are members of the same family.

The eyes are a focal point on the face, and because the pupils work independently of other neural and cognitive systems, a person who is being dishonest or is holding back information will avoid eye contact around one-third of the time more than others. When they meet more than that the pupils tend to dilate or else they will constrict if he or she is hostile to someone. A good rapport with another person entails a gaze that lasts a period that is between these two extremes, with the pupils remaining normal. However, this pattern breaks down if gazing is marked radically different in other cultures. Southern Europeans show a high frequency of eye gazing, whereas the Japanese tend to gaze at the neck rather than the eyes while conversing. The gaze, in other words, must be interpreted in cultural terms during forensic investigations, otherwise we end up with wrongful assessments.

It is interesting to note that crime programs on television, documentary and fictional, often bring facial expression and eye contact research into the plot. One program, *Lie to Me* (Fox 2009–2011), used Ekman's FACS system as the central investigative technique in its narrative. A clinical psychologist was sent out to analyze people and find out information that they might have been hiding. He did this by reading their body language and facial expressions and then, without the suspects realizing it, forcing them to admit to the truth. *Lie to Me* and the scientific research that it brought into its plots, however, did not take cultural variation into account. To wit: in some cultures looking away from those in authority is a sign of respect, not deception. Interpretations of facial expressions, in isolation from other factors, can be virtually useless.

2.2.3 Head Movement

The two most common head movements are the nod and the shake. The former is a positive gesture indicating agreement and the latter a negative one indicating disagreement in western culture; in others, however, the opposite may be true, as Morris et al. (1979) discovered. In some Slavic cultures, nodding means disapproval, while shaking from left to right means approval. The head position is also indicative of specific meanings in western culture. Some of these are as follows:

– the "head up" position (with the head remaining still) characterizes the person who has a neutral attitude about what he or she is hearing;
– the "head tilt" position is usually assumed instead by the person who is interested in what is being said or in who is speaking;
– the "head down" position signals a negative or judgmental attitude;
– the "hands behind the head" position conveys confidence and authority.

Interpreting head movements correctly is, again, an important part of assessing truth or falsity during investigations. When combined with microexpression, eye contact, and other bodily-based forms of communication it can lead to more accurate appraisals of interrogations. To put it in more technical semiotic terms, while the facial signifier, or physical form, of some expression may occur across the world, its signified, or meaning, may vary considerably. Determining how bodily semiosis is to be interpreted is, therefore, a crucial part of FS[1]. Some psychologists and anthropologists consider nonverbal semiosis to be a more fundamental form of communication than vocal language (Bremer and Roodenberg 1991, Armstrong, Stokoe, and Wilcox 1995) and thus much less likely to vary across cultures. Discoveries in neuroscience have, in fact, shown that nonverbal signs are produced and processed differently from words. Spoken language is processed in the cerebral cortex, a more developed area of the brain that is unique to human beings. In contrast, nonverbal cues – such as smiling, staring, and clenching the fists – are processed in the more primitive limbic system.

2.3 Body Language

Facial expressions, eye contact patterns, and head movements are all part of what has come to be called body language – a coordinated system of meaning-making and communication that can complement, supplement, or even substitute vocal language (Knapp 1978: 94–95). As Duncan and Fiske (1977: xi) observe, and as we have seen, body language "can be construed as having a definite organization or structure." Actually, the three areas just discussed (facial expressions, eye contact, head movements) are generally treated as separate domains of investigation, with posture, touch, gesture, and the zones people maintain between them while conversing being considered as more proper to the study of body language.

2.3.1 Posture

Posture is a major area of research in kinesics, communicating information about one's sense of self, moods, motivation, and attitudes. A pose, like a facial expression, can be broken down into a series of specific units conveying various meanings. These are mixed signs, being partly involuntary and partly learned or acquired in social context. The goal of FS[1] would be to separate the involuntary or unmarked poses, from the culture-specific ones or marked ones. For example, some research exists to show that the following are unmarked, that is, they tend to occur across cultures with moderate variation (Latiolais-Hargrave 2008):
1. Slumped posture = low spirits
2. Erect posture = high spirits, energy and confidence
3. Leaning forward = open and interested behavior
4. Leaning away = defensive or disinterested behavior
5. Crossed arms = defensive behavior
6. Uncrossed arms = willingness to listen

Most other poses are marked culturally, and thus shaped by historically-acquired behavioral signifiers (Synnot 1993). In the human species, posture is not only a reflex of biology, but also a product of history and tradition. It entails interpretation, as does everything else in human semiosis.

2.3.2 Touch

The study of touch patterns falls more specifically under the rubric of *haptics* (from Greek *haptikos* "grasping," "touching"). These form a mixed sign system. Using the hands to shield oneself from an attack is an innate kinesic sign. So too is raising the hand to warn someone. But most other haptic signs are culture-specific. These include patting someone on the arm, shoulder, or back to indicate agreement or praise, linking arms to designate companionship, putting an arm around the shoulder to indicate friendship or intimacy, holding hands to express intimacy, hugging to convey happiness, and so on.

It is unclear why haptic communication varies so much across cultures. The reason may have a basis in cultural perceptions of the body's meanings. Some people perceive the skin to be a surface "sheath." Others regard the body as a "container" and thus think of themselves as "contained" in their skin. The zones of privacy that define Self-space in these cultures, therefore, include the clothes that cover the skin. Others feel instead that the Self is located down within the body shell, resulting in a totally different expression of haptic behaviors. People in such cultures are in general more tolerant of crowds, of noise levels, of the touching of hands, of eye contact, and of body odors than others.

2.3.3 Gesture

When a child tells a lie, he or she will tend to cover the mouth with one or both hands immediately afterwards. This gesture is used unwittingly later in life as well. Often the adult pulls the hand away at the last moment, touching the nose instead. The latter gesture is more sophisticated and less obvious, but it still reveals mendacity.

There seems to be a universal tendency in us to cover the mouth with the hands when we see, speak, or hear untruths. The most common form is the "mouth guard," with the hand concealing the mouth and the thumb pressing against the cheek as the brain instructs the hand to suppress the deceitful words that are being said in a symbolic manner. Sometimes the gesture may involve only several fingers over the mouth or even a closed fist. Some people try to disguise this gesture with a false cough. Sophisticated versions of this sign are the nose, eye, and ear touch gestures. The first consists of several light rubs below the nose; the second of a rubbing motion just below the eye; and the third of putting the hand over the ear. Other signs are the neck scratch, with the index finger scratching below the earlobe or on the side of the neck, and the collar pull, whereby the collar of a shirt is pulled away from the neck by a finger or the entire hand. While covering is a gestural strategy across the world, the specific forms are, again, subject to substantial variation across cultures. Again, it will be a research task of FS[1] to separate the unmarked or universal gestures from the contextually-shaped or marked ones and develop a relevant taxonomy for the purposes of criminal investigations.

Not all hand-to-face gestures imply deceit in some way. A few common ones that do not in western culture are as follows:

- The "fingers in the mouth" gesture, whereby the fingers are placed in the mouth, indicates generally that the person is under pressure.
- The "hand on the cheek" gesture, with the hand supporting the head, is normally a sign that the person is bored.

- The "evaluation" gesture, whereby a closed hand is made to rest on the cheek, often with the index finger pointing upwards, signals that the person is probably losing interest but nevertheless wants to appear interested for the sake of courtesy.
- The "chin-stroking" gesture, with one hand moving to the chin and stroking it, is a sign that the person is making a decision.

Kinesic research has shown that the open palm is associated with truth, honesty, allegiance, or submission in many cultures across the world. This might explain why, in most legal and juridical systems, the right palm is held in the air when someone is giving evidence in a court of law, as he or she takes some pledge or oath to tell the truth. When people wish to be totally honest or open they will hold one or both palms out to the other person, saying something like "to be perfectly honest" or "to be open with you," to accompany the gesture. When someone hides the palms (usually behind the back), as do children when they are lying, the person is generally trying to hide something or is not being open about something. At that point the body's lie detector system kicks in and a recognizable incongruence manifests itself with reactions (L-signs) such as fidgeting, sweating, and the like. Most people find it difficult, if not impossible, to lie with their palms exposed.

Rubbing the palms together is a way of communicating positive expectation. This is why someone who throws a pair of dice in gambling rubs his or her hands first. It is also the reason why a master of ceremonies tends to rub his or her palms as he or she announces to the audience "we have been looking forward to our next speaker." The speed at which a person rubs the hands signals the degree of expectation he or she brings to the situation – the greater the rubbing the more the expectation.

Clenching the hands together in a central, raised, or lowered position (depending on whether the person is standing or sitting) is a confidence gesture. But it can also be a frustration gesture if the clenching is robust to the point of turning the knuckles white.

"Steepling" is the term used by Birdwhistell (1970) to indicate the gesture of touching the fingers together to form a "steeple." It can be raised or lowered depending on the body's orientation, but it invariably communicates confidence and authority. It is a kind of "know-it-all" gesture. The raised steeple is used when the steepler is doing the talking and the lowered one when he or she is listening.

Gripping the hands, arms, and wrists behind the body generally conveys superiority or confidence. The palm-in-palm gesture (behind the back) is the most common of the gripping gestures and should not be confused with the wrist-gripping gesture which is, instead, a signal of frustration or an attempt at self-control. One hand grips the other wrist or arm as if to prevent it from striking out. The further the hand is moved up the arm, the angrier is the person likely to be.

Thumb displays – with the other fingers in a pocket or under a jacket lapel, and the thumbs protruding out – are used to communicate confidence, domination, superiority, and even aggression. These become most obvious when the person gives a contradictory verbal message. When a lawyer turns to a jury and says "In my humble opinion..." as he or she displays the thumbs, tilting back his or her head, the effect on the jury is a negative and counteractive one – it makes the jury feel that the lawyer is insincere or pompous. To appear sincere, the lawyer should approach the jury with one foot forward, an open palm display and a slight sloop. These convey humility and honesty.

The folding and crossing of the arms send out specific kinds of signals. Folding them generally implies that the person has negative thoughts about the interlocutor and is thus paying less attention to what he or she is saying. Folding both arms together typically undergirds an attempt to hide from an unfavorable situation. It is also a negative sign in some situations, indicating that the person disagrees with what someone is saying. If the arms are gripped tightly it reveals a negative but restrained attitude. A variant of this sign is the partial arm gesture, with one hand holding the other near or at the elbow. This shows lack of self-confidence or humility. It is used typically by someone about to receive an award.

American linguist David McNeill (1992, 2005) showed that during conversation gesture is an unconscious complementary sign system to vocal language. He videotaped a large number of people as they spoke, gathering a substantial amount of data on the gesture signs that accompany speech, which he termed *gesticulants*. His findings suggest that these are used in concomitance with words because they exhibit images that cannot be communicated overtly in vocal utterances. Psychologically, they are traces to what the speaker is thinking about. This kind of research is of obvious relevance to lie detection. If one can decode the gesticulants correctly, one can determine what the person being interrogated may be really thinking.

McNeill's gesticulant category is, actually, what Ekman (1973) calls an *illustrator*. There are other illustrators, including the following:
- *Emblems*: These are gestures used to translate words or phrases. Examples are the *Okay* sign, the *Come here* sign, the hitchhiking sign, waving, and obscene gestures.
- *Affect Displays*: These communicate emotional meaning. Examples include the hand actions that accompany expressions of happiness, surprise, fear, anger, sadness, contempt, disgust, and so on.

- *Regulators*: These are designed to regulate or control the speech of someone else. Examples include the hand movements for *Keep going, Slow down,* and *What else happened?*
- *Adaptors*: These indicate some need or reveal some state of mind. Examples are scratching the head when puzzled and rubbing the forehead when worried.

Because they are partly involuntary and partly learned in context, research on gesture within FS[1] will have to determine which are which, so that interpretations of interrogations can be tempered with the insight that they will vary from individual to individual, depending on situation and context. According to psychologist Meier-Faust (2002), kinesic information can be used to assess the intensity of emotion involved during vocal communication and, thus, to examine if the two – body language and vocal language – are complementary (consonant) or not (dissonant). Dissonance can be defined simply as a variance between the expected and documented sign patterns of complementarity and the meaning of a message. Dissonance produces L-signs; consonance does not.

2.3.4 Proxemics

The study of the zones people maintain between their bodies during conversation comes under a different rubric than body language study, even though it still studies the meanings we assign to the body. The rubric is called *proxemics*, a field that researches how individuals and groups perceive and organize the zones they maintain between each other as they interact. This field was founded by the American anthropologist Edward T. Hall in the late 1950s, who developed it substantively over the subsequent thirty years (Hall 1959, 1963a, 1963b, 1964, 1966, 1968, 1974, 1976, 1983). It became a branch of semiotics with Eco (1968) and Watson (1970). As a soldier during World War II, Hall had noticed that people maintained recognizable distances among themselves during conversations, coming soon to realize that many (if not most) breakdowns in communication were attributable to infractions of these zone patterns. The unconscious differences in the ways that people of diverse cultures perceive interpersonal zones and in the ways they behave within them play a powerful role in influencing the outcomes of face-to-face interactions. Hall measured and assessed these critical interpersonal zones with statistical techniques. The zones can be measured with great accuracy, varying according to age, gender, and other social variables.

Some proxemic patterns seem to be universal. For example, the immediate physical zone around a human being constitutes a sphere of privacy. The size of the zone will vary somewhat from culture to culture, but all cultures perceive this zone as an intimate one. The next is within a person's reach, but falls outside the privacy zone. This is the zone in which handshaking can occur. The intimate zone (from 0–18 in.), Hall surmises, is rooted in our biological past, and is thus based on our innate sense of territoriality, which involves establishing boundaries. In the close phase (from 0–6 in.) the senses are activated and the presence of the other is unmistakable. This phase is typically reserved for lovemaking, comforting, and protecting; the far phase (from 6–18 in.) is the zone in which family members and close friends interact under normal conditions. The actual dimensions may vary somewhat, but the intimate zone and its phases seem to have a universal validity.

The study of proxemic zones has only little relevance to FS[1]. The main implication is that behaviors have been found to change in specific ways if the intimate zone is violated during interactions. Breaching this zone during interrogation will put a suspect into a state of nervousness or discomfort, making it more likely that he or she will be emotionally inclined to tell the truth or at least emit L-signs even if he or she is a skilled liar.

2.4 First-Order Forensic Semiotics

As argued throughout this chapter, lying produces specific kinds of bodily signs, which we have called L-signs. The study of these signs is a major focus of FS[1]. As Latiolais-Hargrave (2008: 20) notes: "Most individuals only focus on the verbal part of an encounter, but during an average 15 minute meeting approximately 400 different non-verbal messages are being exchanged." Birdwhistell (1952) estimates that not more than 35 percent of messages exchanged in face-to-face interaction are purely verbal. As we have seen, nonverbal signs are more reliable than speech as vehicles for deciphering the intentions of speakers, because, by sheer quantity alone, the nonverbal dimension of human interaction offers a larger source of information for detection purposes. In a phrase, body language is a major key to unlocking a suspect's inner psychological and emotional states.

2.4.1 The Body as a Lie Detector System

The unconscious or unwitting bodily signs that appear spontaneously during conversations reveal what a person is thinking. Most of the time, it is impossible to lie without the body reacting in some predictable way. There is almost always incongruence between body signage and verbal content as one lies, adverting an interlocutor that something suspicious is going on. In effect, our brain registers a kind of tilt when it perceives this incongruence.

Nevertheless, there are many people, such as actors and skilled orators, as well as inveterate criminals, who can control their bodily system, counteracting its natural instincts, to give the impression that they are telling the truth. Knowing how to use smiles, nods, and winks to cover up lies takes skill, but it is possible to do. But even expert liars cannot suppress all L-signs. As kinesic research has shown, facial muscular twitching, dilation and contraction of the pupils, an increased rate of eye blinking, and a general lack of composure in posture are L-signs that can rarely be contained, no matter how skilled a liar may be at body-language control. These are monitored by the brain's "lie detector" apparatus. Obviously, to lie successfully, the body must be hidden from sight. It is easier to lie in writing or on the phone than it is in a face-to-face encounter.

There is one possible exception to all this and that concerns the case of the pathological or compulsive liar for the reason that the body has adjusted to the pathology attenuating many of the lie indicators. Severe forms of pathological lying fall under the medical category of *pseudologia fantastica*. The individual may or may not be aware that he or she is lying, relating fantasies more than facts and events. Interestingly, research has found that pseudologia fantastica emerges in juvenile delinquents, becoming a strategy of such individuals later on in life (King and Ford 1988). Currently, there is no known way to identify a pathological liar other than previous experience with the individual or contrasting testimony.

L-signs are marked forms. By filming subjects during and after questioning sessions the veracity of their statements can be analyzed through kinesic analysis. In accordance with the Principle of Synchronization, if the analysis matches the results of other lie-detection techniques (polygraph tests, FACS analysis, and so on), then one can conclude with a high degree of certainty that some form of deception is involved. The objective of FS[1] would be to compile, describe, and classify the marked and unmarked signs that appear on the body during interrogations. These can then be used to make sense of what a suspect says during interviews. It is difficult to sustain deceptive behavior for a long period of time. Even veteran criminals, who tend to be effective liars by conscious control over their kinesic movements, will still unconsciously betray their intent because of exasperation. All this is the reason why, today, suspects sit in a chair with their entire body and face visible under a bright light while the interrogations are taped. By literally putting the criminal "in the spotlight" the possibility of detecting deception increases considerably.

2.4.2 Interviewing

Awareness of the power of kinesic research to detect lying, many police forces and forensic units throughout the world are adopting various interviewing styles based on the implications deriving from this type of research. For example, in 1984 Frederik Link and Glenn Foster devised an interview system, which they call the *Kinesic Interview Technique* (KIT), that incorporates many of the kinesic concepts discussed in this chapter. Link taught the technique to military police schools, agents of the FBI, and other federal government agencies – a fact that in itself suggests that it is believed by the authorities to be reliable. Foster used the technique in connection with the polygraph and other lie-detection devices, finding that it produced highly synchronous results. KIT allowed investigators to notice and interpret basic behavioral signs of stress during interviews. But, again, the forensic semiotician would issue a word of caution, because of cultural markedness phenomena that shape the interpretation of certain signs. Looking people in the eyes when spoken to, especially by authority figures, is considered bad manners by some people, not a sign of evasion and guilt.

Another interview technique based on kinesic notions that has been adopted by police forces is the so-called *Reid Technique* system, named after John Reid (1991). The interviewer session in this case is designed to stimulate facial expressions, poses, hand movements, and the like directly which, as we have seen, can reveal a lot about the emotional state of the suspect. Because they are prompted there may, however, be a possibility that they are purely reactive signs rather than real L-signs.

Taken together, the groups of indicators (L-signs) that can be compiled with the use of technology, semiotic theory, kinesics, facial analysis, and the like can indicate if there is the presence of above-average emotional distress and possible lying in criminal interrogations. These are now implicit in what has come to be called the *Behavioral Analysis Interview* (BAI), developed by police. During a 20–30 minute interview, the investigator asks background questions such as name, address, age, marital status and occupation. As we have already discussed, this kind of interview strategy permits the investigator to establish the suspect's "normal" responsive bodily reflex behavior. Then by changing the nature of the questions to be more accusatory, the investigator can start to detect the appearance of L-signs in a systematic fashion and interpret them in a semiotic way, taking culture and other aspects of the signs into account.

Chapter 3
Signs of Identity

Ex-Professor Moriarty of mathematical celebrity is the Napoleon of crime, Watson.

Sir Arthur Conan Doyle (1859–1930)

As discussed previously, modern forensic science and crime fiction emerged at the same time towards the end of the nineteenth century. The thinking method employed by C. Auguste Dupin or Sherlock Holmes to solve crimes, which Peirce called abduction, is what unites the two. This method is used by the detective to make sense of the clues left at a crime scene and then to connect them cohesively so that the perpetrator can be identified. It is basic fictional detective method; and it is basic forensic science. As Peirce (1931–1958, volume 7, p. 231) observed, abduction is more powerful than the other logical processes (induction and deduction) even though it really is no more than guessing:

> No new truth can come from induction or from deduction. It can only come from abduction; and abduction is, after all, nothing but guessing. We are therefore bound to hope that, although the possible explanations of our facts may be strictly innumerable, yet our mind will be able, in some finite number of guesses, to guess the sole true explanation of them. That we are bound to assume, independently of any evidence that it is true. Animated by that hope, we are to proceed to the construction of a hypothesis.

Peirce was drawn to the Sherlock Holmes stories, because Holmes' solutions to crimes come from hunches rather than just simple conclusions based on evidence. In *Study in Scarlet* (1886), for example, Holmes claims that his solution to the crime came about by "intuitive clue gathering." When Watson asks Holmes to explain what he means, he replies: "Ah, that is good luck. I could only explain the balance of probability. I did not expect to be so accurate." Without scientific tools like DNA fingerprinting, Holmes solved crimes on the basis of reasoning alone. The new tools make criminal investigations more solid, but they have not changed the kind of inferential guesswork involved that makes such investigations an art. Interestingly, the creator of Sherlock Holmes, Sir Arthur Conan Doyle, was a medical student at the University of Edinburgh in 1877 where he was impressed by one of his professors, Dr. Joseph Bell, a pioneering forensic pathologist. Doyle became Bell's assistant and was thus able to observe his mentor's crime detection skills in action. Bell would often make remarks on the walking style and linguistic accent of strangers, using these signs to identify them in terms of their provenance and profession. Incredibly, Bell was generally right. So impressed was Conan Doyle that he modeled his fictional sleuth after Bell who would supposedly say, as does Holmes, "It was elementary," after diagnosing a patient.

In this chapter, we will look at the tools used in forensic science in more detail and at the relevance of forensic semiotics to the task of uncovering the identities of perpetrators. The analysis of fingerprint, DNA, and other kinds of evidence is the starting point in a criminal investigation. At first, these clues denote something specific about a crime scene; upon further analysis, they start engaging the detective's abductive intellect, as he or she starts connecting them to potential suspects. At that point they become "signs of identity" that establish traces or links to specific individuals. There is a growing sense (and perhaps even movement) to make explicit the use of semiotic notions in crime detection. Crime scenes consist of clues that need to be interpreted as sign structures – What does it stand for? Why did the perpetrator use this particular object? There are, actually, several examples that suggest a nascent police movement that advocates, or is at least contemplating, the use of semiotics in interpreting specific aspects of crimes (Nicaso and Danesi 2013).

3.1 Prints

The collection of prints of all kinds, from fingerprints to tire tracks, is critical evidence used in developing an hypothesis about a crime and who may have been its congener. They are key signs of identity. Early civilizations were well aware of the value of fingerprints for identification purposes (Beavan 2001). The ancient Babylonians impressed their fingers into clay tables for business reasons, presumably to be able to track and identify someone should the need arise. In 200 BCE, Chinese rulers used thumbprints for identification purposes on documents sent to government officials, believing that they were more reliable than other forms of identity. In the seventh century, an Arab merchant named Soleiman described how a debtor's fingerprints were placed on a bill and given to the lender as legal proof of the debt.

Forensic scientists collect various types of prints, not just fingerprints. DNA is now classified as a type of fingerprint, given that it identifies someone with virtual certainty. Also collected, if they are present at a crime scene, are footprints, shoeprints, tire prints (or tracks), and even voiceprints.

3.1.1 Fingerprints

As already discussed, the first systematic use of fingerprint analysis can be traced to 1877, when William James Herschel, a British administrator in India, used it to identify prisoners. Dr. Henry Faulds, a Scottish missionary, employed fingerprints in 1879 to capture a thief in Japan, publishing the case in an 1880 issue of the journal *Nature*. Faulds (1905) eventually put forward a typology of fingerprints based on ridge patterns that is still used somewhat today. It was, as mentioned, Sir Francis Galton who made fingerprinting a central part of criminal investigations with his 1892 book *Finger Prints*, in which he demonstrated that each human being had unique fingerprints. In the same year, Argentine policeman Juan Vucetich adopted Galton's system to solve a case. The case concerned a mother called Francisca Rojas who murdered her two sons, cutting her throat in order to deflect the blame from herself and to put it on an intruder. But, Vucetich found her bloody fingerprint at the crime scene, which he presented as evidence. This evidence led to her conviction. The Argentine police immediately adopted fingerprint analysis as a basic criminal investigation procedure, spreading to police forces throughout the world.

Visible fingerprints can be photographed *in situ*, but latent (invisible) prints on nonabsorbent surfaces, such as wood or metal, must first be developed (made visible) with colored powder. The powder is dusted onto the surface, because it sticks to the oils in the prints. The fingerprints are then lifted from the surface by pressing a piece of sticky tape against the powder. They are photographed from the tape. Different chemicals are used in a crime lab to develop fingerprints left on absorbent surfaces, such as paper or cloth. These react with substances in the perspiration left in a fingerprint and form a colored image of the print. Some fingerprints can be developed only with a laser, which causes the perspiration in a fingerprint to shine with a yellow color so that it can be photographed.

One of the first scientists to classify fingerprint patterns was the nineteenth century Bohemian pathologist Jan Purkinje. Already in 1823, he classified them into transverse curves, oblique loops, ellipses, central longitudinal stria, almond whorls, circles, oblique stripes, spiral whorls, and double whorls. Some of his categories are still used today. The main ways to classify fingerprints are as follows (as discussed briefly in the opening chapter):

-   according to arch patterns, in which the ridges extend from one side of the finger to the other, rising in the center;
-   according to loop patterns, in which the ridges begin on one side of the finger, curve back sharply, and end on the same side;
-   according to whorl patterns, in which the ridges have a circular form;
-   as combinations of loops, whorls, and arches;
-   in accidental patterns with no specific forms.

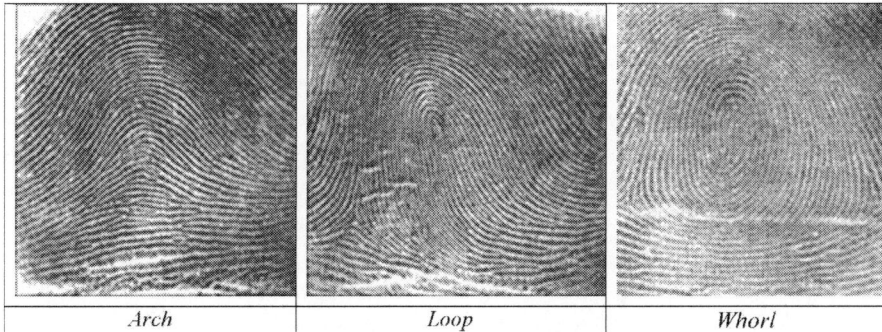

Figure 9: Fingerprint patterns

It has been found that arches make up about 5 percent of all patterns, loops about 60 percent, and whorls around 35 percent. Fingerprints are now scanned electronically into databases. Australia was the first country to establish an automatic fingerprint identification system in 1986. The FBI established their Automated Fingerprint Identification System (AFIS) in 1991. AFIS gives investigators access to a large database of fingerprints almost instantly. The system scans prints collected at a crime scene and plots them in such a way as to make it possible to compare them to prints within the database for a match. AFIS has the capability of latent searching, electronic image storage, and electronic exchange of fingerprints and responses. The process of automatically matching one or many unknown fingerprints against a database of known and unknown prints can help identify a person suspected of committing a crime or linking a suspect to other unsolved crimes.

Fingerprints are natural signs. They are, more specifically, locator indexes. An *index* is a sign that locates the referent in relation to some situation or source (chapter 1). For example, a pointing finger is a sign that literally helps us locate something in space in relation to our position to the referent. Smoke is an index of fire, pointing to where the location of the fire is. Fingerprints, therefore, can be defined as indexes pointing to a unique human source. Actually, all clues are indexes, to varying degrees, since they can be used either to point to a perpetrator directly or to locate him or her indirectly (by further investigative procedures). In other words, evidentiary clues must be turned into indexes that point in a certain direction. This is what Dupin and Holmes certainly knew, and forensic scientists practice without likely knowing that they are engaged in semiotic analysis. An index is a locator sign telling us, if properly interpreted, who, what, or where to look.

Fingerprints appear throughout crime fiction as an intrinsic part of the plot, showing again that fiction and reality in the area of crime investigation constantly overlap and reflect each other. In his 1883 memoir, *Life on the Mississippi*,

Mark Twain tells of a murder in which the killer is identified by a thumbprint – a fact that he included in his novel *Pudd'nhead Wilson* (1893). In *The Norwood Builder* (1903), Sherlock Holmes turns to a bloody fingerprint to help him confirm his suspicions and thus to identify the murderer. The 1997 movie *Men in Black* shows Agent J delete his ten fingerprints by putting his hands on a metal ball that removes them, aware of their ability to identify him. There are very few fictional crime narratives that do not include fingerprint evidence as part of the plot or the presentation. The fingerprint has, in effect, become a metaphor of crime itself, constituting a trace not only to a specific criminal but also to the uniqueness of human criminality among species.

3.1.2 DNA

As discussed (chapter 1), today DNA fingerprinting, based on the analysis of genetic material taken from samples of biological substances, has become a primary form of evidence wherever it can be collected. It is also used to solve cold cases or to exonerate those convicted of crimes they did not commit. The documentary movie *After Innocence* (2005) followed seven convicted men and their emotional journey back into society, which was made possible because DNA evidence cleared them of the crimes they were purported to have committed. The term *DNA fingerprinting* was used for the first time by British geneticist Alec Jeffreys in 1984, putting forward the notion that the DNA could be used in criminal cases, given its indexical power to trace its human source (Wambaugh 1989: 202). Jeffreys was involved in one of the earliest cases using DNA evidence in 1986, which he used to verify the confession of an individual suspected of two rape-murders. DNA testing exonerated him. In 1987, Robert Melias was the first person in Britain to be convicted of a crime on the basis of DNA evidence. In the same year, the criminal conviction of rape suspect Tommy Lee Andrews was recorded in the United States. From a blood sample, Andrew's DNA was matched with semen found in the victim.

Many famous cases have been solved because of DNA evidence and perhaps none more so than the case of Gary Ridgway (previous chapter). From 1982 to 1998 Ridgway murdered 48 women (mainly prostitutes), dumping many of his victims in the Green River in the state of Washington. After giving a saliva sample to investigators from an early investigation, which was stored by the police, the advent of the technique called *Polymerase Chain Reaction* (PCR) allowed the police to test the saliva. It matched Ridgway's. Faced with this result, Ridgway pleaded guilty and was sentenced to life imprisonment. PCR is a technique that amplifies (multiplies) DNA, allowing scientists to create millions of copies in a short period of time (under two hours). PCR was developed by forensic scientist Edward Blake in 1985, revolutionizing the process of DNA testing.

DNA fingerprinting is also called *DNA typing* or *DNA analysis*. The power of the technique as a means of identification lies in the fact that no two unrelated individuals will possess identical DNA. So, investigators may compare the DNA found at the crime scene with DNA from a suspected criminal. On the basis of this comparison, the suspect can be included or excluded as a possible source of the crime-scene DNA. Forensic scientists can analyze DNA found in the cells of almost any body fluid or tissue, including bone, blood, semen, hair, or teeth. In an early technique, known as *Restriction Fragment Length Polymorphism* (RFLP) analysis, a chemical called a restriction enzyme is used to cut the DNA into fragments for comparison. The PCR technique uses the enzyme polymerase to create copies of specific sections of a DNA molecule. These may then be used for comparison to determine whether an individual contributed to an evidence sample.

Law enforcement agencies have used DNA evidence to create databases of genetic profiles of convicted criminals. Britain's Forensic Science Service is the first to have developed a national criminal DNA database. It also maintains a database of forensic science literature and various crime documents. The *National DNA Indexing System* (NDIS) is maintained by law enforcement agencies in the United States. It is part of a national database of DNA profiles called the Combined DNA Index System (CODIS), which allows law enforcement laboratories to compare DNA profiles of convicted offenders with samples from crime scenes. CODIS uses markers to identify an individual – these are shown below:

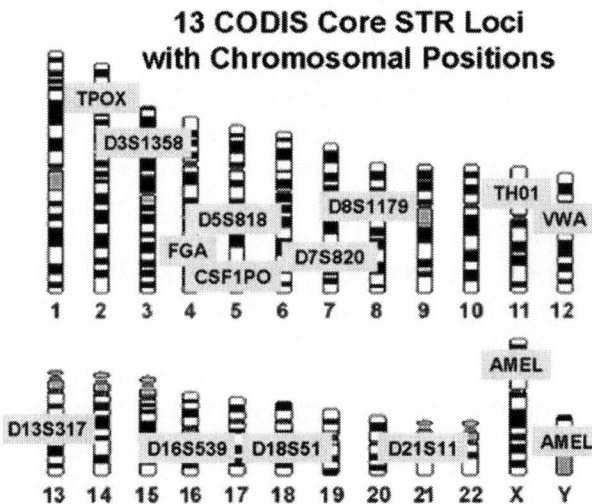

Figure 10: CODIS

It is estimated that over 70 percent of court cases are decided on the basis of this kind of DNA evidence, known as *nuclear* DNA. But now forensic scientists are also using *mitochondrial* DNA, when the biological evidence is degraded or small in quantity. While nuclear DNA is inherited from each parent equally, mitochondrial DNA comes only from the mother. A recent technology, called *Low Copy Number* DNA, is being used to provide a profile from samples containing only a few cells. Britain's Forensic Science Service has introduced a computer-based software system, called *DNAboost*, which allows investigators to work with poor-quality or miniscule DNA evidence, as well as with a mixed profile, a sample with more than one person's DNA on it.

The relevance of DNA science to FS[1] and, in turn, of FS[1] to criminal identification procedures is the fact that the DNA is a natural index. For lack of a better word, such a sign can be called simply an *identisign*, or I-sign for short. The DNA and fingerprints are I-signs. They allow for the identification or location of their human sources. This is not just a clever terminological exercise. When a piece of evidence is named more precisely it allows for insights to be gleaned from it. A clue is a sign, standing for something in some way. The tools of semiotic analysis allow for the decipherment of clues to be connected to other clues of like nature – indexes to indexes, icons to icons, and so on. This constitutes an informed search for the meaning of the clues that can only bolster an investigation.

3.1.3 Footprints and Shoeprints

Footprints are the impressions made by ridges on the soles of the feet. Like fingerprints, they remain unchanged throughout a person's lifetime. No individual's footprints have been found to be identical to those of another person. They are thus I-signs – signs of identity that, together with other I-signs, can be used to determine who a perpetrator is. When fingerprints cannot be obtained because of severe burns or other injuries, footprints become more crucial to an investigation. Many hospitals will take footprints of newborn infants for identification shortly after birth and keep the prints on file for future reference. These records have sometimes been used to match the footprints found at a crime scene with a possible human source. Needless to say, in colder climates, footprints have diminished value as I-signs, because people would wear shoes of some kind. They are more relevant in hot areas of the world where people often go barefoot.

Shoeprint evidence is more commonly found at crime scenes. Even clean, dry shoes can leave an impression on a hard surface by creating electrostatic charges. By simply sprinkling the same dusting powder used for fingerprints over footprints the powder creates a visual image of the impression. Residual static charges do not last very long and can be easily upset, so crime scene investigators rely more on the deformation of surface areas. Shoe impressions on materials such as soil, sand or snow can produce a largely three-dimensional footprint. Like other kinds of prints, shoeprints can be used to identify a wearer directly or indirectly through investigative processes. The impressions made by shoes provide information of various kinds – such as foot size, brand of footwear, likely manufacturer, and so on (Bodziak 1995).

The indentations by any type of footwear can be photographed and matched, if the case arises, to shoeprints found at other locations – that is, one set of prints found at the scene of a crime can be compared to another set of prints found at a separate crime scene, in order to determine if the same perpetrator was involved in both crimes. The photographs can be scanned into computers for analysis. Crime scene technicians will also make a casting of the shoeprint, by pouring a dense liquid into the indentation. After the liquid solidifies, the cast becomes an exact replica that is available for future use.

Forensic scientists can also make other inferences about a suspect based on shoeprints. The size, for example, makes it possible to estimate the person's height; weight can be estimated by measuring how deep the print is with respect to how solid the soil is and whether or not the ground is damp. All of these are I-signs (or more correctly I-signifiers) that can help to reveal or find a trace to the perpetrator's identity.

3.1.4 Tire Prints

Skid and tire marks are indexes that can be used to deduce the sequence of events at a crime scene that may have occurred and thus indirectly determine who the perpetrator might be. Initially, a tire mark can tell an investigator the brand of tire used. Further inspection can also reveal defects and the wear on a tire tread caused by nails, gravel, patches and alignment problems. All these signs can be combined to help identify a unique set of tires or at least a brand of tires. A skid mark is the mark a tire makes when a vehicle wheel stops rolling and slides or spins on the surface of the road. These are used for estimating the maximum and minimum vehicle speed.

Without going into details here, suffice it to say that tire prints constitute the same kind of evidence as any kind of print, requiring a similar type of analysis (discussed already several times above). For example, investigators use latent-recovery techniques of tire impressions that are very similar to fingerprint recovery techniques. Powder is applied with a brush to make the print more visible, and then tape or a lifting device allows the investigator to make a visual record of the impression. As in the case of footprints or shoeprints, casting is also used. A substance is poured into the tire impression, which is allowed to solidify, after which a cast of the impression takes shape.

3.1.5 Voiceprints

Voiceprinting Analysis (as already discussed and to be discussed further in the next chapter) is based on the fact that each human voice produces unique sound patterns and can thus be used for identification purposes. Voiceprints are made by running a tape recording of a voice through an instrument called a sound spectrograph. A voiceprint shows the duration of spoken words and the loudness, pitch, and quality of the voice.

Some forensic scientists question the reliability of this kind of evidence, since there are too many variables involved – unlike fingerprinting and DNA evidence. Admittedly, voiceprints are difficult to interpret and are not as accurate for use in court, as are fingerprints and DNA. The voice can, moreover, easily be camouflaged by individuals who can imitate voice patterns effectively, such as mimics or impersonators. But voiceprints can still be used in accordance with the Principle of Synchronization, enunciated in the previous chapter – namely, if they point in the same direction as do other I-signs then their reliability increases. Even intuitive and anecdotal considerations bring this out. We can instantly recognize someone we know after a simple "Hello" on the phone. Our identification can only be confirmed, however, when the interlocutor gives us more information about himself or herself. Several police departments in the United States use voiceprint evidence in criminal cases, seeing it as a reliable method of identification when used in combination with other kinds of evidence.

3.2 Other Types of Evidence

Other types of evidence can be used to help determine the identity of a perpetrator, including trace, firearm, and blood evidence. Forensic investigators also use facial reconstruction to either identity a victim or a suspect. Trace evidence includes fibers, sand, wood splinters, and particles of glass and paint. Larger evidence includes bullets, shell casings, and firearms found at crime scenes. Together, these constitute what can be called indirect I-signs; that is, they do not point directly to a perpetrator, but can be used to search him or her out through specific investigative procedures that may take place in a crime laboratory with special instruments or else by using the I-signs to locate him or her in a roundabout way, as we saw in the case of nail polish (chapter 1), by possibly finding its manufacturer and then the retail stores to which the product was shipped, hoping that its sale at some store was caught on video or can help locate eyewitnesses. Clothing items, fabrics, and other such items can be used in this way.

The U.S. has one of the best forensic databases for recovered bullet and cartridge cases, called the National Integrated Ballistics Information Network (NIBIN), established in 1997 by combining the databases of the FBI and the Bureau of Alcohol, Tobacco, Firearms, and Explosives (ATF). The computerized images of ballistic evidence found at a crime scene can be compared rapidly with images in NIBIN to make potential matches and thus to be able to locate the owner of a firearm. Gunshot residue is also highly useful as indexical evidence found at a crime scene. Traces of gunshot residue cling to the perpetrator's clothes and body, so that samples can be taken and a scanning microscope used to locate the particles. These can also reveal the distance between the shooter and victim, since the spread will be wider from a farther distance. Test firings on similar fabrics will give an even more accurate estimate of the distance.

The first court case to allow the use of trace evidence goes back to England in 1784 when a certain John Toms was convicted of killing Edward Culshaw in Lancaster. A recent dramatic example of how trace evidence has led to unraveling the identity of a perpetrator is the case of serial killer Wayne Williams who was convicted by carpet fibers from his house and vehicle. Williams murdered more than 25 males, including children, in Atlanta from 1979 to 1981. One victim had a yellow-green fiber in his hair that matched a carpet in Williams' home. To rule out the possibility that other houses had such a carpet, the FBI traced the fiber to a textile company in Boston whose records showed that the owners of only 82 houses in the state of Georgia had bought that color. Another victim had a single rayon fiber on his shorts that resembled carpeting in Williams' automobile. This time the FBI had the car company help them calculate that there was a one in 3,828 chance of the victim being in contact with a vehicle having this carpeting. During the trial, 28 fiber types from 12 victims were linked to Williams.

3.2.1 Blood Evidence

Before the advent of DNA fingerprinting, crime scene investigators used blood typing, or the process of identifying a person's blood group by serologic testing of a sample of blood, as a primary form of identification evidence. Today, blood evidence has other kinds of investigative uses. *Bloodstain pattern analysis* (BPA) involves collecting bloodstains, submitting them to DNA analysis, and also photographing them to reconstruct the violent act by drawing on the scientific disciplines of biology, chemistry, mathematics, and physics. Upon exiting the body, bloodstains go from bright red to dark brown, as a result of oxidation. These can then be measured for the period of time that the bloodstains have been separated from the body, thus allowing for an accurate estimation of the time frame in which the crime occurred.

A drop of blood tends to form into a sphere in flight rather than taking on a teardrop shape. This is a result of the surface tension that binds the molecules together. This fact is important for the calculation of the angle of impact (or incidence) of blood when it spatters on a surface. That angle helps determine the point from which the blood originated. The angles of impact of a number of stains, especially those from opposite sides of the pattern, allow for the investigator to triangulate the scene so as to chart the path that the droplets traveled. The point of convergence is the intersection of two bloodstain paths, where the stains come from opposite sides of the impact pattern.

There are three main types of stains: (1) *contact transfers*, which occur when a bloody cutting instrument transfers blood onto a surface, such as a wall or counter; (2) *passive blood stains*, which occur when blood drips or pools on a surface; and (3) *projected stains or blood spatter*, which occur when blood is flung or sprayed onto a surface. Blood spatter is further broken down into velocity patterns, which indicate the speed of the item that caused the injury, not the speed at which the blood flew from the body. A bullet causes a high-velocity blood spatter stain, which is characterized by tiny droplets of blood. Larger droplets are caused by the low-velocity spatter that might be associated with a stabbing motion. The droplet may form a "castoff stain," which reveals the action of a knife moving from left to right in a curve, or it may form a "drip stain," which indicates that the blood fell straight down. The type of stain present at a crime scene will thus tell an investigator what type of impact caused the blood to flow and spatter, where the victim was when the blood flowed, and where the perpetrator may have gone after committing the crime.

In semiotic terms, putting together evidence like this constitutes a text, allowing investigators to reconstruct a certain picture of the crime event. Again, this is not a simple renaming of a forensic situation. Semiotics has studied the structure of texts extensively and this type of study can help illuminate many aspects of crime scene reconstructions, in the same way that we reconstruct a plot after having read a novel. Texts are read along three semiotic axes. Vertically, they are made up of specific forms that stand for certain things as if in a classificatory system; horizontally, they combine these forms in a particular way that shows their interrelation; and reticularly they bear a message or a meaning through associative processes. The vertical axis is the denotative aspect of a text, the horizontal provides the connotative meaning, and the reticular one its potential interpretation. So, a blood spatter scene at first denotes something – the use of some weapon to cause an injury. The way the spatter is displayed connotes how the blood flow occurred and thus what weapon was used, what the direction of the flow was, and so on. Finally, the reticular (or associative) axis indicates the sequence of events that brought about the spatter; this is then mapped against other crime scenes so that a relevant interpretation can be made.

Needless to say, BSA analysis has become part of pop crime fiction. Detective-cum-serial killer Dexter Morgan is a blood spatter analyst for the fictitious Miami Metro Police Department. And Catharine Willows is a blood spatter analyst on *CSI*. Overall, the reconstruction of a scene can be called an I-text, rather than a simple I-sign, standing for "identification text."

3.2.2 Facial Reconstruction and Forensic Sketching

Facial reconstruction techniques are also part of identity-establishing procedures. When a skull is recovered from an unknown victim, forensic sculptors may be engaged in reconstructing the face, either through the use of actual clay or, nowadays, through computer reconstructions, or both. In digital reconstruction a scan is taken of the skull as it rotates on a turntable and the computer program creates a digital skull that can then be manipulated on a screen. As the scan is merged with the actual skull it adjusts to facial features and tissue patterns resulting in a face that resembles the victim. The hair and eyes are estimated and added to the image to produce a lifelike representation – that is, an icon in semiotic terms.

Forensic sketching is another major technique of identity-reconstruction. Traditionally, sketch artists produced a composite drawing of a suspected perpetrator on the basis of oral descriptions by witnesses. Today, computer programs allow for the reconstruction of a criminal's facial features, although this may be used in tandem with the artistic sketches. Forensic sketching can also help find people who have been missing for years with a program that produces an "age progression" model of the face. The forensic artist uses knowledge of the growth of bone structure to create a computer model that will show how the face might have aged. Known as *Electronic Facial Identification Technique* (E-Fit), it stores hundreds of facial features, using an algorithm to mutate a screen image as a witness provides a description. The witness then chooses the closest likeness, and the program evolves the face according to additional details provided.

3.3 Analyzing the Evidence

Since the mid-1900s, many new trace-evidence, ballistic, blood analysis, and facial reconstruction technologies have been developed for use in crime laboratories. These include the *spectrophotometer* and the gas *chromatograph*. The former records light and heat rays that the human eye cannot detect. It shows the pattern of the rays when they strike an object. Criminalists can detect forgeries or illegal erasures on documents with a spectrophotometer by comparing the pattern of rays. A gas chromatograph separates the various components of a substance. The amount of each component is then measured to determine, for instance, the amount of alcohol in a person's blood. Criminalists, or crime lab experts, are responsible for accurately explaining the significance of all kinds of evidence, from facial reconstructions to blood spatter and DNA evidence. They present their findings in written reports and may also testify in court. The whole process is really one of interpretation of the I-signs and I-texts (evidence cues, test results, and so on), as they have been called in this book, with the use of science, technology, and, of course, basic detective or abductive logic.

Crime historians identify Edmond Locard as establishing the first forensic laboratory in Lyon, France, in 1910. Locard had been an assistant to the famous physician, Alexandre Lacassagne, dubbed by some to be the "father of forensics." Locard stressed that every contact leaves a trace, now known as the *Locard Exchange Principle*. He used his crime lab for the first time to solve the case of a bank clerk who murdered his paramour. The clerk gave a seemingly perfect alibi, but confessed to the crime after Locard discovered minute scrapings of skin under his fingernails containing the pink dust of a woman's face powder.

The first U.S. crime laboratory was set up in Los Angeles in 1923. Today, the nation has about 250 crime laboratories. The FBI crime laboratory, organized in 1932, is one of the finest in the world. FBI experts examine about 900,000 pieces of evidence yearly. Some crime laboratories examine only one type of evidence. For example, the U.S. Postal Inspector's Department Laboratory examines documents associated with such crimes as mail theft and forgery of money orders. Below is a relevant timeline of crime labs:

- 1910: Edmond Locard opens up the first laboratory in Lyon
- 1923: The Los Angeles Police Department establishes the U.S.'s first lab in 1923
- 1932: The FBI launches its Technical Laboratory in Washington, D.C.
- 1935: The Metropolitan Police Laboratory is established at Hendon Police College in London
- 1936: The Royal Canadian Mounted Police opens its first forensic lab in Regina, Saskatchewan
- 1957: India establishes its first Central Forensic Laboratory in Calcutta
- 1975: Ireland founds its Forensic Science Laboratory in Dublin
- 1991: The United Kingdom's Forensic Science Service opens up in London
- 2005: The South African Police service establishes its new Criminal Record and Forensic Science Services lab
- 2006: Pakistan establishes a forensic lab in the National Police Bureau in Islamabad

The FBI lab requires a brief commentary, since it has had a worldwide influence in shaping forensic science. In 1967 the lab established one of the first electronic databases, called the National Crime Information Center (NCIC) and in 1978 it pioneered the use of laser technology to detect latent fingerprints. In 1991 it put into place a Computer Analysis and Response Team (CART) to examine computers for investigations. A year later it set up a database of unique markings from bullets and shell casings. Then, in 1996 it established the Hazardous Materials Unit, followed in 1997 by its National DNA Index System (NDIS) allowing crime labs throughout the world to share DNA profiles, as we saw. It also established a special unit in its lab called the *Evidence Response Team* (ERT), which enters a crime scene to collect evidence and return it to the lab. But all technology can do is to improve upon the interpretation of crimes. As the fictional detectives certainly knew, ultimately it is the detective, as author of the crime scene text, who must interpret the situation.

3.3.1 Famous Cases

Some famous cases show how trace and other forms of identification evidence can help identify the perpetrator of a crime. The case of serial killer Ted Bundy, who may have killed 50 women in the 1970s, was pinned down by the prosecution's photograph of a bite mark discovered on the left buttock of one of his victims. The forensic odontologist testified that Bundy's teeth matched the bite mark exactly. This was the key piece of evidence that ultimately led to his conviction. The same technique was also used to identify victims. The skeletal remains of Chandra Levy were discovered in 2002 in a park in Washington, D.C. She was identified only after the odontologist traced the teeth of the skull back to Levy, a former government intern whose affair with a representative brought the case to the media's attention.

The case of the "Night Stalker" brings out the importance of fingerprint evidence. Twenty-five-year-old Richard Ramirez terrorized Los Angeles from 1984 to 1985, sexually attacking and murdering over a dozen female victims. After the last attack, a passing witness wrote down his car's license plate number. The vehicle was located and fingerprints taken. The Los Angeles Police Department had just established the AFIS system and matched Ramirez's prints almost instantly, leading to his arrest after police put out a photo of Ramirez through the media. When members of the public recognized Ramirez from the photo, they overpowered him in a violent struggle. He was saved from being hanged by the arrival of the police.

Another classic crime case that shows how fingerprinting was used as a crucial I-sign is the so-called "Black Dahlia" case that goes back to the 1940s. In early 1947 the nude body of a young woman was discovered in Los Angeles. The victim had been cut in half and had undergone many other mutilations. Detectives could not identify her at first. They took her fingerprints and gave them to the Los Angeles Examiner, which sent them to the FBI, whose fingerprint database at the time had already 104 million prints. From this they were able to match the victim's fingerprints to Elizabeth Short, 22, who had been fingerprinted for a job and for an arrest for underage drinking. Hundreds of police took part in the investigation, treating Short's acquaintances as possible suspects. Because of the intense media coverage, more than 50 individuals confessed to the murder. Despite the intense effort, no serious suspect has ever been identified. It remains a cold case to this day.

3.3.2 Forensics: Real and Fictional

What semiotics adds to the science of collected evidence is the insight of how signs cohere into meaning patterns that can then be analyzed through the process of sign-analysis – figuring out the signifieds of signifiers allows the analyst to project the evidence onto the broader domain of culture and experience. The works of Poe use trace evidence, as do those of Conan Doyle (Thomas 1999, Connelly 2009). Poe was actually quite influential in pioneering the techniques of current forensic science. As Connelly (2009: xix) observes, not only forensic science but its incorporation into pop crime culture has its origins in Poe: "If you look at best-seller lists, movie charts, and television ratings, they are simply dominated by the mystery genre and its many offshoots. The tendrils of imagination behind these contemporary works can be traced all the way back to Poe." As semiotician Jean Fisette (2007) has argued, the importance of crime fiction in the development of Peirce's semiotics is unmistakable. Perhaps this is why there is so much collaboration between real forensic scientists and crime fiction or documentary writers. They think in the same way and thus, in addition to potentially suggesting techniques to each other, they reveal how semiosis works in human life.

In both real and fictional forensic investigations the same kinds of evidence and tools are used, indicating that the tools and techniques of forensics have metaphorical value, that is, they suggest much more than the specifics of a particular criminal case – they reach out farther into the human psyche. Here are some examples:

- *Blood*: There is no murder crime scene without blood. Blood is a primary sign of what crime represents in psychological terms. There are always dramatic and tragic connotations to blood evidence that emphasize the gravity of the crime and raise the stakes for the detective to solve it.
- *Flashlight*: The flashlight (and other visual devices) of real forensics follows the tradition of the magnifying glass used by fictional detectives such as Sherlock Holmes. It is a tool of illumination. It brings clarity and focus to one object at a time, literally and figuratively. Many crime narratives have the detective entering the crime scene in darkness, with the flashlight representing a means of finding one's way around the space. While serving as a suspenseful technique, it also has a Platonic sense: shining a light on an object is a symbolic gesture for the elucidation of truth.
- *Signatures*: Criminals often leave personalized I-signs and I-texts of their visit – a letter, initials, a word, an image or object that is left deliberately. A signature intensifies the rivalry between the criminal and detective. All other clues in the investigation refer back to this most important sign.
- *Body*: The body of a deceased victim is a marketplace of signs for the forensic investigator. Traumas indicate the nature of the crime afflicted. Like the scene itself, a body is the subject of multiple conjectures by a detective, who constantly refers back to it in light of new evidence.
- *Disturbance*: A detective often walks into a room to find chairs overturned, glass shattered and objects strewn about. This is a sign of struggle and violence, allowing for a textualization of the crime that is no longer in the present.

– *Prints*: Fingerprints and specimens of DNA are the imprints of a perpetrator's presence at the scene. Finding different kinds of fingerprints often complicates an investigation rather than help solve it. These can mislead the detective into identifying the wrong person who, though present during the crime, did not commit it.

The osmosis between reality and fiction in the case of crime is unmistakable. This theme will be taken up in subsequent chapters. For now, it is sufficient to say that the discipline that can best describe this osmosis is semiotics. It is at this point that FS[1] turns into FS[2], which ultimately seeks to understand the *raison d'être* of crime in the human species.

Poe himself called the brain of his master detective, C. Auguste Dupin, a dual brain, that combined accurate reckoning and insight thinking. In his *Murders in the Rue Morgue*, he labeled this blend of thinking a "bi-part soul," which, he suggested, produces the mind of a "poet-mathematician."

As the fictional crime writers certainly knew, each sign present in a crime scene has a plethora of possible meanings behind it which need to be constrained in the context of the scene, using inferential reasoning, as well as scientific information. Even if the first assumptions prove to be false, the placement of the sign in relation to the other signs may help guide the investigators to a logically connected system of interpretation.

3.4 Inferring the Criminal's Identity

The movie *Silence of the Lambs* (1991) introduced the figure of the criminal profiler to the world and, at the same time, helped establish profiling as an investigative tool in forensic science and criminology. Perhaps nowhere in crime detection is abduction as evident as it is in profiling. Directed by Jonathan Demme, *Silence of the Lambs* is an essay on this abductive craft. Clarice Starling, a young FBI profiler, is recruited by her superior to help capture a brutal serial killer. She enlists the help of another incarcerated serial killer, Hannibal Lecter, to gain insights into the present serial killer's motivations. She investigates several of the killer's prior murder victims in the hopes of catching him before his next murder. Clarice goes against traditional practices in her pursuit of the killer. In one scene, she finds a cocoon in the throat of a victim. Together with other clues implanted on the bodies of the victims, she finally figures out who the perpetrator is. The serial killer is christened "Buffalo Bill" because of the gruesome features of his crime. Clarice revisits the first victim's house near the end of the movie, looking for one last piece of evidence, and this is the missing piece in the semiotic jigsaw puzzle.

As the movie shows, the profiler uses knowledge of the criminal's *modus operandi* (MO) and signatures. MO is the manner or characteristic way in which the perpetrator commits the crime. It can change or evolve over time as he or she learns from experience and becomes more efficient at committing crimes. But it tends to remain the same across the perpetrator's spree of crimes. The signature is the sign or signs that a perpetrator leaves to identify himself or herself, much like the act of signing one's name on a piece of paper. The signature is a sign-trace to personality, and thus a special kind of I-sign.

Another tool available to profilers today is called *Crime Mapping* (Kerr 2012). Using the Geographic Information Systems (GIS) the tool allows profilers to locate crime hot spots, along with other trends and patterns. They can overlay this with other datasets such as census demographics, locations of pawnshops, schools, and so on to better understand the underlying causes of crime and help the police devise strategies to deal with the problem. Research into computer-based crime mapping started in 1986, when the National Institute of Justice funded a project by the Chicago Police Department to see if crime mapping and profiling really worked. Such research shows that profiling is, indeed, a useful tool, but that one must use it with a great dose of caution.

Also called geographic profiling, the questions that it seeks to answer include: What leads a serial killer to a victim and how do they end up in the same place and at the same time? What geographical patterns can be found in the case at hand? As Kerr (2012: 7) observes:

> To create a useable geographic profile, a number of elements have to be taken into consideration. The distance of an offender is prepared to travel to commit his crimes is critical and, of course, this means that the method of transportation to the crime scene is also important. The less freedom an offender has – the need to travel by public transport, for instance – the more restricted his area of operation will be. Attractiveness of an area or a road must be taken into account. It could be that a particular road is, for instance, more isolated. Or, remarkable as it sounds, it might be that one road that looks prettier to the offender than others.

Perhaps the most important practice in profiling is the use of historical cases of crime in order to extract from them common aspects. For this reason, Douglas, Ressler, Burgess, Hartmann and D'Agostino (1986, 1997) interviewed a number of convicted serial killers to assess their methods and personality traits. This allowed them to construct a framework based on an *organized*-versus-*disorganized* personality dichotomy. The relevant features of this dichotomy are worth paraphrasing here:

Table 3: Personality typology

Disorganized	Organized
IQ below average, 80–95 range	IQ above average, 105–120 range
socially inadequate	socially adequate
lives alone	lives with partner
usually does not date	dates frequently
absent or unstable father	stable father figure
family emotional abuse	inconsistent family physical abuse, harsh
lives and/or works near crime scene	geographically/occupationally mobile
minimal interest in news media	follows the news media
usually a high school dropout	may be college educated
poor hygiene/housekeeping skills	good hygiene/housekeeping skills
keeps a secret hiding place in the home	does not usually keep a hiding place
nocturnal (nighttime) habits	diurnal (daytime) habits
drives a clunky car or pickup truck	drives a flashy car
returns to crime scene for reliving crime	returns to crime scene to see what police know
may contact victim's family to play games	usually contacts police to play games
no interest in police work	a police groupie or wannabe
experiments with self-help programs	doesn't experiment with self-help
kills at one site, considers mission over	kills at one site, disposes at another
usually leaves body intact	may dismember body
attacks in a blitz pattern	attacks using seduction
depersonalizes victim	holds a conversation
leaves a chaotic crime scene	leaves a controlled crime scene
leaves physical evidence	leaves little physical evidence
responds best to counseling interview	responds best to direct interview

These traits have been corroborated extensively by both interviewing serial killers and by looking at well-known cases (Vronsky 2004: 320–323). We shall return to the whole concept of criminal profiling in chapter 5. The gist of the theory is that the characteristics of a crime scene mirror the personality traits of the perpetrator. In a fundamental way, the fictional detectives were expert profilers, able to draw assessments of criminals on the basis of the I-signs they left at scenes. The potential power of profiling has come out in several famous cases, of which the Wayne Williams case (mentioned above) stands out dramatically. At first it was thought that a white supremacist was the killer, since all the children murdered were black. But a profiler indicated that it could not be a white man or group. Vronsky (2004: 342–343) summarizes the case as follows:

> They thought it was unlikely that a white supremacist group was committing the murders because the bodies were partially hidden, dumped in abandoned buildings or in the backs of vacant lots. A more public display of the bodies would have served white supremacists better. Because the crimes were committed in back neighborhoods, it was likely that the offender was black. A white killer would have stood out in the neighborhood and would have been noticed ... Furthermore, statistically speaking, serial killers tend to kill victims within their own race.

Criminal profiling does not aim to solve a case, or produce a definitive identity of a perpetrator. It is a contributory technique, like semiotics itself, that can assess scenarios as being likely or not, on the basis of known personality traits, situational features, statistics, and other tools of inference.

3.4.1 Copycat Crimes

The movie *Copycat* (1995), starring Sigourney Weaver as a profiler, brought out the critical role that imitation plays in crime. When a new series of murders spread fear and panic across her home city of San Francisco, the detective and her partner in the movie solicit Weaver's expertise. As the murders continue she starts to realize that the elusive assailant draws inspiration from notorious serial killers including Albert De Salvo, David Berkowitz, Peter Kürten, Jeffrey Dahmer and Ted Bundy who had become media celebrities, garnering as much attention, if not more so, than actors. The copycat killer also perpetrates the crimes in the same order of the list of serial killers that Weaver had presented at a lecture she gave at the university the night of her attack. The copycat killer was in the audience. When she figures this out, she predicts where and when he will strike next, leading to the denouement.

Copycat crimes have led to the notion of the *Copycat Effect*, or the tendency of sensationalistic publicity about violent murders or suicides to result in more of the same through imitation (Coleman 2004). Most of the persons who mimic crimes seen in the media have prior criminal records, prior severe mental health problems, or a history of violence, suggesting that the effect of the media is indirect. But there are some cases which, like the movie *Copycat* suggests, show that people are simply looking for a moment in the spotlight as serial killers. This topic will be taken up in the final chapter. Crime seems to empower some people, affording them an identity that they desire and that they cannot attain, perhaps, in any other way.

Chapter 4
The Language of Crime

All slang is metaphor, and all metaphor is poetry.
G. K. Chesterton (1874–1936)

One of the most famous, and controversial, cases in recent crime history involved the use of forensic linguistic analysis. In 1996, in Boulder Colorado, six-year-old JonBenet Ramsey was found dead by her father in the basement of his house. The police were already at the home and allowed him to carry the body upstairs, thus destroying crime scene evidence, or at least compromising it. The reason they were there is because a ransom note had been discovered in the house before the father found the body, and the Ramseys, thinking it was a kidnapping, called in the police immediately (despite a warning in the note not to do so). The note indicated that JonBenet had been kidnapped and would be returned safely only if 118,000 dollars were paid. Strangely, it was the exact amount of money the father had received as a bonus the year before. The autopsy of the little girl revealed that she had eaten pineapple a few hours before her death, and a photo taken the day of her disappearance showed a pineapple in the kitchen with a spoon in it. But neither parent recalled feeding the fruit to their daughter. Also, police found no sign of forced entry into the house, but a basement window was broken and unsecured.

A forensic linguist was subsequently called in and he determined that the ransom note could only have been written by the mother, leading to unsubstantiated speculations by the police and the media. It turned out eventually to be a false conclusion. Early on, the investigation became a media spectacle, with people taking sides on who killed JonBenet – a family member or an intruder. One reason why there was so much public interest in the case was, no doubt, the images of the little girl as a beauty queen contestant that were broadcast across the television universe. Long before *Toddlers and Tiaras* and similar television programs, American society used the case to debate precocious sexuality and, more generally, the sexualization of childhood by popular culture. As this case showed once again, crime is a social and moral phenomenon, not just a juridical or legal one. Like sin it arouses everyone's moral sensibilities. Blaming someone, with or without substantial evidence, is a knee-jerk reaction.

A blood sample from the little girl's underwear indicated that it came from two people and a DNA test in 2003 revealed that some of the blood came from an unknown male. In 2008, District Attorney Mary Lacy cleared the Ramseys of all wrongdoing and issued an apology to them, even though the mother, Patsy

Ramsey, had died two years earlier from ovarian cancer. The question of the authenticity of the ransom note was never established, nor was its author. The case remains unsolved.

The analysis of written texts in criminal investigations falls within the domain of *forensic linguistics*. Since semiotics and linguistics share a large territory of research and theorization, it is thus correct to assert that it also falls within the domain of forensic semiotics. Both linguistics and semiotics, in their modern form, originated with Saussure's *Cours de linguistique générale* (1916), as mentioned in the opening chapter. This chapter will look at the general features and investigative areas of forensic linguistics (semiotics), including the type of analysis that can help determine the authorship of notes such as the one in the JonBenet Ramsey case. The topic of criminal cants (dialects) and their role in criminal culture will be examined as well. Finally, metaphor analysis, which is based on recent work in cognitive linguistics, will be described as a means to unravel the meanings of criminal-produced texts.

4.1 Forensic Linguistics

Forensic linguistics is brought in whenever a case involves some aspect related to the use of language either to identify a perpetrator or to shed light on some facet of a criminal investigation. Some of the relevant areas include (Coulthard and Johnson 2007, Olsson 2008, 2012):

- *voice identification*: determining whether the voice on a tape recording is that of the suspect by analyzing its phonetic traits;
- *author identification*: inferring who wrote a particular note, letter, or other text by comparing it to known writing samples of a suspect or by comparing it to databases;
- *discourse analysis*: analyzing the utterances of criminals to help determine what they really mean;
- *linguistic proficiency analysis*: determining whether a suspect has competence in a language and thus if he or she knows what the content of his or her utterances really is;
- *dialectology*: figuring out which dialect of a language a person speaks and what this might entail; this includes the study of criminal cants, or forms of language used by criminal gangs.

The techniques of forensic linguistics are not accepted universally by criminalists and the police. Like other kinds of identification techniques (chapter 2), they may be reliable only in certain situations or to limited extents. For example, linguistic proficiency analysis is generally seen to have low reliability, because many criminals can imitate various forms of speech and, also, because some dialectal forms are really slang forms, and these have a whole set of different implications. On the other hand, voice identification, if done by a qualified phonetician who understands the limitations of the methodology, is accepted as being relatively reliable, although it sometimes does not meet the evidentiary standards of the courts, especially when the analysis is done by a technician who may have little training in linguistic science (Tiersma and Solan 2002).

Author identification is often hampered by the fact that documents in a criminal case (ransom notes, threatening letters, and so on) are too short to make a reliable profile or identification of the author. Moreover, identifying the specific linguistic features that are reliable indicators of authorship, against those that are not, remains an area of debate even within forensic linguistics. Research is ongoing, however, and the availability of large corpora of speech and writing samples suggests that the field is advancing, especially with the use of powerful algorithms that help sift through the data and classify it effectively. Most analyses of authorship conducted with computer technologies are sufficiently reliable to eliminate someone as an author, or select an author from a small group of suspects.

Discourse analysis is a very broad field, and can provide helpful insights to criminal profilers. For example, a suspect's use of the pronoun *I* rather than *we* might indicate noncomplicity in a crime. Forensic linguists have also found that when a suspect is recorded as saying "yeah" or "uh-huh" in response to a suggestion, the suspect is not necessarily agreeing with the suggestion, but may simply be providing feedback to indicate that he has understood the utterance, as we routinely do in ordinary conversation. Courts thus have a mixed record as to whether or not they allow discourse analysts to testify as experts, but even when they are not allowed to do so they may be useful to the lawyers in preparing a case. Discourse analysis is also employed to examine language as it is used in cross-examination, evidence presentation, judgments, police interrogations, police testimonies in court, the summing up to a jury, interview techniques, the cross-examination process in court, and in other areas. A branch of semiotics, called *legal semiotics*, is concerned specifically with this kind of subject matter, connecting it as well to traditions in the law and how these affect interpretations of legal proceedings and even the nature of justice itself (Schane 2006, Hutton 2009, Wagner and Broekman 2010).

Proficiency testing and dialectology are both time-tested and relatively non-controversial areas of linguistics proper, but they remain contentious within forensic science as investigative tools. Because of the influence of the mass media and population mobility, dialects are becoming less distinct than they once were, and people often mix dialectal features in their regular speech as part of style, rather than as true dialectal communication. Determining a person's origin by means of his or her dialect is also complicated by the fact that many languages straddle a geographical border or are spoken in multiple countries. However, with dialectological analysis it is possible to determine that a person is not from a specified country or may or may not be the one who authored a certain text. But even such inferences must be made carefully, taking into account the limitations of the approach.

Overall, with the techniques of forensic linguistics, someone can often be eliminated as a suspect with a reasonable degree of confidence; it is much harder to prove him or her guilty beyond a reasonable doubt. Thus, it is not surprising that most linguistic expertise in criminal cases has been for the defense, where reliability is less essential. Nonetheless, such expertise can be useful to the police, especially during the early investigatory stages.

4.1.1 Voiceprinting

As already discussed in previous chapters, voiceprinting analysis is a potentially useful investigatory tool, because it can help indicate if someone might be lying based on the stress patterns in the voice. The method used in evaluating such patterns is called the *Psychological Stress Evaluator* (PSE). Relevant research has found that the voice will reach a higher pitch when someone is lying, emitting inaudible vibrations called *micro-tremors* that can be recorded (Tanner and Tanner 2004). Stress causes the vocal muscles to tighten and the micro-tremors to decrease, producing flattened lines on the screen of a computerized speech synthesizer. In other words, a voiceprint is an I-sign and can be used in the same way as other I-signs to help determine identity. A recent version of this method, called the *Computer Voice Stress Analyzer* (CVSA), has proven to be more reliable than the PSE. The CVSA checks for voice shifts during interrogations, and appears to complement the findings produced by other truth-telling devices to a high degree of consistency, putting it in line with the Principle of Synchronization (chapter 2).

Voiceprinting has helped solve a number of famous cases. The most well-known one is the Gloria Carpenter case, whose body was found in her bath in Modesto in 1973 with a mark around the neck indicating that she had been strangled by a nylon stocking. Detectives went to a local bar and found her drinking partner, John Wayne Glenn, who admitted to taking her home while vowing that he did not enter her apartment. There was no concrete evidence linking him to the crime, but detectives persuaded him to take the PSE test. The results showed significant stress in his voice. This convinced them that Glenn was involved. They returned to the apartment and after meticulous investigation finally turned up a palm print that belonged to him. Glenn confessed, even though the PSE evidence could not be used in court. It did however encourage the detectives to pursue further investigation and ultimately identify the perpetrator.

The technology used in voiceprinting analysis, called spectrography, was first developed by Bell Laboratories in the 1940s for military purposes. The forensic use of voice analysis did not start until the late 1960s following its utilization by the Michigan State Police. From then until the present day, voiceprinting has been used in the investigation of many criminal cases. It is part of a larger forensic approach, which includes such tactics and technologies as tape filtering and enhancement, the reconstruction of conversations, and so on. The fundamental premise on which all this is based is the fact that voiceprints are unique, shaped by the sizes of the oral and nasal cavities of individuals, as well as the quality of the vocal cords located in the larynx. The cavities are resonators, reinforcing some of the overtones produced by the vocal cords. On spectrographs these produce formats or *voiceprint bars*. The likelihood that two individuals would have the same formats appears remote. Also, the articulators (the lips, teeth, tongue, and jaw muscles) are controlled in different and unique ways by different speakers, producing the kinds of sounds and patterns that we can easily recognize as belonging to a specific individual. Again, the likelihood that two people may have developed identical articulatory patterns is very low. Below is an example of a computerized voiceprint:

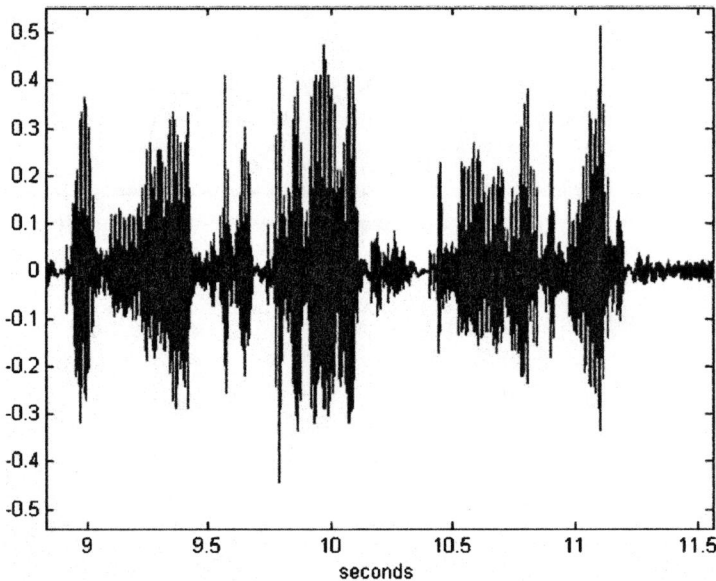

Figure 11: Voiceprint

The FBI has examined thousands of voiceprint cases and found the reliability to be high. For this reason, the police now conserve spectrograms as a permanent record alongside fingerprint, DNA, and other kinds of I-sign evidence. Voiceprinting investigation can take place in a controlled environment, such as in police interrogation rooms, or informally, such as in the case of face-to-face encounters with hidden recording devices, or in the use of recorded phone conversations.

4.1.2 Forensic Linguistics and Social Media

Forensic linguistics is becoming a very useful tool in the current Internet Age because of the rise in the use of mobile devices and of social media sites, such as Facebook and Twitter. Above all else, these can be accessed easily for investigating crime directly (Potter and Kappler 2006). Like everyone else, criminals now use social media for their personal motives and objectives. The police thus have an instantly-accessible platform for investigating crimes, criminals, and criminality like never before in the history of forensic science.

The Internet can be mined to examine the amount and types of crime committed, who commits crimes, and what crimes are now part of social problems. Data-mining software allows investigators to scan posts and chats for criminal activity. If the scanning algorithm detects suspicious behavior, it flags it and then determines if further steps are required. The mining techniques include the automatic grouping of documents or files, categorizing them into directories, and analyzing patterns and interrelationships within them. One particular technique, called filtering, involves making profiles of people's interests and then comparing these against related information from various sources. Forensic linguistics can then use the profiles for identifying suspects on the basis of the content. Even those who do not go online leave "data trails" through the use of credit cards, social security numbers, and so forth.

The importance of the new digital technologies in criminal activities was dramatized by disturbing post-9/11 revelations that cellphones were used to organize, implement, and execute the events. Untraceable pay-as-you-go cellphones have also been used by criminals and terrorists alike, as was discovered in the aftermath of the Madrid and London bombing incidents. And, of course, the Internet is now used systematically by terrorist groups to send out their messages, many of which are encrypted and, thus, require investigation by cryptologists, or experts in the science of code interpretation.

4.2 Handwriting, Content, and Style

Forensic linguists are often called in by the police to help them determine if and how documents are altered and to analyze handwriting. The U.S. Secret Service and Germany's Bunderskriminalamt use the *Forensic Information System for Handwriting* (FISH) – established by German authorities in the 1980s, which now has more than a hundred thousand samples of handwriting in its database. Research using FISH has established that no two individuals have the same combinations of handwriting characteristics. For this reason handwriting constitutes a type of I-sign that can be traced back only to one individual. FISH scans a block of text and plots the handwriting as arithmetic and geometric values. These can then be used to infer who the writer of a document is most likely to be by comparison with samples in the database.

Another feature of written texts is their content and the style used to write them. Both of these can also help identify a suspect and to determine what his or her state of mind might be (or might have been). The examination of content is called *Content Analysis* and the examination of stylistic patterns is called *stylometry*.

4.2.1 Handwriting Analysis

Handwriting is a complex psychomotor skill that results from the combination of sensory, neurological, and physiological processes. The output of these processes produces a specific form of handwriting that is characterized by specific signifiers such as:
–   the shape of individual letters, including their size, slant, and style of connectivity;
–   peculiarities and inconsistencies of spelling;
–   preferred characters, such as the use of "&" instead of "and";
–   peculiarities of grammar and punctuation.

A feature of handwriting that is especially important is the signature. When the two-year-old son of aviator Charles Lindbergh was kidnapped and murdered, the letters in the ransom note were compared to the signature of Bruno Hauptmann, suggesting that he was the note writer and thus the probable perpetrator. Faking signatures, and handwriting style generally, is also part of forensic investigations. In forged writing, pen lifts can be detected in odd places where the forger was likely checking his writing and retouching the script. Tracing can be detected by observing the presence of indentation patterns.

The comparison of handwriting features with other relevant samples enables forensic linguists to identify or exclude someone as the source for any questioned writing. Sometimes investigators will appeal to the public to help them, asking them if they recognize the handwriting of a note. This happened in the case of David Berkowitz (the Son of Sam) case when a deputy sheriff went on television to show two threatening letters he had received. They had a similar style of handwriting to others signed by the Son of Sam in other correspondence. But lay people typically do not recognize the subtleties in the writing that may differentiate it – including the size and slope of the letters, the spacing between words and letters, the position of the words on the baseline, height relationships, initial and ending strokes, and line quality.

The study of handwriting patterns is called *graphology*. Among the facts-on-file that graphology has established is that handwriting is affected by illness, old age, and stress. Also, no two individuals share the same combination of handwriting characteristics given sufficient quantity and quality of writing (Horton 1996 and Boot 1998). Identical twins share the same environmental influences and the same DNA. Therefore, one would expect their handwriting to be at the very least highly similar. However, this is not the case. Some of the broader claims of graphology, connecting handwriting to emotional states and personality however lack scientific corroboration – such as the assertion that lines slanting upward indicate enthusiasm, and those slanting downward discouragement. But apart from these caveats, graphology has proved to be a reliable detector of identity in some criminal cases (such as the Lindbergh one). Already in the late 1800s, the French psychologist Alfred Binet (1888) asked seven graphologists to distinguish writing samples of intelligent individuals from samples of average people. All performed better than chance would allow, and one scored correctly on 92 percent of the cases. In the 1940s, the Russian psychologist Alexander R. Luria (1970) studied the use of handwriting to determine the location of brain injuries, finding it to be a fairly accurate predictor.

Today, forensic linguists use handwriting-recognition software that translates handwritten notes into computer codes. The software works with light pens and electronic writing pads, which enable the user to write words or draw pictures directly on the computer.

To get a concrete sense of how handwriting analysis can be used forensically, consider the following note left by David Berkowitz, the Son of Sam killer, found in Berkowitz's car upon his arrest on August 10, 1977 (from Gibson 2004: 10):

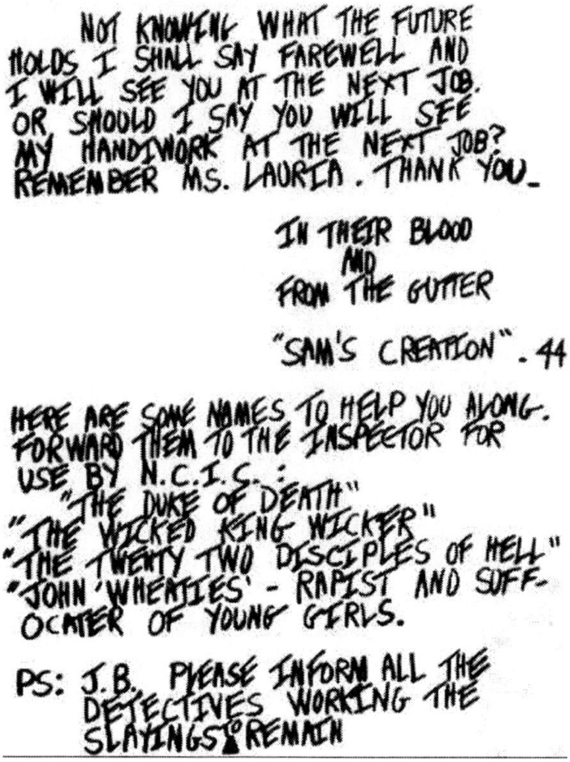

Figure 12: Son of Sam note

Even before reading the note's contents, several features of the handwriting immediately stand out. First, Berkowitz uses only capital block letters, a sign suggesting a display of masculine strength. The leftward slant to the top of the letters "T" and "I" follows the overall leftward slant of the writing. This suggests an unconscious leaning towards the "sinister" (from Latin meaning "left") – a theory reinforced by the contents of this and his other letters and notes. Berkowitz seems to convey an unbridled but repressed masculine sexual power that he needs to express in a sinister fashion. This is why he refers to his killing spree as "handiwork" and to killing as a "job," making them part of his plans as if they were ordinary events. He refers to himself with several crucial epithets that reinforce this interpretation: "The duke of death," "The wicked king of wicker," "the twenty two disciples of hell," "John Wheaties [an obvious use of irony] – rapist and suffocator of young girls." As the police eventually found out, the name "Sam" was a reference to Berkowitz's neighbor, Sam Carr, who Berkowitz believed to be a sort of demon. He claimed that Carr's black Labrador retriever passed on to him the dark commands that motivated him to kill. Significantly, Berkowitz himself, under interrogation, referred to his handwriting style as intended to produce a "ghoulish effect." In effect, he made his handwriting style match his demonic fantasies and apprehensions in an iconic way.

4.2.2 Content Analysis

The Berkowitz letters reveal a high degree of paranoia and an intense antipathy towards women. As McNab (2010: 117) writes: "Most of the evidence seemed to point to Berkowitz being a sufferer of paranoid schizophrenia," even though the court judged him to be sane.

The meanings that can be gleaned from Berkowitz's letters are analyzed under the rubric of Content Analysis (CA). Actually, this is a term with multiple meanings, depending on the discipline that employs it. It is used, for instance, to refer to an approach in psychology and anthropology that aims to identify, classify, and analyze the content (meaning or interpretation) of messages. It is also used in the social sciences generally to indicate a quantitative approach based on counting the number of times some item appears in a text and the reasons for this. The term is also sometimes employed to indicate a technique for analyzing the transcripts of interviews. In literary analysis, as in forensic science, it can also refer to a study of the authorship and authenticity of texts, based on their stylistic features. Using frequency counts of words, syntactic structures, and the like, one can infer what emphases are present in a text, what word collocations signify, and so on (Krippendorff 2004). These can then be used to determine authorship, if one knows that a certain writer has a predisposition for certain words, turns of phrase, and so on. A number of serial killers have been identified, or at least typecast at the start, through CA.

It was CA that led to the identification and arrest of the so-called Unabomber, Theodore Kaczynski, a lone anti-technology terrorist, who mailed and planted bombs from the late 1970s to the mid-1990s targeting technology-based victims. On April 24, 1995 Kaczynski sent a letter to the *New York Times* promising "to desist from terrorism" if the *Times* or the *Washington Post* published his manifesto, *Industrial Society and Its Future*, in which he argued that his bombings were extreme but necessary to draw attention to the erosion of human freedom that has come about as a result of the rise of modern technologies. The manifesto was published and it was his brother who recognized its style and contents as pointing to Theodore. The brother brought written sheets that Theodore had left in the house to the police who made the identification more compelling through statistical CA.

The content of a letter is a kind of textual I-sign that can also provide a profile of the perpetrator. Below is a letter written by Berkowitz. It was addressed to Captain Joseph Borelli in 1977 and handwritten in mostly block letter capitals [not reproduced here] (from Gibson 2004: 11). In it, he announces himself as the Son of Sam:

```
I am deeply hurt by your calling me a wemon [sic] hater! I
am not. But I am a monster. I am the "Son of Sam." I am a
little brat. When father Sam gets drunk he gets mean. He
beats his family. Sometimes he ties me up to the back of
the house. Other times he locks me in the garage. Sam loves
to drink blood. "Go out and kill," commands father Sam.
Behind   our   house   some   rest.   Mostly   young—raped   and
slaughtered—their blood drained—just bones now. Papa Sam
keeps me locked in the attic too. I can't get out but I
look out the attic window and watch the world go by. I feel
like an outsider. I am on a different wavelength then [sic]
everybody else—programmed too [sic] kill. However, to stop
me you must kill me. Attention all police: Shoot me first—
shoot to kill or else keep out of my way or you will die!
Papa Sam is old now. He needs some blood to preserve his
youth. He has had too many heart attacks. "Ugh, me hoot, it
hurts, sonny boy." I miss my pretty princess most of all.
She's resting in our ladies house. But I'll see her soon. I
am the "Monster"—"Beelzebub"—the chubby behemouth. I love
to hunt. Prowling the streets looking for fair game—tasty
meat. The wemon of Queens are prettyist of all. It must be
the water they drink. I live for the hunt—my life. Blood
for papa. Mr. Borrelli, sir, I don't want to kill anymore.
No sur, no more but I must, 'honor thy father.' I want to
make love to the world. I love people. I don't belong on
earth. Return me to yahoos. To the people of Queens, I love
you. And I want to wish all of you a happy Easter. May God
bless you in this life and in the next. And for now I say
goodbye and goodnight. Police: Let me haunt you with these
words: I'll be back! I'll be back! To be interpreted as—
bang bang bang, bank, bang—ugh!! Yours in murder, Mr.
Monster
```

Figure 13: Son of Sam letter

A feature that instantly stands out is the misspelling of words, especially those associated with referents that apparently are emotionally-charged ones for Berkowitz, such as *wemon* (*women*). In the letter, Berkowitz provides a snapshot of his upbringing, identifying it indirectly as the source of his criminal behavior. Also noticeable is his own self-analysis as someone who is "programmed to kill" because of Sam – thus providing a self-styled psychological profile. Allusions to vampirism ("he needs some blood to preserve his youth") and Satanism ("Beelzebub") mesh with his ironic self-description as a "monster" and a "chubby behemouth." The metaphor of the hunt is an especially revealing one, tying his motives to a feral sense of female-hunting, given his inability to attract women in a socially-acceptable way. Sardonically, he claims to love the world and does not want to kill anymore, but taunts the police with "I'll be back."

Other content features to note are the following, all of which are exculpatory through references to the influence of upbringing and internal fantasies:

- *Childlike language*: "I am a little brat". This matches the block capital letters, which suggest childish handwriting, but sinister and menacing, at the same time.
- *Victimization*: "He beats his family." "Sometimes he ties me up to the back of the house. Other times he locks me in the garage". These suggest that his childhood memories haunt him, victimize him, and motivate his current behavior.
- *Dissociated blame*: He blames "Sam" for his murders because it is he who commands him to "Go out and kill," thus attempting to exculpate himself as a victim of uncontrollable forces. So, he warns: "to stop me you must kill me. Attention all police: Shoot me first – shoot to kill or else keep out of my way or you will die!" ... "I don't want to kill anymore. No sur, no more but I must, 'honor thy father'. I want to make love to the world. I love people. I don't belong on earth. Return me to yahoos. To the people of Queens, I love you. And I want to wish all of you a happy Easter. May God bless you in this life and in the next. And for now I say goodbye and goodnight."
- *Gives a reason to kill*: "Papa Sam is old now. He needs some blood to preserve his youth". Using vampiristic imagery, Berkowitz explains his reasons for killing as prompted by an urge for bestiality that he takes out in real life through murder.
- *Separation from the world*: "I feel like an outsider. I am on a different wavelength then everybody else – programmed too kill".
- *Alludes to multiple personalities, animalism, Satanism, and classical characters*: "I am the "Monster" – "Beelzebub" – the chubby behemouth. I love to hunt. Prowling the streets looking for fair game – tasty meat ... I live for the hunt..." "Yours in murder, Mr. Monster". Berkowitz shows his engagement with the dark side of fantasy, provoked, so he claims, by his repressed upbringing.

- *Taunts the police*: "I miss my pretty princess most of all. She's resting in our ladies house. But I'll see her soon … Let me haunt you with these words: I'll be back! I'll be back! To be interpreted as – bang bang bang, bank, bang – ugh!!". Berkowitz desires to enter into a sinister dialogue with those in authority who, he claims, have made him do what he does.

The syntax is disorganized and rambling, revealing the disorientation and chaos he experiences inside of himself. As his follow-up letters demonstrate, the repetition of images, people, objects (blood, dogs, urine) allow him to objectify his criminality as a largely symbolic force, thus dissociating himself from blame, deflecting it on "Sam," who exhorts him to "Go out and kill." This is an ersatz confession, a baring of the unconscious, in order to justify his killing. The constant use of the pronoun "I" shows that he sees himself as unique. His return to childhood is implicit in sentences such as "I am a little brat." There is also a frantic cry for help: "He beats his family. Sometimes he ties me up to the back of the house. Other times he locks me in the garage".

As it turns out, the forensic CA put forth here was actually corroborated by Berkowitz himself after he was arrested. Berkowitz wanted to attend his victims' funerals but could not because of police surveillance, feeling a deep connection to them as victims. There was complete investment and involvement in every aspect of his crimes, showing that he was not really out of touch with reality. To be able to plan, commit and keep tabs on each murder, Berkowitz showed calculating lucidity amidst his madness. As investigators eventually found out, he was abandoned as an infant, adopted by Pearl and Nathan Berkowitz. Pearl died when he was sixteen, an event that greatly anguished him. He researched his birth parents, portraying his victimization as follows: "I was an accident, unwanted. My birth was either out of spite or by accident." He became sexually incompetent and was "prone to fabricate elaborate lies about his bedroom prowess, all the while intent upon revenge against the women who habitually rejected him" (Newton 1990: 312).

Another famous example of the use of CA concerned the case of the "Zodiac Killer" a serial killer in Northern California in the late 1960s and early 1970s, whose identity remains unknown to this day. The killer himself originated the nickname of "Zodiac" in a series of letters that taunted the local Bay Area press. These included four cryptograms of which only one has ever been decoded. The following letter was sent by the killer on August 1, 1969, to the *San Francisco Examiner, San Francisco Chronicle* and the *Vallejo Times-Herald* (from Gibson 2004: 97):

Dear Editor:

This is the murderer of the 2 teenagers last Christmass at Lake Herman & the girl on the 4th of July near the golf course in Vallejo. To prove I killed them I shall state some facts which only I & the police know. Christmas 1. Brand name of ammo Super X. 2. 10 shots were fired. 3. The boy was on his back with his feet to the car 4. The girl was on her right side feet to the west.

4th of July 1. Girl was wearing paterned slacks. 2. The boy was also shot in the knee 3. Brand name of ammo was western. Here is part of a cipher the other 2 parts of this cipher are being mailed to the editors of the Vallejo times & SF Examiner. I want you to print this cipher on the front page of your paper. In this cipher is my identity. If you do not print this cipher by the afternoon of Fry 1st of

Aug 69, I will go on a kill rampage Fry. night. I will cruise around all weekend killing lone people in the night then move on to kill again, until I end up with a dozen people over the weekend.

Figure 14: Zodiac letter

The Zodiac wants to prove he is the killer, staking a grisly claim to fame. He brags and plays with the police by employing cryptography and misspellings (to trip up forensic linguists) to conceal his identity. As it happened, the Zodiac stopped killing a few years later leaving the police and the public in the dark about his identity which, itself, seems to have been an intrinsic component of his overall plan. As his letters showed, he was enjoying the "game" and wanted to prove how organized his mind was. The possibility of the killer being insecure and a loner who hated people is implicit in this statement: "I will cruise around all weekend killing lone people in the night then move on to kill again, until I end up with a dozen people over the weekend."

One of the more intriguing aspects of the Zodiac case is that some of the letters that the Zodiac sent contained cryptographic text. The killer demanded that his letters, with the coded text, be printed in the newspapers otherwise he would kill many more people. The newspapers eventually published the letters. One of the encrypted texts, consisting of 408 symbols, was cracked by a husband and wife team, but in the code the Zodiac had not encrypted his name. In November of 1969, the Zodiac sent a letter with a 340-character code to the media that has never been deciphered. It is reproduced below. Note that at the bottom it includes the symbol – a circle with a cross in the middle – that the Zodiac adopted as his emblem:

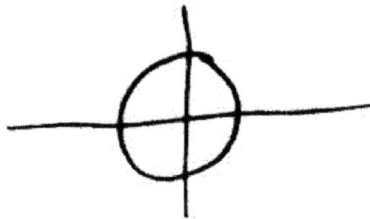

Figure 15: A cryptic message from the Zodiac

The meaning of the circle-and-cross symbol has been debated for decades – there are even websites devoted to speculating about its interpretation. To a semiotician, a composite symbol such as this one would be seen as blending two sets of connotations – those associated with the circle and those with the cross. Without going into details here, suffice it to say that both have mythic connotations, making a perfect symbolic counterpart to the pseudonym of Zodiac. Astrological charts were constructed in a circular form and continue to be so devised to this day. The outer circle of the chart marks the Zodiac itself, which is a coordinate system for the plane, not a picture of the star configurations with the same names. Each of the twelve Zodiac signs is 30° of the total 360° circle. Inside the circle, the positions of the planets are marked. Also, there is a twelve part division of the astrological Houses. The cross has mythic connotations. Like the circle it is one of the first figures drawn spontaneously by children, suggesting archetypal qualities. So, the symbol used by the Zodiac seems to be nothing more than a logo that matches his name. It constitutes a form of visual eponymy. As Lunde (2012: 142) remarks, "it also chillingly echoes a telescopic sight."

The Zodiac's use of cryptography raises the question of whether or not he was inspired by Edgar Allan Poe, who employed secret writing in his stories. There is no evidence whatsoever to link them, but there is a compelling implication for this because in many ways the episodes and facts surrounding the Zodiac story read like the plots in Poe's detective stories. The Zodiac may have been an avid reader and aficionado of Poe's works. Like other literary figures of his time, Poe had a keen interest in cryptography, believing that breaking ciphers was required in order to stimulate the use of the imagination together with reason and logic. In the December 1839 issue of *Alexander's Weekly Messenger*, he challenged readers to write to the newspaper using substitution ciphers that readers of the magazine cared to submit. This is exactly what the Zodiac did, as if he were sending it to Poe himself via the San Francisco press. Poe used cryptography as a central part of the plot in his story *The Gold Bug*. Perhaps the Zodiac wanted to bring the darkness of Poe's plots to the world in which he lived.

4.2.3 Style

The study of style in writing, known as *stylometry,* can complement both handwriting analysis and Content Analysis in helping to identify a perpetrator. In contrast to CA, stylometry involves measurements and quantifications of various kinds. For example, the *Mean Length of Utterance* (MLU) is carried out by determining the average number of morphemes (meaningful linguistic units) in sentences, utilizing the following counting procedures:

- Repeated words are counted only once.
- Fillers (*um, oh*) are not included.
- Hesitation and other kinds of discourse markers are instead considered to be countable units: *No, yeah, hi.*
- Compound words (*pocket book*) are counted as single units, as are altered words (*doggie, stylish*).
- Verbs are counted as units, ignoring their predictable grammatical features, such as conjugation.
- Functor words (*to, a*) are ignored.

The MLU of individuals tends to be fairly constant – that is, we make up sentences that, on average, have the same length. This constitutes a type of grammatical I-sign that certainly can be used with CA for forensic purposes.

Another important aspect of style is lexical habits. People consistently use certain words consistently as part of their discourse style, and are barely conscious of so doing. These offer the stylometrist a means of establishing the identity of the author of some text. However, this is not as reliable as other methods of identification because an individual's style is always susceptible to variation from environmental influences, including other speakers, the media, and changes in language itself. Nevertheless, vocabulary style tends to be fairly stable and immune from outside influences even as people age. The documents (ransom notes, threatening letters) of relevance to forensic linguistics can thus be easily examined for lexical habits with the use of computers. The information gleaned from this may be adequate to eliminate a suspect as an author or narrow down an author from a small group of suspects. The statistical techniques used in stylometry include factor and multivariate analysis, Poisson distribution analysis, and the discriminant analysis of functor words (Buckland 2007). These rely on the assumption that each speaker has a unique set of habits.

Returning to the JonBenet Ramsey case with which we started off this chapter, it is relevant that the ransom note seemed to have been written on paper taken from a legal pad present in the house. Together with the fact that the cord twisted around JonBenet's neck was broken off from one of the mother's paintbrushes. These may have influenced the forensic linguist to see more into the note than was there. In fact, the style of the note, when looked at closely, does not seem to relate to anyone in the household and the handwriting analysis produced ambiguous results from various other linguists.

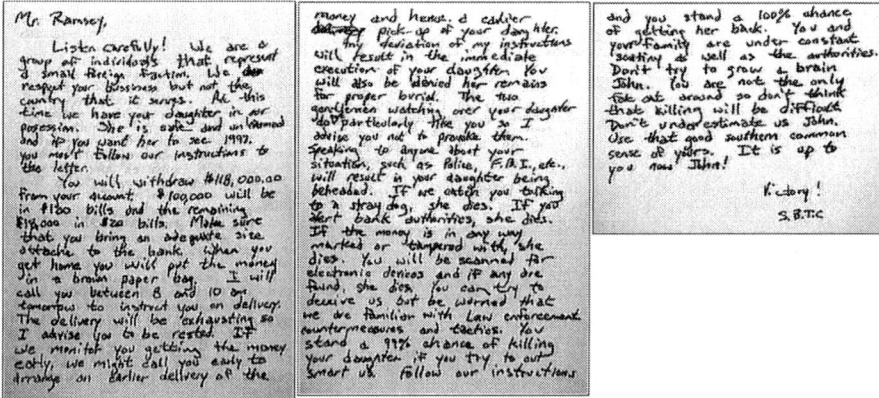

Figure 16: JonBenet Ramsey ransom note

A handwriting analysis of the note – comparing the handwriting style to that of notes written by Patsy Ramsey – as well as a stylometric analysis have been inconclusive. As for CA, it is sufficient to point out that, despite the comments of various investigators to the contrary, there is nothing that would connect the note to the parents (Holmes and Holmes 2008). One of the problems is that the profiler was not a recognized expert. It was an academic with no investigative experience. He cited Patsy Ramsey's ties to the Pentecostal religion as part of the proof for his theory that she killed her daughter, based primarily on the fact that the note is signed S.B.T.C., which he claimed stands for an acronym that represents the words *Saved By The Cross*. While this may be true, the killer could have used this information to his advantage, in the same way he used knowledge of the father's bonus check in asking for the specific sum of 118,000 dollars. The author is more likely to be someone who knew the family well and enacted a kind of vendetta against them by murdering the beloved daughter.

4.3 Criminal Speech

The kind of language that members of criminal gangs use constitutes what linguists call a *cant*. Cants are invented for secretive communication, allowing criminals in gangs or in prisons to communicate with each other so that others will not be able to understand. The study of cants is not considered to be part of forensic linguistics proper, but for the purposes of FS[1], which has a broader social and conceptual objective, the study of cants can be used to interpret criminal behavior through the lens of language.

The first dictionary of a criminal cant was published in 1819. It was compiled by an English nobleman, named James Hardy Vaux. Vaux had spent his early life in London and Liverpool and had become a criminal because of his addiction to gambling. He probably recorded the cant spoken by English criminals and wrote the dictionary in order to gain a pardon, which he received in 1820. Historical documents show that various criminal cants were spoken centuries prior to Vaux's book, many going back to the medieval period. Whether communicating orally, in writing, or spraying painted words on walls or buildings, criminals and criminal gangs have always used language for identity, group solidarity, and even for historical documentation (Coleman 2008). It is quite likely that the word *cant* originates in the Irish (Gaelic) word *cam* or *gam* meaning "disguised, bent or twisted."

4.3.1 The Nature of Cant

Facing unique dilemmas of whom to trust, and of how to make themselves trusted without being detected, many criminals develop their own type of speech to communicate with their collaborators. The subtlety and ingenuity of each cant is truly remarkable. Starting in the late 1800s, Italian criminal gangs communicated with a truly inventive method, using *pizzini*, little pieces of paper on which they wrote their messages (Nicaso and Danesi 2013). Many times the messages were encrypted with special words that could only be decoded by the intended receivers. Over time, these became increasingly sophisticated, and continue to be used today because, unlike electronic forms of communication, the *pizzini* are hand delivered and thus less likely to be intercepted.

The use of what came to be called "thieves' cant" was particularly popular in the sixteenth century when the leading Elizabethan playwrights and pamphleteers of the day, such as Thomas Harman, Thomas Dekker, and Christopher Marlowe, invented a literary genre known as the "Literature of Roguery," writing about the "underworld" and incorporating underworld slang in plays and other publications (Chandler 1907). Thomas Harman claimed to be a Justice of the Peace, including samples of thieves' cant in his *Caveat for Common Cursitors* (1566). He maintained that he collected his information from vagabonds that he had interrogated at his home in Essex. If so, then this might be the first case of the use of forensic linguistics in the history of criminology. In 1591 Robert Greene produced a series of five pamphlets on various aspects of the criminal underworld, followed by pamphlets by Thomas Middleton (*The Black Book*, 1604) and Thomas Dekker (*The Bellman of London*, 1608 and *Lantern and Candlelight*, 1608). Cant was included in these works together with (alleged) descriptions of the social structure of beggars, the techniques of thieves, and descriptions of the underworld, making them quite popular. Many of these pamphlets borrowed from earlier works. Shakespeare used cant in his *As You Like It* (1623) and *The Winter's Tale* (1623), bringing realism into his plays through the language he crafted for his lowlife characters. Examples of words in the thieves' cant as used by pickpockets in England are found below (from Lunde 2012: 129):

- *bung:* the targeted purse
- *cuttle-bung:* the knife used to cut the purse
- *drawing:* taking the purse
- *figging:* pickpocketing
- *foin:* a pickpocket
- *nip:* someone who cuts the strings of the victim's purse
- *shells:* the money in the purse
- *smoking:* spying on the victim
- *snap:* a pickpocket's accomplice
- *stale:* an accomplice who distracts the victim
- *striking:* the act of pickpocketing

Criminal organizations like the Mafia, the Japanese Yakuza, the Chinese Triads, as well as street gangs of various kinds, all have their own form of slang and accompanying (or even substitutive) gesture language.

Because of its secretive nature, cant is known technically as a *cryptolectic* language, which aims to disguise communication of a gang or criminal clique from outsiders. Because it constitutes an "our thing," cant creates a sense of unity among its speakers. Knowing the cant of gang members can allow investigators to effectively understand and communicate with them. It has been shown that those who can speak the cant are more likely to gather more information about a criminal or about gang activities. Knowledge of cant terms could also lead to a better interview. By using and understanding a particular cant, investigators can build a rapport with their interviewees. Familiarity with their language is a signal of confidence.

4.3.2 Nicknames

Personal names are signs that have both indexical and symbolic value: they are indexical in that they collocate a person in some relational way (in relation to a kinship group, to a particular social context, and so on), and they are symbolic in that they are based on specific traditions (Nuessel 1992). The study of *names* falls under the branch of both semiotics and linguistics called *onomastics* (from Greek *onoma* "name").

Nicknames are part of a generic criminal code – a subcode of cant, so to speak. They are more likely to stand out than real names because they are more colorful and vivid. For criminals, they are part of how they define themselves, alluding to something in a gangster's character, appearance, or background that is thought to have import or significance. The Mafioso Lucky Luciano, born Salvatore Lucania, was called "Lucky" because of the noticeable large scars around his neck that permanently recorded his fortuitous escape from death after being slashed and left dead by criminal rivals. The nickname of "Scarface" was given to Al Capone because he was involved in an altercation that left him with three noticeable scars on his face. A criminal is a "nobody" until he devises a nickname for himself – Son of Sam, Zodiac, BTK, and so on. Nicknames promote distinctiveness.

Sometimes gang names are based on those of their leaders. One of the most renowned gangs named in this way is the Sabini Brothers, formed in 1939 in London (Nicaso and Danesi 2013). The gang took its name from five brothers who were half Scottish and half Italian. Another London gang, named after two brothers, the Richardsons, terrorized the streets in the 1960s. The main rival gang of the Richardsons was named after two brothers as well, the Krays, which became one of the most notorious gangs in Britain. At first the gangs, like military armies, collaborated, but eventually they came to distrust each other, leading to gang warfare on the streets of London. The rivalry was captured by the 1990 British movie *The Krays*, which revolved around the claim made by the Krays that their violence did not target common people, but was limited to "their own kind." Some gangs name themselves after territories or places. The Dover Road Gang, for instance, named itself after a London street that they took over as their territory. The *Yardies* went to Britain from Jamaica. They got their name from the fact that they originated in the impoverished back streets of their native Jamaica. In Jamaican, the word "yard" can mean home or patch of territory.

Many nicknames are essentially character profiles, as we saw with Son of Sam, which Berkowitz used to describe his sense of victimization. They constitute a form of antonomasia, or the substitution of an epithet or title for a proper name. Because of its psychological connotative power, in some cases it is a marker of self-importance and braggadocio. Many criminals try to live up to their names, perhaps fulfilling the omen present in them. An example is the Sicilian Michele "The Cobra" Cavataio, a brutal killer who got his nickname from his deceitfulness and the fact the he carried a Colt Cobra revolver. He acted and lived his life as a snake might, sneakily yet viciously when disturbed. The

Palermo bosses had decided to get rid of him in 1969 because he was seen to be a loose cannon. In a gunfight, Cavataio was eventually killed. Here are some other nicknames of famous Mafiosi that show how they are intended to bring out some feature of the Mafioso's character, appearance, or personality:

- Vincent "Chin" Gigante (who had a prominent chin)
- Richard "Shellackhead" Cantarella (from his hair pomade)
- Vincent "Vinny Gorgeous" Basciano (who always dressed in dapper clothes and slicked his hair in style)
- Earl "Squint" Coralluzzo (because he squinted a lot)
- Anthony "Fat Tony" Salerno (for his corpulent body)
- Thomas "Tough Tommy" Contaldo (because of his brutality)
- Salvatore "Sammy the Bull" Gravano (who had a neck like a bull and was a capable fighter)
- Ettore "Killer" Coco (for his ruthlessness)
- Thomas "Tommy Karate" Pitera (used martial arts in his vicious killing sprees)

Interestingly, some names are ironic, describing some weakness, such as Earl "Squint" Coralluzzo and Carmine "Papa Smurf" Franco. It is not clear how Franco got his nickname. But photographs show a grandfatherly-looking man and seemingly wise like the cartoon character Papa Smurf. Forensic linguists and other crime experts have found that the nickname is given early on in a mobster's career, sometimes as far back as childhood. Interestingly, in 2011 as over a hundred mobsters were rounded up by American authorities, nicknames such as Vinny "Carwash," Tony "Bagels," and Junior "Lollipops" stood out ludicrously.

4.4 Metaphor Analysis

In contemporary linguistics, the study of metaphor or figurative language has become a central focus. The approach to language as a system of concepts grounded in figurative language is known as *Conceptual Metaphor Theory* (CMT). Although the term surfaced in the early 1980s, the theoretical notions that it embodies have a long history behind them, starting in the ancient world and elaborated more systematically throughout the twentieth century in psychology, semiotics, and linguistics. The theory has significant implications for the study of criminal language and of the writings that criminals execute, since, if it is correct, metaphorical utterances are systematic and thus can be used to reveal unconscious thinking.

4.4.1 Background

In the middle part of the twentieth century, the American philosopher Max Black (1962) introduced a distinction that was to become fundamental in subsequent work, namely that a specific metaphor, such as *Your friend is a snake*, is really an exemplar of the more general conceptual category that links people and animals. The former is now called a *linguistic metaphor* and the latter a *conceptual metaphor*. A watershed 1977 study then showed that conceptual metaphors pervaded common everyday speech. Titled *Psychology and the Poetics of Growth: Figurative Language in Psychology, Psychotherapy, and Education*, it found that speakers of English uttered, on average, a surprising 3,000 novel metaphors and 7,000 idioms per week (Pollio, Barlow, Fine, and Pollio 1977). It became saliently obvious that metaphorical discourse could hardly be characterized as a deviation from literal speech, or a mere stylistic accessory to literal conversation. Two collections of studies published shortly thereafter, *Metaphor and Thought* (Ortony 1979) and *Cognition and Figurative Language* (Honeck and Hoffman 1980), and a groundbreaking book by George Lakoff and Mark Johnson, *Metaphors We Live By* (1980), set the stage for CMT.

The latter book laid out the notions upon which the theory was subsequently elaborated, researched, expanded, and applied. Recall the example above of *Your friend is a snake*. The friend could have been portrayed as any other animal, such as a *gorilla*, a *pig*, a *puppy*, and so forth. The result would have been a different metaphorical portrait of his or her personality. In other words, each linguistic metaphor instantiates a more general concept: *people are animals*. *People* is termed the target domain and *animals* the source domain. The source domain is the set of animal concepts that allow us to grasp the target domain of human personality. The source for understanding the latter is not, however, limited to our experience of animals; it can be anything from a substance (*Your friend is a softie*) to electricity (*Your friend is always wired*). Each linguistic metaphor implies a different psychology behind our evaluation of human personality. Portraying a friend as a monkey, for instance, forces us to imagine a human person in simian terms.

The bulk of the research in CMT has shown that metaphorical language is a product of systematic associative thinking. Lakoff and Johnson trace the cognitive source of conceptual metaphors to what they call image schemas (Lakoff 1987, Johnson 1987, Lakoff and Johnson 1999). These are mental outlines that convert concrete experiences (like perceived animal behaviors) into source domains for understanding abstractions (like human personality). Whatever their neural substrate, they not only permit people to recognize patterns in the world, but also to anticipate new ones and to draw inferences from them. These are all imprinted in specific linguistic metaphors. For example, the experience of orientation – up vs. down, back vs. front, near vs. far, and so on – underlies how we express such concepts as happiness (*Lately my spirits are up*), responsibility (*You have to face up to your problems*), among many others. The common experience of how containers work and what they allow us to do, on the other hand, underlies such concepts as the mind (*My mind is full of good memories*), emotions (*My heart is filled with hope*), and so on.

There are two other figures of speech that are considered to be cognitively different from metaphor in CMT – metonymy and irony. Metonymy is the process of representing a concept with something that is associated with it: *She loves Hemingway* (= the writings of Hemingway); *The automobile is destroying our health* (= the collection of automobiles); and so on. In parallel with the notion of conceptual metaphor, the term conceptual metonym can be adopted to refer to generalized concepts based on metonymy rather than metaphor: *the face for the person* (as in *He's nothing more than another pretty face*); *a body part for the person* (as in *Get your butt over here!*); and so on (Danesi 2004).

Conceptual metonyms reveal that we evaluate certain concepts as representative of larger concepts or referents. There are various reasons for this, but the relevant discussion is beyond the purposes of this chapter. Suffice it to say that experience, context, and other factors play a role in the type of metonymic process. Irony is limited in CMT to designating a strategy whereby words are used to convey a meaning contrary to their literal sense – for example *I love being tortured* would be interpreted as ironic if it were uttered by someone experiencing unwelcome pain. The intent of the speaker, including his or her prosody (tone of voice, accent, and so on), the speaker's relation to the listener, and the context are all factors that establish the ironic meaning of an utterance. If the above sentence were uttered by a masochist, then it would hardly have an ironic meaning.

All three figurative processes (metaphor, metonymy, irony), however, show association as the underlying cognitive mechanism, so all three have the structure of *X is Y*, either by mapping one domain onto another (conceptual metaphor), using one domain to stand for another (metonymy), or using one domain contrastively for another (irony).

4.4.2 Criminal Texts

The use of CMT in examining texts forensically has been rarely, if ever used, to the best of my knowledge. But it is potentially a very useful technique, which can be called, simply, *Metaphor Analysis* (MA).

Let us return to the Son of Sam case. Berkowitz sent the following letter on May 30, 1977, to Jimmy Breslin, a journalist for the New York *Daily News*. Interestingly, Berkowitz used the return address "Mother, the Cemetery, 174 Coligni Avenue, New Rochelle, NY 10801," which is itself a conceptual metaphor for his state of mind. The text of the letter is replete with conceptual metaphors that can be used to reconstruct his frame of mind (from Gibson 2004: 12).

Hello from the gutters of N.Y.C. which are filled with dog manure, vomit, stale wine, urine and blood. Hello from the sewers of N.Y.C. which swallow up these delicacies when they are washed away by the sweeper trucks. Hello from the cracks in the sidewalks of N.Y.C. and from the ants that dwell in these cracks and feed in the dried blood of the dead that has settled into the cracks. J.B., I'm just dropping you a line to let you know that I appreciate your interest in those recent and horrendous .44 killings. I also want to tell you that I read your column daily and I find it quite informative. Tell me Jim, what will you have for July twenty-ninth? You can forget about me if you like because I don't care for publicity. However you must not forget Donna Lauria and you cannot let the people forget her either. She was a very, very sweet girl but Sam's a thirsty lad and he won't let me stop killing until he gets his fill of blood. Mr. Breslin, sir, don't think that because you haven't heard from me for a while that I went to sleep. No, rather, I am still here. Like a spirit roaming the night. Thirsty, hungry, seldom stopping to rest; anxious to please Sam. I love my work. Now, the void has been filled. Perhaps we shall meet face to face someday or perhaps I will be blown away by cops with smoking .38's. Whatever, if I shall be fortunate enough to meet you I will tell you all about Sam if you like and I will introduce you to him. His name is "Sam the terrible." Son of Sam

Figure 17: Another Son of Sam letter

Here is what an MA of various parts of the text would reveal:

Table 4: Metaphor Analysis

Metaphorical Referent	Underlying Concept
gutters, dog manure	"My life is a sewage dump"
stale wine, urine and blood	"My life is reduced to rudimentary biology"
sewers – swallow up these delicacies	"I am contained in a sewer"
cracks in the sidewalk	"I live in a fragmented world"
Sam's a thirsty lad ... fill of blood	"People's blood is my life-giving substance"
the void has been filled	"I feel empty inside"

In the remainder of this letter he alludes to himself as a "Duke," among other epithets, which are all linguistic metaphors bringing out his unconscious need to rise above the banality and emptiness of his life to accomplish something that will get noticed. A similar analysis of his other notes, some of which were discussed above, shows that the unconscious conceptual metaphors in them are a trace to his state of mind.

In effect, MA is really a complementary technique to CA, focusing more on underlying conceptualizations that the criminal harbors and which come out in specific expressions. As part of forensic semiotics, the technique of MA would consist in:

- checking through for the conceptual metaphors in a criminal's texts (oral and written);
- checking for thematic consistency, that is, how the conceptual metaphors form a cohesive verbal portrait of the criminal's state of mind.
- mapping the MA against findings by forensic psychologists, profilers, and other kinds of criminal investigative experts to see if they fit in with the overall portrait.

Chapter 5
The Criminal Mind

Crime is terribly revealing. Try and vary your methods as you will, your tastes, your habits, your attitude of mind, and your soul is revealed by your actions.

Agatha Christie (1891–1976)

The television program *Criminal Minds* attracted large audiences on several major channels and networks in the mid-2000s. The plots revolved around the activities of the Behavioral Analysis Unit (BAU), a fictional version of a sub-section of the FBI called the Behavioral Sciences Unit (BSU), also named the Behavioral Sciences Services (BSS). A team of criminal profilers is called in, from episode to episode, by local police departments to assist them in solving crimes usually involving unknown serial killers (referred to as the "unknown subjects" or "unsubs" for short). The team members use the craft of profiling, along with all available evidence, to track down the unsub. As the show intimates, criminal profiling is an important investigative tool used by the FBI for capturing serial killers. The team uses evidence from the specific case at hand, matching it to historical precedents (famous cases of real serial killers). This allows them to draw an appropriate psychological profile as a means to solve the case. Each program is both a thriller crime story and a quasi-documentary on criminal profiling.

Criminal Minds is a spinoff of *The Silence of the Lambs*, the film that first brought criminal profiling to the attention of a large audience and into the realm of popular culture. But even before that, another movie, *In Cold Blood* (1967), from the book by Truman Capote (1966), painted a terrifying psychological portrait of the criminal mind through the filmic technique of analepsis (flashback). The film suggested that some people may be "natural born killers," incapable of differentiating between moral and immoral states of mind.

The topic of criminal profiling and of the criminal mind generally is of obvious interest to forensic semiotics, since one of the basic tenets of semiotics is that there is an intrinsic connection between semiosis and behavior. The nature of this connection is often the thematic subject of *Criminal Minds* and of serial killer stories and documentaries, showing how killers leave specific kinds of signs behind, signs that reveal the *raison d'être* of their actions. This chapter will look at criminal profiling in the light of its implications and relation to semiotic analysis, focusing on serial killers. For the sake of accuracy, it should be mentioned that the term *profiling* is a generic term. The technical term is *criminal investigative analysis*.

5.1 Forensic Psychology

Criminals, like ordinary people, are, by and large, creatures of habit. Criminal profiling is based on this common-sense principle. Some criminals, such as serial killers, are guided by particular kinds of motivations that may have their source in childhood. Profiling is a branch of forensic psychology and, like general psychology itself, is an interdisciplinary area that can be of practical use to criminal investigations. The profile is constructed on the basis of historical cases, research on personality types (such as the one described in chapter 3), which are matched to the case at hand. A suspect can then be subjected to tests and interrogations to verify the profile, modify it, or in some cases even reject it. The instruments used include the usual lie-detection ones (chapter 2) and the ones developed within forensic linguistics, such as Content Analysis.

Today, profilers have at their disposal a wide range of techniques, such as geographic profiling, which was devised at Simon Fraser University in British Columbia in 1989 (Kerr 2012). The idea is to go beyond the points on a map to understand the significance or logistics of the places selected by the offender. Geographic profiling uses the locations of crimes that appear to be connected to estimate the offender's likeliest base of operation or residence. As Kerr (2012: 7) puts it:

> In our daily lives we follow patterns. Using experience and familiarity with the locations of the things we need for our daily lives, we create mental maps of our surroundings, maps that provide us with information about our individual access routes to things we need such as food, school, work, and transport. A killer's mental map will take into account the thing he needs – convenience and ease of access and escape for a murder or body-dump site, for example. A criminal's primary residence is usually integral in his mental map. As we take the easiest routes to and from places where the things we need are located, we establish patterns.

Psychological theories of personality are also used by profilers extensively, such as the disorganized-versus-organized typology discussed in chapter 3. The FBI *Crime Classification Manual*, first published in 1992, was perhaps the first police manual to adopt such a typology, placing habitual murderers into one of these two categories, or into a mixed one (that is, a serial killer who exhibits a mixture of disorganized and organized personality traits).

There are, of course, other ways to classify personality features, as McNab (2010: 9) points out:

> Typical categories in this regard include "visionary" and "missionary" – together known as the Holmes typology, after the authors Ronald M. and Stephen T. Holmes (2008). The visionary killer acts because he believes that he is commanded to do so by an external force, such as God, while the missionary (or "mission-oriented") killer does so because of a desire to exterminate a certain group of people, such as homosexuals and prostitutes.

As we have seen, in this framework David Berkowitz (chapter 4) would be labeled as a visionary killer (since he claimed that he was being controlled by demonic forces), while Gary Ridgway (chapters 2 and 3) would be considered to be a missionary killer (since he killed mainly prostitutes). Other motives include sexual excitement, power, or an enjoyment of sadism. Yet, however much we try to understand killers, there is always something of a mystery about them. To a semiotician, the overriding motivation for any form of behavior, including criminal behavior, is what can be called the search for meaning or the need to fill a meaning vacuum. Even in the case of serial killers who seem to be "natural born killers" the quest for meaning is still there, constituting, perhaps, the need to assert oneself in some base instinctive way through murderous actions. So, the forensic semiotician would look for the meaning gaps in a killer's life and attempt to reconstruct his or her motivations through the expressions related to these gaps.

5.1.1 Born or Reared to Kill?

There are several assumptions involved in profiling that merit critical discussion. The first one, as just discussed, is that there is a part in all of us that is predictable and thus that we inherit some of our personality and character traits through the genetic channel. This means that some people may be born killers, no matter what upbringing they may have had. In the movie *Natural Born Killers* (1994), directed by Oliver Stone, this theme is explored brilliantly, concluding that the source of the serial killer phenomenon in the modern world is a culture of violence that breeds a lack of respect for morality structures. The connection between culture and crime seems to come out in the relevant research, suggesting an interaction between environmental and genetic factors. Some of these are as follows (McNab 2010: 8):

- The vast majority of serial killers are male (over 90%).
- They come typically from abusive or dysfunctional family backgrounds.
- They perform violent or destructive acts from an early age, such as torturing animals, arson, and so on.
- They grow up with distorted sexual preferences.

As McNab (2010: 8) observes, "There remains the sense, however, that this is not the whole picture, that within each serial killer is a deeper abnormality, or predisposition to violence." McNab may be correct, but it is impossible to determine to what extent nature and culture interact in the genesis of the criminal mind. All we can do is speculate. *Natural Born Killers* seems to put its eggs into the cultural basket, implicitly condemning the contemporary world of glorified violence that encourages killing as retributive justice. The rise of mass and serial murders is thus connected to the rise of the influence of the mass media on human behavior. The film is part portrait of the criminal mind, part cultural satire. A young couple is united by their common love of violence. Together, they embark on a frenetic and gory killing spree that grabs the attention of a sensation-hungry tabloid media. Their fame is ensured by a newsman for his show, *American Maniacs*. There is little doubt that the two killers are psychotic, but so is the media and the culture that glorifies them.

Describing what the criminal mind is all about is the task of forensic psychology. Of specific interest to the field is the way the brain of the criminal works in opposition to the brains of non-criminals. This is where devices such as the EEG come into play. The EEG tracks electrical waves moving through the brain. As we saw, it is used as a technique in brain fingerprinting, in the form of the Memory and Encoding Related Multifaceted Electroencephalographic Response (MERMER), which maps people's responses to certain stimuli. MERMER is effective because it skips over the control mechanisms of the brain and purportedly fleshes out only the information stored in the brain that is beyond intentional control. The technique can help a profiler find out what kinds of memories motivate a suspect's actions, matching them to evidence at a crime scene. It also allows researchers to look for intrinsic patterns in the minds of criminals that may be different from those of normal minds.

As an aside, it should be mentioned that MERMER is also used sometimes as a lie-detection method. The images produced by an individual's reactions to simple stimuli are used to establish a baseline response pattern. The brain wave alters when an image is recognized, and guilty suspects cannot suppress their reactions as they can sometimes with a polygraph. A computer is then used to analyze the reactions. It has been found with a significant degree of accuracy that innocent suspects have no MERMER when they are shown a crime scene that they do not know; guilty ones do. This technique was instrumental in getting a confession from serial killer James Grinder in 1999 in Missouri. The inventor of the technique, Dr. Lawrence A. Farwell (2001), a Harvard research associate, gave the test to Grinder, showing him images connected to an unsolved murder. Grinder's brain reactions confirmed a MERMER match. The suspect subsequently pleaded guilty.

5.1.2 Behaviorism

In some ways, criminal profiling and forensic psychology generally are a throwback to behaviorist psychology, which was based on the notion that only observable behaviors can be studied scientifically. Behaviorism was introduced in 1913 by the American psychologist James B. Watson, who believed that changes in behavior resulted from conditioning, a process whereby a new response is associated with a certain stimulus, becoming part of habitual thought. That premise is, clearly, a primary assumption of criminal profiling. The basic method in behaviorism is to analyze complex forms of behavior by observing, measuring, and then analyzing the responses of human subjects to various stimuli under controlled conditions.

The key notion of behaviorism is that of the conditioned response, developed initially by the Russian physiologist Ivan Pavlov in 1902 in his work with dogs. Pavlov presented a piece of meat to a hungry dog, producing in the dog the expected response of salivation. He called it the dog's *unconditioned response*, because it is part of the animal's instinctual behavior, not acquired from context. Then Pavlov rang a bell at the same time that he presented the meat stimulus a number of times. He discovered that the dog eventually salivated only to the ringing of the bell, without the presence of meat. Clearly, the bell ringing, which would not have triggered the salivation instinctively, had brought about a *conditioned response* in the dog. This suggested that in all species, conditioning is a critical factor that leads to habit-formation. This is why criminal profiling looks at the upbringing of the perpetrator and any other influences from the environment (such as media-induced copycat crime) in order to better understand the criminal personality.

Watson subsequently proposed that human conditioning could be studied in a laboratory, since all complex forms of behavior can ultimately be broken down into simple muscular and glandular processes and can thus be observed and measured directly. In one of his well-known studies, he struck a metal bar loudly each time a child touched a furry animal. The sound scared the infant, who gradually became frightened just at the sight of the animal. Watson maintained that any response in a child could be evoked if the environment could be controlled. In the first decades of the twentieth century, the American psychologist B. F. Skinner (1938) became famous for his studies on how rewards (positive conditioning) and punishments (negative conditioning) can influence behavior. His work had significant impacts on theories of crime and models of penology, even though behaviorism had fallen into disfavor among psychologists generally in the late 1960s. Skinner's ideas are still used in techniques such as behavior modification theory to help children who are facing mental challenges in learning school subjects. They are also used as basic techniques in some kinds of criminal interrogations where negative and positive forms of reinforcement are used to flesh out the truth or relevant information from someone. And it is employed by criminologists in their attempt to understand how simulated violence in the media might condition certain people. However, forensic psychologists focus not only on conditioning forces in the shaping of criminality, but also on how biological, psychological, and social factors may intermingle in producing the enigmatic criminal mind.

5.1.3 Cognitivism

A basic premise in criminal profiling, as we have seen, is that perpetrators of crimes are driven by similar patterns of compulsion, and thus will tend to commit a series of crimes in a similar manner. This premise has a basis in both behaviorist and cognitivist theories of the mind. Cognitivism is the school of thought in psychology that most mental phenomena and human faculties are hard-wired at birth and thus that some, if not many, criminals are born to be criminals.

A primary technique of cognitivists is to "get to" the "unobservable" mental phenomena by modeling them on computers. The underlying assumption is that the functions of the mind can be understood if they are modeled by software designed to simulate them; so, by noting what the computer cannot do, we can infer what makes the brain unique. Ulrich Neisser (1967: 6) put it as follows at the dawn of the movement:

> The task of the psychologist in trying to understand human cognition is analogous to that of a man trying to discover how a computer has been programmed. In particular, if the program seems to store and reuse information, he would like to know by what "routines" or "procedures" this is done. Given this purpose, he will not care much whether his particular computer stores information in magnetic cores or in thin films; he wants to understand the program, not the "hardware." By the same token, it would not help the psychologist to know that memory is carried by RNA as opposed to some other medium. He wants to understand its utilization, not its incarnation.

Neisser realized, however, that the computer metaphor, if brought to an extreme, would actually lead psychology astray. So, only a few pages later he issued the following warning (Neisser 1967: 9): "Unlike men, artificially intelligent programs tend to be single-minded, undistractable, and unemotional ... in my opinion, none does even remote justice to the complexity of mental processes." The term *cognition*, rather than *mind* or *behavior*, is employed to eliminate the artificial distinction maintained by behaviorists between inner (mental) and observable (behavioral) processes. Although cognitivism's goals are much broader than what has been outlined here, and include experientialist approaches to the mind, the basic axiom that we inherit our traits remains constant (Gardner 1985).

Profilers employ a blend of behaviorist and cognitivist notions to access the criminal mind and to draw profiles of unsubs. They also look to neuroscience to understand how the criminal brain functions under certain conditions. Modern imaging equipment such as PET scans and fMRI technologies are a means of exploring how humans process information and develop thought patterns. In effect, modern-day profiling is a non-partisan, inter-theoretical discipline that, like semiotics, looks at the signs of crime as revealing the broader referential system of culture as the overall conditioning system.

5.2 Criminal Profiling

Criminal profiling consists of several steps or phases. First, the assumption is made that a criminal, especially a serial killer, will behave and think like other criminals have in the past, and a computer model of the behavior exhibited in the case at hand is mapped against historically-analyzed behaviors. Specifically, the modus operandi (MO) of a criminal is analyzed and considered against a general MO of other criminal behaviors that seem connected to the same kinds of crimes. Often, criminals leave a *signature* that can be used to infer who the perpetrator might be in terms of age, background, sex, physical appearance, and even the make of automobile he or she might drive. The signature – leaving messages at a crime scene, taking or leaving souvenirs at a crime scene, and so on – reveals personal needs and fantasies. Profilers also investigate victims – known as *victimology* – in order to understand why the victim was selected. For example, if several prostitutes are murdered, the perpetrator may be a customer or a fanatical moralist and thus his background, age, experiences, and so on are seen as connected to certain personality types.

5.2.1 Basic Profiling

Profiling grew out of studies commissioned by the FBI's Behavioral Science Unit (BSU), which was opened in 1971. Today, the unit keeps a database of profiles of perpetrators and victims, and then draws ever more general profiles of criminals in order to develop individual profiles for going after criminals. Profiling actually goes back to a police surgeon in England, named Dr. Thomas Bond, who performed an autopsy on Mary Kelly, Jack the Ripper's seventh and final victim. Bond claimed that, on the basis of the signs gleaned from the autopsy, the killer was a daring, physically strong, mentally unstable, and quiet loner. Jack the Ripper's identity has, of course, never been determined, but Dr. Bond's assessment caught the attention of the police. Then, in the 1940s and 1950s, nearly 40 bombings occurred in New York City, perplexing the police. Dr. James Brussel, a psychiatrist, provided the police with his own profile that predicted, strangely, that the perpetrator wore a double-breasted suit and lived with an unmarried sister or aunt in Connecticut, New Hampshire, or Maine. When the police caught up with the perpetrator, George Metesky, in 1957, he surprisingly fit the profile (Vronsky 2004: 323–324).

Among the features that go into a profile, the following are of primary importance:

- *Geographic origin:* Geographical profiling, as we have seen, involves mapping where the crimes occurred, in order to draw a map of where the perpetrator may live or at least operate.
- *Ethnic group:* The ethnicity of the perpetrator is often apparent through vocabulary choices and the particular type of syntax used in written or voice messages. Symbols and signatures left at a crime scene are also used in drawing up a probable ethnic origin.
- *Age:* Written messages may also reveal patterns in language use and style that are associated with an age group.
- *Gender:* Language is gender-sensitive, with women's and men's speech differing in vocabulary, grammar, and style. This can be used to determine who wrote a note.
- *Education level:* Written notes leave traces of educational level, of course. In the absence of notes, the type of crime scene that emerges, as organized or disorganized (as already discussed), is also suggestive of education level.

As can be seen, profiling is based on the observation of patterned semiotic and linguistic behavior. This makes it, ipso facto, a branch of forensic semiotics. A partnership between forensic psychology and forensic semiotics would be an advantageous one helping to establish behavioral and cognitive patterns in criminal behaviors under the general theoretical frame of "meaning," as discussed above. For example, the suggested technique of Metaphor Analysis (chapter 4) might allow a profiler to confirm or disconfirm a profile. It may also provide insights into the motivations and emotional state of the perpetrator, by decoding the underlying conceptual metaphors in a suspect's language.

5.3 Inside the Criminal Mind

Criminals live, by and large, in a "live wire" world of their own making. As the history of crime reveals, many find their "work" exciting, a form of entertainment and escape from boredom and routine. Reynolds (2006: 192) notes that this type of mindset may result from affluence and a fixation on material prosperity – the more affluent societies tend to produce more criminals than poorer ones:

> Their entertainment value is obvious, but we may also need threats to our security in order to fully appreciate it. In the process, we speculate about things we cannot explain, and often become fixed on threats and events well removed from our day-to-day lives. It's more comforting that way, which perhaps explains why the greatest concentration of secret society concerns rests in urban Europe and affluent North America, whose residents have the most to lose materially and spiritually.

Crime rates are indeed higher in affluent areas of the world. One of the reasons for this may have a psychosocial source, which can be called simply endemic boredom, which the existentialist philosophers called *ennui*, inhering in a deep abiding sense of uselessness and weariness. There is no documentary evidence (writings) of boredom until the nineteenth century, where it is discussed perhaps for the first time in Charles Dickens' novel *Bleak House* (1862). Boredom is connected to meaningless habits in everyday life, emerging as an emotion in the Industrial Period, as the Dickens' anecdote implies. In fact, some sociologists see the ultimate source of pathological boredom as capitalism, which requires the imprinting of *habitus* in the human mind – a term coined by French philosopher Marcel Mauss (1934) and elaborated further by Pierre Bourdieu (1977) to refer to the ways in which people living in capitalist systems are controlled by those in power or in the upper echelons of society and by the profit motive, above all other kinds of goals and objectives. Social success depends largely on the individual's ability to absorb the habitus of the cultural mainstream, leading to automatonic and mindless behavior. This whole line of thought derives ultimately from the notion of *alienation* – a term coined by Karl Marx (1959) to describe a sensed estrangement from other people, society, or work that is purportedly endemic to capitalist urban societies, which are described as morally shallow and depersonalizing. French social theorist Émile Durkheim (1912) suggested that alienation stemmed from a loss of moral and religious traditions in a secularized and materialistic world. He used the term *anomie* to refer to the sense of irrational boredom and purposelessness experienced by a person or a class as a result of a lack of moral standards and values (Durkheim 1912). Anomie may, in fact, be a factor in producing the high crime rates that modern-day societies reveal.

Alienation takes different forms and may have different consequences. Alienated individuals may become disoriented or hostile, feel helpless, withdraw within themselves, or reject established values – a fact that the history of profiling has consistently revealed. But this theoretical framework does not explain the motivations of many criminals, who are hardly bored and apathetic individuals. The real achievement for the serial killer is to get people to notice him and yet remain undetected – a fact that deeply upsets us as unresolved cases such as that of the Zodiac killer continue to make obvious. Alienation theory would also not explain copycat crime. From the point of view of FS[1], one factor to be taken more seriously into consideration is mimesis. Mimesis is a powerful form of imitation because it is grafted from social models. Portrayals of criminal thugs on the screen have given rise to an unconscious "criminal culture," as Oliver Stone suggested in his movie, and these produce a mimesis effect that, although sporadic in populations, is still significant. Mimesis filters out unsavory reality, allowing for a life model that the criminal uses to counteract his or her plight, real or imagined.

5.3.1 Raskolnikov

The personage who can be used to discuss and debate the validity of some of the theories of criminality is not a real criminal, but a fictitious one – Rodion Romanovich Raskolnikov, the main character in Fyodor Dostoyevsky's great novel *Crime and Punishment* (1866). Raskolnikov is a poor student, who nevertheless sees himself as different from the plebeian and bourgeois masses and consequently comes up with a personal theory which maintains that extraordinary people, like himself, have a right to commit any crime, since this paradoxically will improve humanity's lot, shaking people, in effect, from their habitus. To prove his theory, he kills an old, wicked pawnbroker and tragically her half-sister who happened to come by chance onto the scene. Right after the crime, Raskolnikov becomes ill and stays in his room semi-conscious for days. As soon as he can, he goes out and reads about his crime in the newspapers. He encounters police inspector Porfiry who is investigating the crime, and almost confesses to him on the spot. Porfiry becomes suspicious and decides to pursue him doggedly. He interviews all those who had anything to do with the pawnbroker. He interviews Raskolnikov as well, who starts believing that Porfiry definitely suspects him. A short time before, Raskolnikov had serendipitously met Sonya Marmeladov, the daughter of a dead man whom he had helped previously. So, he decides to go to her for solace and support, asking her to read to him the Bible story of Lazarus – a story of rebirth. He suddenly promises to tell her who murdered the old pawnbroker, in a qualm of conscience. After talking with Sonya, Raskolnikov confesses to the murder and is sentenced to eight years in a Siberian prison. With Sonya's support, Raskolnikov begins his rebirth.

Sigmund Freud's investigations of the mind were published after Dostoyevsky had written this novel. But the novel's portraits of the dark side of the human psyche clearly prefigure his notion that there are unconscious forces in us that drive us to commit certain acts. Porfiry's investigations into the Freudian motives behind the crime and of Raskolnikov's mental state would become mainstream criminal profiling decades later. Just before the publication of *Crime and Punishment*, Dostoevsky had written his short masterpiece *Notes from the Underground* (1864). The protagonist of that story starts by saying: "I am a sick man. I am a spiteful man. I am an unattractive man." This sense of worthlessness, or alienation, exposing a need to "be someone" is what motivates Raskolnikov to kill in *Crime and Punishment*. Raskolnikov's character is, in effect, a fictitious psychological profile, showing that crime is not an instinctual or genetic trait, but the result of broader psychosocial factors that produce criminal impulses.

5.3.2 The Criminal

It was Cesare Lombroso (1876), as mentioned (chapter 1), who first tackled the problem of criminal traits. Lombroso studied convicted criminals and their behavior, thus anticipating the age of the profiler. He attempted to describe what could be construed as distinctive criminal traits, believing that criminals constituted a distinct "subspecies" of society – they were marked with recognizable body features, such as above or below average height, projecting ears, thick hair, thin beards, enormous jaws, a square chin, large cheekbones, and other visible features. Although most of Lombroso's claims have been shown to be false, forensic research has actually confirmed his basic hypothesis – that many criminals share common traits. The diverse statistical and psychological studies of criminals has shown the following, as already pointed out above, which can be summarized here:
- They are most often males.
- They are usually in their mid-to late teens or in their twenties.
- They tend to come from difficult family backgrounds.
- They have family friends convicted of crimes.
- They tend to do poorly at school.
- Women commit fewer violent crimes and are less likely to be involved with gangs.
- Also, it has been found that substances such as alcohol and drugs are not criminal triggers, even though some criminals deal with drugs as part of their trade.

Overall, the criminal mind seems to be the product of a nature and culture partnership that has become twisted. Upbringing undoubtedly has a role in shaping a criminal mind, as Freud suspected. So does social system, as alienation theory and, as writers such as Dostoyevsky, have persuasively argued. And so too does the search for meaning to one's life, as Raskolnikov certainly knew.

Nations vary in the incidence and perception of crime and criminals. Conditions that affect the amount and type of crimes committed include the proportion of people living in cities, the proportion of young and old people in the population, and the degree of conflict among various groups in society. Added to this are the factors discussed here, such as alienation and mimesis. Comparisons of crime rates of different countries indicate that increases in crime accompany increases in the rate of social change (Newman 2010). The crime rate stays relatively stable in traditional societies where people believe their way of life will continue. Crime rates are particularly high in industrial nations that have large cities. These rates include crimes of passion and those that are premeditated, such as serial killing. It seems that in tribal-like societies, the system of elders and of kinship ties is used to settle issues of infidelity and dishonor. In urban centers this is, of course, not always possible, and this may be a reason for the spike in crimes of revenge.

5.3.3 Copycat Crime

The movie *Copycat* (1995), discussed already, is a filmic essay on the theory of mimesis, showing how some individuals come to be serial killers through the copycat effect (Coleman 2004). The issue of copycat crime raises deep questions about the relation between crime and the media, which will be taken up in the final chapter. Incredibly, it has been documented that movies do indeed induce copycat crimes. Following is a sampling.

Natural Born Killers has inspired the greatest documented or alleged number of copycat killings. The most famous was committed by the couple Sarah Edmonson and Benjamin Darrus, who drank LSD and watched the film several times before going out and shooting victims soon after. The same movie was apparently also a spark for the Columbine massacre, with the phrase "going NBK" (*Natural Born Killers*) in the journal entries of Eric Harris and Dylan Klebold signaling the start of their rampage. The decapitation of a 13-year-old Texan girl by a 14-year-old boy who wanted to be famous like the protagonists in the movie became a media event.

Other movies that have purportedly inspired copycat crimes include *The Collector* (1965), *A Clockwork Orange* (1971), *Taxi Driver* (1976), *The Basketball Diaries* (1995), *The Matrix* (1995), *Wedding Crashers* (2005), among others. A scene in *Money Train* (1995) involved an attendant in a New York subway tollbooth being set on fire. Soon after the movie was released a copycat killer filled a booth with lighter fluid and ignited it, killing the tollbooth attendant. What these show to the semiotician is the power of mimesis in producing criminal behaviors. The copycat crimes are, in semiotic terms, icons of the originals. Iconicity is a powerful form of semiosis, as discussed. In this case it is an aberrant form.

5.4 The Serial Killer

Copycat is also about pop culture's fascination with the serial killer. Starting with Jack the Ripper, the rise of the serial killer as an anti-hero in popular culture raises several fundamental questions. In his in-depth study of the serial killer, David Canter (1994) went beneath the skin of both fictional and real serial killers, finding little difference, in public perception between the two, even though real-life serial killers are quite unlike their fictional counterparts. The real ones are lucky, rather than clever, banal rather than interesting, and seldom play mind games with the police. But the fact that they are perceived as identical is evidence that there is a powerful synergy, again, between fiction and reality.

This has produced a "serial killer culture," as Vronsky (2004: 19) aptly calls it, which has become absorbed by this type of crime, showcasing it in media coverage, movies, television programs, and websites:

> You cannot turn on the TV without major network news magazine shows like *Dateline* or *20/20* running previously broadcast episodes or updates shows on some serial killer. Tune into the Discovery Channel for the "science of catching serial killers." Go to the History Channel and you will find the "history of serial killers."

The rise of criminal profiling as a forensic technique is connected directly with the rise in serial killings and with the mimesis or copycat effect. Serial murders have always existed; obsession with them is a modern phenomenon brought about by media culture. To quote Vronsky (2004: 31) again:

> Jack the Ripper with his five victims is immortalized, but the Louisiana-Texas axe murderer with forty-nine victims is entirely forgotten. The primary difference is that London was the center of a huge newspaper industry while Louisiana and Texas were not. The story of Jack the Ripper was retold and entered popular myth and literature – while the Louisiana-Texas axe murderer faded from public consciousness. Serial murder "epidemics" are as much about reporting as they are about killing.

5.4.1 Culture

Among the movies inspired by the case of the Zodiac killer, 1971's *Dirty Harry* and David Fincher's 2007 *Zodiac* are particularly relevant. In the first movie a killer, named "Scorpio," is killed by Dirty Harry Callaghan, a ruthless cop played by Clint Eastwood. The Zodiac was never identified and captured, leaving people in a suspended state of uncertainty. The movie captured the killer and enacted retributive justice upon him. It thus allowed people to experience a form of catharsis – if the real killer cannot be found, at least we got him in fictional form. The second movie tapped into our fear of the unknowable that the Zodiac Killer evoked in his heyday, and continues to evoke today in those who recall the period of his killing spree. The film follows the exploits of a cartoonist and a newspaper reporter who have become obsessed with tracking down the Zodiac. It examines the actual murder investigation, focusing on the most renowned and puzzling feature of the Zodiac's craft – his cryptic messages which, as suggested in the previous chapter, may have been part of a homage he may have been paying to Edgar Allan Poe.

These movies bring out the grip that the figure of the serial killer has on modern society and the blurring of the lines between fiction and reality that this society has engendered. Alfred Hitchcock's silent 1926 masterpiece, *The Lodger*, established the serial killer movie as a distinct genre. By the 1980s, the genre became highly popular. That is the era when Hannibal Lecter made his first screen appearance in *Manhunter*. After *Silence of the Lambs* in 1991 and Fincher's *Se7en* in 1995, the figure of the sadistic serial killer gained the status of a mythic anti-hero. One of the key questions that Fincher's *Zodiac* raises, in fact, is whether or not the proliferation of real serial killers is a consequence of pop culture's fascination (and archetypal fear) of them. Serial killers seem to love the media attention they get for their crimes, even admitting to committing them for their own macabre "fifteen minutes of fame." Did we create this monster? Perhaps, the movie answers, because fear is a primal emotion. The current television frenzy over serial killers, and the proliferation of movies such as the *Saw* and *Hostel* ones are, arguably, contemporary expressions of our fascination with the archetype of the Shadow. As Carl Jung (1971: 12) wrote: "Everyone carries a shadow and the less it is embodied in the individual's conscious life, the blacker and denser it is." The fascination with serial killers, real and fictional, may have a therapeutic source – the elimination of our own shadows by projecting them onto others. As Jung (1971: 12) put it: "The projection-making factor (the Shadow archetype) then has a free hand and can realize its object – if it has one – or bring about some other situation characteristic of its power." He also believed that "In spite of its function as a reservoir for human darkness – or perhaps because of this – the Shadow is the seat of creativity."

5.4.2 Nature

The role of social factors on criminal behavior and especially on the rise of the serial killer has today many sustainers within criminology. However, there are many others who beg to differ, seeing serial killers as natural born killers who possess "evil genes" that compel them to commit their senseless crimes. Using data from brain imaging studies, Barbara A. Oakley (2008), for example, has put together a persuasive case suggesting that infamous serial killers, such as Slobodan Milosevic, have some form of antisocial personality disorder that they have been born with. The killers are charming on the surface but harbor evil thoughts constantly that she attributes to a pathological form of narcissism combined with emotional disturbances that lead them to believe they are actually altruistic.

In other words, serial killers do what they do mainly because of an inherent dysfunction, which has a neural source. But this may simplify the explanation of crime somewhat. There are certainly criminals who have been examined as having an unlucky dose of risk genes. But the same ones often have had impoverished experiences in their upbringing. And many others who do have the risk genes do not end up becoming serial killers. Looking at crime across cultures and across time, it is obvious that crime cannot be explained easily without taking cultural, social, and historical factors into account. There are nasty people, and there have always been so. But nastiness does not necessarily lead to criminality.

5.4.3 Serial Killers: A Few Case Studies

A survey of famous serial killers might shed light on the debate. We start with one of the best-known cases is that of Jeffrey Dahmer, who kept the remains of thirteen dismembered males in his apartment. Dahmer admitted that he saved the frozen body parts to eat later. How could someone end up as a cannibal in our modern age? Was it in his genes?

Dahmer was raised by a broken family and was sexually abused at the age of eight by a man in his neighborhood. This was the most likely source of his unusual behaviors, such as the fact that he decapitated and dismembered a dog in his youth, mounting the head on a stick next to a wooden cross. The symbolism of this act speaks of anger – against the events in his life that kept him from growing up normally alluding to a religious subtext. An early indicator that Dahmer was undergoing a deep internal stress was at age seven when he gave a bowl of tadpoles to a teacher as a sign of affection. When the teacher gave the bowl to one of Dahmer's friends, he killed the tadpoles with engine oil as a sign of revenge. He became an alcoholic by the age of thirteen and while in high school confessed to having sexual fantasies with corpses. He killed his first victim the year his parents divorced in 1978, suggesting that the break-up of his family was another likely factor in aggravating his aberrant view of the world. Dahmer confessed to fifteen murders and pleaded insanity. He was found sane and sentenced to fifteen consecutive life terms. Addressing the court, Dahmer revealed his inner turmoil by claiming "I knew I was sick or evil or both." Had the same human being, Jeffrey Dahmer, been raised by a "normal" family and not been sexually abused, would he have done what he did? In this case, the evidence seems to fall heavily on the side of childhood experiences as the primary factor in the shaping of the criminal mind.

The case of Ted Bundy is a fascinating one that stands out as favoring the evil gene theory. Bundy was described in childhood as a "great kid." He was a Boy Scout, ran a paper route, was on the high school track team, and ran his own lawn-mowing business. In other words, he seems to have had the exact opposite kind of childhood experiences to those of Dahmer. He even went on to serve as a chairman at the Seattle 1968 presidential convention for Rockefeller. He earned a degree in psychology in 1972, entering law school shortly thereafter, working as a night janitor to pay the bills. Bundy even wrote a rape-prevention pamphlet for a Seattle crime-watch group. He was handsome and six feet tall, contrasting with pre-conditioned perceptions of criminal appearance. But Bundy was one of the most heinous serial killers of history. He was convicted of killing two sorority girls and a woman named Kimberly Leach. But he may have killed over 40 women. Wooed by his charm, many women declared their love for him while in prison, believing that he was falsely accused. He was convicted and executed in 1989. Ted Bundy's case is not unique. He came apparently from a crime-free family background. But he "had it in him," as evil gene theory would have it.

But not all was truly perfect in Bundy's upbringing. His twenty-two-year-old unmarried mother lived with her parents, who assumed the role of his parents. Actually, Bundy grew up thinking that his real mother was his sister. Moreover, the grandfather was abusive and racist. As a result, McNab (2010: 41) writes, "Ted expressed himself with violent tempers, and even terrorized relatives by placing kitchen knives under their bed clothes." He was also bullied at school, managing to conceal his violent personality with a surface charm and confidence. So, upon further consideration, the Bundy case is hardly one that supports the natural born killer theory. We will never understand serial killers without taking theories of conditioned violence and cultural definitions of violence into account. Dahmer and Bundy were looking for meaning to their lives and, not having had a normal family upbringing (at least as perceived culturally), developed a distorted sense of normalcy which was then channeled into their murder sprees.

So, were Bundy and Dahmer evil murderers, or were they victims of the world in which they grew up in childhood? Consider the case of the "BTK" killer, Dennis Rader, in Wichita, Kansas. Rader murdered ten people, chosen at random, by binding, torturing, and killing them (hence BTK). He claimed that it was a "monster" that "entered my brain," and that "I will never know, but it is here to stay ... Maybe you can stop him. I can't." Rader clearly enjoyed his handiwork and under interrogation suggested that his lack of success was a type of reverse sublimation, transforming his impulses into sadomasochistic actions, rather than acceptable ones. Rader taunted the authorities, like the Son of Sam and the Zodiac, showing that he suffered from what we have called here a lack of meaning, craving for recognition. He sent letters to his victims, including a poem, "Oh Anna, Why Didn't You Appear," about a targeted victim who escaped death by arriving at her home later than Rader expected.

A consideration of the cases of many other serial killers leads to the general conclusion that serial killers are, by and large, made, not born. They do not kill for financial gain, for advancement in society, or for some other "normal" human motivation. They kill to restore a sense of meaning to their lives, enacting their pent-up rage and agony in a horrific way. They do not know their victims and, in most cases, do not want to know them, thus avoiding the affective states that would otherwise emerge in them.

5.4.4 Psychoanalysis

Most murders are the result of lust, anger, revenge, and greed and are thus all explainable in straightforward ways, rather than in complex psychological or semiotic ones as was done above. Killing of this type reaches back to the dawn of civilization. But serial killing falls into another category. Someone like a Rader or a Bundy kill for the thrill of the kill. They do not hate or know their victims, as mentioned. They are sociopaths, and as Oakley suggests, we should just call them evil. Rader's case showed that he associated his meaningless life with lack of excitement and, unable to attract partners to take part in his sadistic sexual fantasies, he went out and made them himself. The unconscious quest for significance seems to have spurred him on.

The clinical notion of the unconscious comes from psychoanalytic theory, which begins with Sigmund Freud's (1963: 235–236) concept that the psyche has a number of different levels, one of which, called the unconscious, is inaccessible to us:

> It was a triumph for the interpretative art of psychoanalysis when it succeeded in demonstrating that certain mental acts of normal people, for which no one had hitherto attempted to put forward a psychological explanation, were to be regarded in the same light as the symptoms of neurotics: that is to say that had a meaning, which was unknown to the subject but which could easily be discovered by analytic means ... A class of material was brought to light which is calculated better than any other to stimulate a belief in the existence of unconscious mental acts even in people to whom the hypothesis of something at once mental and unconscious seems strange and even absurd.

As Freud maintained, there seem to be "unconscious mental acts" that we do not comprehend, and these might, purportedly, lead a Bundy or a Rader to do what they did. The unconscious is an interesting and relevant concept because it might be the force that shapes our conscious behaviors, which are vulnerable to various emotional and irrational impulses within us that he categorized under the notion of the *Id*. Freud claimed that there is a continual struggle going on in our minds between the *Id*, the *Ego*, and the *Superego*. He described the Id as follows (quoted in Hinsie and Campbell 1970: 372):

> We can come nearer to the Id with images, and call it chaos, a cauldron of seething excitement. We suppose that is somewhere in direct contact with somatic processes, and takes over from them instinctual needs and gives them mental expression. These instincts fill it with energy but it has no organization and no unified will, only an impulsion to obtain satisfaction for the instinctual needs, in accordance with the pleasure-principle.

If this "cauldron of seething excitement" dominates us, then we have an abundance of energy that we cannot use because of social rules and constraints. One might thus explain serial killing in these terms, as an impulse of the repressed Id – hence an "Id Hypothesis." Opposing the Id is the *Superego*, which can be characterized as a conscience-taking impulse that is based in a sense of morality. Charles Brenner (1974: 111–112) discusses how the Superego manifests itself in human behavior and actions as follows:
1. the approval or disapproval of actions and wishes on the grounds of rectitude
2. critical self-observation
3. self-punishment
4. the demand for reparation or repentance of wrong-doing.
5. self-praise or self-love as a reward for virtuous or desirable thoughts and actions.

Serial killers may, arguably, have the Id and the Superego at loggerheads with each other within their unconscious. The Id seeks gratification and has great energy, but cannot be expressed freely because it must submit to the demands of society – demands which might cause considerable mental anguish in killers, as we saw with Rader's phrase that there was a monster in his head – the same metaphor used by Berkowitz, recalling the original meaning of *monster* as "warning." The *Ego* is the sense of awareness that mediates between the conflicting demands of the Id and the Superego. The Ego tests reality and stores up experiences in memory, finding a way to balance the demands of the Id and Superego, allowing people to be free of neurotic compulsions. It seeks to harness the energy of the Id in socially constructive ways. Serial killers seem to be incapable of controlling the Id, rejecting the defense mechanisms that operate at the level of the Superego. Some of the more relevant defense mechanisms as documented in serial killers are as follows:

- *Ambivalence*: the feeling of both love and hatred toward some person at the same time
- *Avoidance*: a refusal to pay attention to things that are disturbing because they are connected to unconscious aggressive or sexual impulses
- *Denial*: a refusal to accept the reality of something by blocking it from consciousness
- *Fixation*: an obsessive preoccupation with or attachment to something or someone
- *Projection*: a denial of negative and hostile feelings in oneself by attributing them to someone else
- *Rationalization*: a means of excusing behavior by offering reasons or excuses
- *Reaction formation*: a situation which occurs when ambivalent feelings create problems, suppressing one element and overemphasizing its opposite
- *Regression*: a return to an earlier stage in development when confronted with stressful or anxiety-provoking situations
- *Repression*: inhibiting wishes, memories, desires that are derived from childhood experiences
- *Sublimation*: transferring sexual impulses and other desires into other kinds of behavior
- *Suppression*: a voluntary attempt to put out of mind something we find upsetting and distasteful

These mechanisms are of obvious interest to criminal-semiotic profiling, because they produce typical symbolic behaviors, as we saw with Berkowitz and Rader, as well as specific conceptual metaphors in criminal texts. Psychoanalysis has traditionally been in a close partnership with semiotics because, as Freud claimed, the former (like the latter) was an interpretive art. In psychoanalytic theory, symbols are critical because they often disguise aggressive wishes and sexual desires. Freud (1901: 286) put it as follows:

> Symbolism is not peculiar to dreams, but is characteristic of unconscious ideation, in particular, among people, and is to be found in folklore, and in popular myths, legends, linguistic idioms, proverbial wisdom and current jokes, to a more complete extent than in dreams.

One Freudian theory that may also apply to serial killers is the *Oedipus Complex*, based on the Oedipus myth, which Freud believed explained the process of development. Freud thought that in all children there is hostility toward the parent of the same sex and an attraction to the parent of the opposite sex; this attraction eventually manifests itself in some neurotic behavior. He wrote about his notion in a letter to a friend (cited in Grotjahn 1966: 84):

> Being entirely honest with oneself if a good exercise. Only one idea of general value has occurred to me. I have found love of the mother and jealousy of the father in my own case too, and now believe it to be a general phenomenon of early childhood. If that is the case, the gripping power of Oedipus Rex, in spite of all the rational objections to the inexorable fate that the story presupposes, becomes intelligible. Our feelings rise against any arbitrary individual fate but the Greek myth seizes on a compulsion which everyone recognizes because he has felt traces of it in himself. Every member of the audience was once a budding Oedipus in fantasy, and this dream-fulfillment played out in reality causes everyone to recoil in horror, with the full measure of repression which separates his infantile from his present state.

Many serial killers may be reliving their Oedipal sexual fantasies in a warped and perverted way. The cases of David Berkowitz and even Ted Bundy could certainly be elucidated in these terms. For Berkowitz, Sam was his imaginary enemy, perhaps blocking his need to engage in normal oedipal interplay, and for Bundy the act that he did not really know who his mother was, until later, may also have had oedipal overtones.

Simon Lesser (1957: 15) observes that psychoanalysis investigates the same themes that our greatest fiction writers deal with, namely "the emotional, unconscious or only partly comprehended bases of our behavior." In a way, Dostoyevsky's *Crime and Punishment* or Poe's tales of murder and terror are really fictional versions of later Freudian theory. They offer deep insights into the non-rational and in some cases irrational forces that shape criminal behavior. Bundy and Ridgway returned to practice necrophilia in order to vicariously relive their crimes through the symbolic presence of the body. To use Deleuze and Guattari's (1987) Freudian notion of "point of subjectification," these can be seen as instances in which subjectivity (the Ego) is reconstructed, as the serial killer reactivates the resonances and excitement associated with the crime and its anti-repression functions. Revitalized moments such as these fulfill the killer's need to reify his subjectivity. This is where the Ego surfaces as a center of control. The bodies are trophies that represent signs of self-awareness. Crime sites become loci where Ego construction can unfold.

This model of serial killers might also explain why fetishism and rituals are consistent signatures of serial killers, connecting them with primordial forms of worship. Dahmer had bodies decomposing in his apartment. Skulls had been severed, cleaned and painted, set atop the victim's two hands, with the palms up, like an altar. This reveals dread, hierophany (engagement with the sacred), and the desire for transcendence through the experience of power over the body. Fetishism is the use of some object connected with the victim through which one relives the crime and its excitement. We will look at this topic in the next chapter. The term *auto-plasticity* is sometimes used by forensic psychologists to describe fetishism, referring to actions and behaviors on the part of serial killers. For the killer, the search for meaning, or meaning-replacement, relies on his fantasies. The souvenirs taken from victims (clothing, jewelry, and so on) are true sexual fetishes, allowing the killer to re-experience the thrill of the murder. In sum, the serial killer may have evil genes within him, but he also stores up images and memories that certainly seem to activate these genes.

Chapter 6
Symbols and Rituals of Crime

Murder is always a mistake. One should never do anything that one cannot talk about after dinner.

Oscar Wilde (1854–1900)

The murder trial of football star and actor O. J. Simpson has become enshrined in both the annals of criminology and popular culture history for the many implications that it had both for forensics and racial relations in the United States, not to mention the interest it engendered as a tale of the fall of an icon into villainy. The importance of crime scene investigations came to the forefront with the Simpson case. As mentioned previously, he was accused of having stabbed his former wife, Nicole Simpson, and her friend, Ronald Goldman. The crime scene consisted of the walkway leading to Nicole's apartment. The first investigators on the scene determined that the two victims were deceased and, with three more officers, they were able to secure the scene, creating a sign-in sheet. A police photographer joined the police officers on the scene but could only take area shots until the civilian forensic scientist arrived.

Detectives then went to O. J Simpson's house, declaring it a crime scene as well. From there the criminalist collected blood spots and a bloody glove. Despite this and other strongly incriminating evidence, Simpson was acquitted in 1995 after a televised trial that lasted more than eight months. This whole episode brought out the importance of two things – first, that the media do influence the outcomes of trials, and second, that crime scene investigations are crucial to the carriage of justice. The fact that the crime scene may have been contaminated, along with the televised scene of Simpson trying on the bloody glove that did not seem to fit him, were some of the factors in the acquittal. The trial was also a social justice one, using Simpson (misguidedly) as a victim of racial profiling and, thus, its subtext was the endemic injustices that African Americans had received in the past.

Crime scene investigations (CSIs) involve, as we have already seen, decoding signs à la Sherlock Holmes. Part of CSI is to identify particular kinds of signs, symbols, as well as any peculiar rituals that a crime scene might present. We have already looked at trace and other kinds of evidence that can be used to identify perpetrators. In this chapter, the focus is on the meanings of the symbolism and rituals that sometimes characterize crime scenes and criminality generally. The fascination with CSIs seems to stem from two sources. First, there is the element of mystery and the sense of reassurance that comes from solving a crime with human ingenuity. The clues found at crime scenes intrigue us like a jigsaw puzzle as the detective, real or fictional, puts them together to solve the crime. Second, unless and until they are found, the killers are phantoms. If we do not know who the perpetrator is, like the Zodiac, something incomplete seems to remain within us. As we saw, sometimes this is resolved by fictional solutions to the crimes (chapter 5).

6.1 Crime Scene Investigations

Edgar Allan Poe tapped directly into our unconscious need to solve mysteries by creating the detective story. Since then, the mystery genre has become one of the most popular of all forms of narrative with television shows and movies show-casing mystery through real crime and detective stories to broad audiences. The plots revolve typically around the crime scene, which is a puzzle that is solved by decoding the signs of crime in it through ingenious reasoning, much like solving a Sudoku or crossword puzzle. Add to this basic textual focus elements of romance, sex, and the other human virtues and vices and you have a veritable mystery drama with a moral tinge to it, much like the mystery plays of the medieval period. Real life CSIs are not as glamorous as are their fictional coun-terparts, even though they utilize the same techniques and are guided by the same forms of reasoning. But like the fictional ones they are interpreted by everyone involved as moral dramas.

A primary crime scene is where a crime, like a murder, has taken place, whereas a secondary crime scene is a site related to a crime, such as a burial site or a vehicle used to transport a body. Needless to say, a crime cannot be reconstructed without a crime scene – a fact that comes up frequently. The case of Natalee Holloway – made famous by the American media – shows how a case can crumble without knowing where the location of the crime is. Authorities on the Dutch Caribbean island of Aruba faced this situation when eighteen-year-old Natalee Holloway, an American student, disappeared on May 30, 2005. The entire island was searched for two years and the police even drained a pond and scoured various locations (beaches, dunes, and so on) in search of the body. The area where she was last seen was combed over and over. In 2007, investigators dug around the home of a suspect, but found nothing. Holloway is still listed as missing.

The central idea of a CSI is to reconstruct the crime. As we saw, fingerprints, tool marks, blood spatters, bullet trajectories, wound patterns, and so on are the signs used in the reconstruction. Some crime scenes, such as those that are part of serial murders, may also present other kinds of evidence, which can be called symbolic and ritualistic. These have a higher connotative value, so to speak, since they are put there intentionally, whereas the trace evidence is a consequence of the commission of the crime.

6.1.1 Signature Analysis

In the case of seemingly similar crime scenes, the initial goal of CSI lies in determining if there is indeed a recurring pattern, known (as discussed) as a *signature*, involved in the commission of the crime. If there is not, then the crime scene can be regarded as novel. If there is, then the particular crime scene is considered to be part of a developing crime text that little by little reveals the criminal's state of mind and intended social message. As Keppel and Birnes (2004) argue, in an implicit semiotic way, signature signs are incredibly useful in linking crimes to specific killers and in revealing their inner states of mind. They are symbols of personality and intent.

The importance of signature analysis was brought out originally by the case of Harvey Glatman. Known as the "The Lonely Hearts Killer," Glatman was a serial killer during the 1950s. He looked around modeling agencies for his victims, contacting them with offers of work for a fabricated magazine, luring them up to his apartment, tying them up and sexually assaulting them as he took pictures of them. He would then strangle them and dump them in the desert. The pictures constituted a unique signature, allowing the police to link all the different murders to an individual unsub. The pictures not only revealed his killing methodology but also the workings of his depraved mind and the kinds of messages he was trying to convey (Keppel and Birnes 2004: 21):

- Some victims were photographed with a forced or concocted look of innocence, insinuating that the victim was in a modeling shoot.
- Some photos showed the victim's impending horror on her face, revealing a sadist's eye view of a sexually-terrorized victim.
- Other photos showed the victim in the position Glatman had put her after strangulation.

As was later discovered, Glatman used these photos to experience the euphoria of violence over and over. Eventually, the police were able to use the photos, tracing them to the killer.

Another famous case of signature evidence is that of the "Lipstick Killer," William Heirens, who killed three people in the late 1940s. His signature was a message scrawled in lipstick at a crime scene – an image that has been used frequently by fictional representations of crime scenes. In one of the murder scenes, Heirens left the following message: "For heaven's sake, catch me before I kill more; I cannot control myself."

There are many such cases in the history of crime and there are many kinds of signatures. Some, however, are recurrent, perhaps revealing a darker side to the human psyche that seeks expression in gruesome ways. Picquerism, or sexual interest in penetrating the skin of another person, was the signature trademark of several serial killers, including Jack the Ripper and Andrei Chikatilo, who sexually assaulted and murdered at least 52 people, including women and children in Ukraine. This type of signature suggests a need to get the immediate submission of the victim and thus, by retrospection, to penetrate the psychology of the perpetrator, suggesting a need for sadism or the derivation of sexual pleasure by inflicting pain, suffering or humiliation on others. Another frequent signature is the posing of bodies – flat on their backs, legs splayed, genitalia exposed in a degrading manner, and so on. These reveal various intentions, including the need for the enactment of twisted sacrificial rituals. Postmortem mutilation and organ harvesting are also signatures of various serial killers, indicating a need to destroy the humanity of the victims and to shock and horrify those who find the body.

Marks of violence can be random as in most crimes scenes or constitute signatures. In both cases, they are iconic signs, allowing investigators to infer what kind of action was committed and how it was committed. Violent signs on the body can also prove or disprove a hypothesis and, in the case of signature signs, help connect a particular crime scene to others. When a wife of a police officer was found dead in front of her house in India in 2004, it was at first ruled to be a suicide. But the post-mortem report found evidence of strangulation, thus turning the case into a homicide. A typology of wounds and traumas is really an inventory of icons that refer to a violent action committed in a specific way. These include:

- *Abrasion:* an injury in which the skin is scraped off by some cutting instrument or fingernails
- *Concussion:* a serious brain injury caused by a hard blow to the head
- *Contusion:* a bruise in which the skin is not broken, often indicative of tight manipulation such as strangulation
- *Fracture:* a break, shattering, or crack in bones usually indicative of some blow to the body
- *Laceration:* a cut that is deep enough to require stitches typically caused by a knife attack or an attack by some cutting instrument
- *Trauma:* a wound or a physical emotional shock to the body

Diagrams of injuries and wounds to a body are often made by investigators in order to create a model of how a victim may have suffered before dying. Models also help provide a picture of the violent activity by working backwards – that is, by showing how the marks entail some action or tool use. They also can be used to connect signatures left at various crime scenes in order to make inferences as to their meanings.

So, where does FS[1] come into all this? First, signature analysis and reconstruction modeling are fundamentally semiotic – akin to reconstructing any text on the basis of partial information through an interpretation of the information and of deciding who the author of the text might be (if he leaves a signature). Second, by naming a particular clue as a type of sign, such as an icon, the investigator can start to envision connections that may otherwise not be apparent. This can be reinforced by looking at the typologies of iconic phenomena and using these to gain insights into a crime scene. Peirce, as we saw, argued that signs revealed three basic types of semiosis: resemblance, relation, and cultural convention. To reiterate here, signs resulting from resemblance are icons, those from relation indexes, and those by cultural convention symbols. Clues such as blood spatter are iconic, and this is why they are used to reconstruct how the killing occurred in terms of direction and force. Fingerprints and DNA signs are indexical, since they point to a specific individual, helping the investigator infer a series of things, including who the perpetrator may have been, where he or she may reside, and so on. Finally, signature clues are symbols, because they reveal some aspect of the killer's personality that is sensitive to cultural or upbringing factors of some kind. Using lipstick to write warped messages is clearly symbolic, since lipstick itself is a symbol of womanhood.

The forgoing discussion has implications for CSI, since the presence of signature signs at some crime scenes requires interpretation above and beyond the purely denotative, involving what they suggest about both the perpetrator and the world in which he lives (Shon and Milovanovic 2006). Signatures in ritual killings can be used to link or discard a particular crime scene with others, because they are iconic and thus resemble previous crimes. And the rituals and symbols involved in serial killing can help determine if there is a theme among the crime scenes and what the state of mind of the perpetrator might be.

6.2 Symbolism

Symbolism is a feature that characterizes many serial killings. It is also the semiotic glue that keeps criminal organizations united. In the initiation ceremony scene in the movie *Eastern Promises* (2007), Viggo Mortensen is seen in his underwear in front of members of a faction of the Russian Mafia. The members are reading the tattoos on his body in order to "understand his character." The tattoos tell Mortensen's life story – he was a thief who had spent time in a Siberian prison, he was non-cooperative in prison, he spent time in solitary confinement. After Mortensen passes the initiation, his body is incised with three new tattoos: a star on each shoulder near the collarbone and a star on his knee, indicating his status as a new member of the clan. Tattoos are important symbols in many criminal cultures. They constitute a signature that allows them to establish identity, present character, indicate autobiographical achievements, and so on. They are I-signs, allowing criminals to claim bragging rights, by indicating their strengths, accomplishments, and even opinions. The same holds for many of the symbolic artifacts left by serial killers at their crime scenes.

6.2.1 Symbols

From the beginning of time, people have created symbols to stand for the values and beliefs they espouse. They speak their own form of language. At many serial murder crime scenes, one finds recurring symbols. These invariably contain a hidden message, which can be interpreted much more effectively if the theories of symbolism are understood by investigators. This is where semiotics comes directly into play. For example, when something is written in blood it suggests something connected to life and rebirth. When religious symbols, such as crosses, are left at crime scenes it generally suggests a need either to reject a strict religious upbringing or else to impose a sense of order to the crime scene, in contrast to the chaotic inner life that the killer may be experiencing.

Symbols are the building blocks of all social systems, imposing order on the world by representing it meaningfully to the members of the systems. They also allow people to develop a sense of belonging. This is why societies have national symbols – the United States has Uncle Sam and the Statue of Liberty, Canada the maple leaf, England John Bull, and France the fleur-de-lis. Symbolic artifacts such as coats of arms, flags, heraldic emblems, university seals, and the like are all "affiliation" signs of specific kinds. Known more specifically as *emblems*, they indicate membership or ownership.

Symbols can also be personalized. Tattooing is one of the most ancient forms of personalized body symbolism. Some anthropologists date it back to around 8000 BCE, but it may go back even farther in time. Almost every culture has practiced tattooing at some time or other. As early as 2000 BCE, the Egyptians used it to indicate social rank and affiliation. The ancient Greeks and Romans used tattoos to brand slaves and criminals. In the Marquesas Islands, a group of islands in the South Pacific Ocean, tattoos are revered signs of honor, and have to be earned by actions. In eastern New Guinea tattoos on young women are signs of beauty, much like they have become in western culture. The list of cross-cultural functions of tattooing could go on endlessly.

The importance placed on the role of tattoos as symbols in character portraiture by the Russian Mafia, as discussed briefly above, was first brought to wide attention by the documentary film *Mark of Cain* (2000), which consisted of interviews of the inmates in a Russian prison. Some of the lines spoken by gangsters in *Eastern Promises* were taken, word-for-word, from the interviews. Each tattoo is a symbol with a specific designation. The tattoo of famous communists like Lenin, Stalin, or Engels on one's chest means that the inmate has received a death sentence. Knuckle tattoos stand for a convicted armed robber; a ring tattoo on a prisoner's finger indicates that the prisoner had been in a juvenile correctional facility. Tattoos of churches stand for beliefs. As one prisoner interviewed in the movie put it: "Each cupola is a conviction." Those who wear tattoos to brag about themselves without having earned them will have them cut off "along with his skin," declared another prison interviewee. A tattoo in criminal culture is not a fashion statement; it is a biographical and achievement statement. As another prisoner put it in the film: "You don't have the right to tattoo just anything."

Some criminal organizations demand that their members cover their bodies completely with tattoos. This is the case with the Japanese Yakuza. The size, shape, configuration, and color of the tattoos indicate not only the wearers' affiliation, but also his ability to withstand pain. Historically, tattoos were signs of nobility and social distinctiveness. Their association to criminals started in the Kofun period (300–600 CE), when they were placed on thieves and murderers by authorities as marks of identification, much like the brand marks put on cattle. At the start of the Meiji period (1868–1912 CE) the authorities banned tattoos in public because of their criminal connotations. So, tattooing continued to be practiced underground. It was legalized after the occupation forces entered Japan in 1945. Many businesses in Japan still ban or at least look down on customers with tattoos. Yakuza members cover their entire bodies with tattoos in large part to indicate that they have a high tolerance for pain and thus a commitment to suffer for the organization. Tattoos similarly constitute the hallmark of membership for many gangs, not just the Russian Mafia or the Yakuza. Wearing unearned tattoos is seen as a punishable offense across the criminal world, with discipline ranging from the painful removal of the tattoo to death. The tattoo must be earned by some action that is deemed to be valiant in criminal terms.

Colors, letters, numbers, like tattoos, are affiliation symbols as well. The Sureños, or Southerners, were the first gang in the California prison system to employ colors and the number 13 along with tattoos to distinguish themselves from other gangs. The meaning of the number is that the letter M is the thirteenth letter of the alphabet, signifying *La Eme* or "The M" in Spanish and thus the Mexican Mafia. Another interpretation of the number is that the letters L (12) and A (1), refer to Los Angeles, the hometown of the Sureños. The other of the largest prison gangs in the California Penal System is the Norteños, or Northerners, also referred to as Nuestra Familia (Our Family). They are bitter rivals of the Sureños due to a split in the 1960s, with the Sureños remaining heavily connected to the Mexican Mafia and the Norteños desiring to break all affiliation with La Eme. This particular gang is symbolized by the color red and the number fourteen, thus offsetting their identity from that of their rivals.

The number thirteen may also indicate membership in the Mara Salvatrucha (MS13), a Central American gang formed for protection against the more powerful Mexican gangs as well as the Mexican Mafia. It is common for gang members to have the phone area code of their hometown tattooed on themselves. The number 12 is associated with the California based white supremacist organization The Aryan Brotherhood, the digit one symbolizing the letter A and the digit two meaning B. Such symbols impart sense and purpose to the gang, much like national symbols, such as flags, do to countries. Knowing the language of symbolism is a key to understanding gang mentality and deconstructing the power of gangs.

6.2.2 The Power of Symbols

Allegiance symbolism has emotional power. Traditionally, psychological and sociological theories explain the appeal of gangs to some young people as being tied to socioeconomic variables. These go back to the 1920s when the first studies on what motivates people to band together in gang configurations emerged. But recent research is starting to show that the symbolism imprinted in clothing, hairstyle, tattoos, and other forms of symbolic self-presentation is more powerful than such variables in attracting individuals to join gangs (Nicaso and Danesi 2013). Symbols are the ersatz means through which some people satisfy their need to belong to some social grouping above and beyond the family or other social structure. These also help reinforce the myth of the "outlaw lifestyle," a lifestyle designed to allow people to live apart from the mainstream world within a parallel culture, with its special appeal. In our culture, "bad boys" have always been popular, both in real life and in fiction. From Robin

Hood to Bonnie and Clyde, they are perceived as personages who realize every-one's desire of live in a state of danger and to establish oneself as different from the masses.

Juvenile groups were called "gangs" for the first time after a 1927 study by Frederic Thrasher, which claimed that the social conditions in the United States at the end of the nineteenth century brought about the growth of street gangs. Many immigrants settled in inner-city enclaves characterized by deteriorating housing, poor employment prospects, and a rapid turnover in population. Thrasher suggested that these conditions led to disorganized neighborhoods where mainstream social rules and mechanisms were weak and ineffectual. The youths thus searched out other means of establishing social order. The gangs provided the opportunity to do so. The gang culture offered the only viable source of status-gaining, given that people in such areas had limited access to the social and legal means of achieving material success. Gang membership reduced feelings of powerlessness by providing access to illegitimate means of achieving success. This concept of the gang and what a gang really is has been questioned somewhat, but it is still the dominant theme in the relevant research.

But social conditions did not explain why non-immigrant gangs also cropped up throughout the United States at about the same time (Meyerhoff and Meyerhoff 1964). And they do not explain why gangs fight each other. Deadly warfare among gangs is a common event, as they vie for the control of territories within which to carry out their imperatives and establish a symbolic stake in the world. Like any social system, the gang is strictly hierarchical, with leaders at the top and foot-soldiers at the bottom ready to obey or else to be ostracized and punished for their nonconformity. Individuals in such groups are held together primarily by a common interest in being perceived as physically aggressive and tough. They see the outlaw lifestyle as the only attractive one to them, empowering then through immediately available means.

Since Thrasher, theories of gang membership have focused mainly on the context of upbringing and of its influence on individuals. Some suggest that people join criminal gangs because they were not sufficiently penalized for pre-vious delinquent acts or because they have been influenced by others. Others suggest that youths become part of gangs in response to the failure to rise above their socioeconomic status, or as a repudiation of middle-class values. Others still claim that in the case of male youths, gang membership is an act of "virility demonstration," as it can be called, a way to show that they have physical prowess and endurance. Other factors include everything from birth trauma, neglect, and ineffective parental discipline to family disruptions, school failure, learning dis-abilities, limited employment opportunities, inadequate housing, and residence in high-crime neighborhoods.

The historical-contextual factor is an important one. This was borne out by a 1991 survey by the National Crime Prevention Council, which found that those who join gangs are primarily young people who live in situations and locales where gang membership is perceived as prestigious or even an obligatory coming-of-age rite. But then this raises a fundamental question: Why are young people who have not been raised in areas historically associated with gangs also attracted to gangs? By the process of elimination, the only reason left, arguably, is the enormous emotional power of gang symbolism. Those who look for the causes underlying gang membership in the social sphere (family background, class, and so on) are only partially correct, guided more by the tradition of research in this domain than actual facts.

Boredom is also a factor that cannot be underestimated. Gangs provide youths with status, recognition, security, and opportunities for excitement when these needs are not met by everyday life. The conditions of contemporary culture, in other words, are volatile because of the need to express oneself in creative ways. This would explain why the gang phenomenon is not proscribed to inner-city contexts, but is found virtually everywhere, including the suburbs. The common explanation for suburban gangs is that affluence, rather than poverty, promotes alienation, isolation, and apathy (Johnstone 1981). But all this ignores the empowerment that comes from belonging through symbolism (tattoos, colors, and so on). If the symbolism that society provides is perceived as empty then people will search for ways to devise their *sui generis* forms of symbolism.

Mimesis too is a powerful factor. Showcasing gang cultures on the screen has undoubtedly had an abiding effect on people, who have become accustomed to seeing gangs as inevitable social groupings in some contexts. In other words, popular culture has had as much an effect on gang membership as have socioeconomic and psychosocial factors, if not more so.

But as is always the case, theories can never really penetrate the essence of something like gangs, not to mention criminality in general. The connection between marginalized people and criminal activity is a complex one. There is an obvious relationship between feeling outside of the society one is immersed in and seeking out a sense of belonging that is clearly delineated through systems of symbolism that may serve as a substitute for other systems present in a community. But there is also the broader factor of family structure and the changing role of this structure in the modern world, Dirsuption of this structure may entail the need for young people to seek out a more tribal configuration to gain a sense of belonging – a sense that families may no longer provide. In the end, it is not possible to use one disciplinary approach to the study of criminality of any kind, from serial murders to gang activities. The usefulness of forensic semiotics is that, being an interdisciplinary science, it allows for the balancing of various theories around a central force – the need for symbolism.

6.3 Ritual

Ritual is evidence that there is much more to human life than instinctual survival. Religious ritual, for example, weaves a feeling of bonding on believers and on specific groups (and even entire societies). But rituals and attendant rites can, over time, suffer from the erosion of significance. So, some individuals enact their own versions to restore significance in an ersatz fashion. This may be an underlying cause of the use of rituals by some serial killers. Simply put, they assign significance to their gruesome actions. As sociologist Emile Durkheim (1912) pointed out, in a secular and materialist world, some people seek to replicate existing religious forms in a *sui generis* fashion. In the case of ritual serial killers, these forms are replicated in a twisted and ghastly fashion.

In Freudian terms, the use of ritual in this way can be explained as distorted sublimation. Actually, the original conceptualization of sublimation as an inner psychic force comes from Friedrich Nietzsche (2000). Nietzsche wrote that we all want to gain power over our unruly drives and instincts, believing that the self-control exhibited by artists and people who practice self-denial for religious reasons was actually a higher form of power than the physical bullying of the weak by the strong. Nietzsche's ideal was the *overman* (or superman), a passionate individual who learns to control his or her passions and use them in a creative manner. Criminals might see themselves as *overmen*, as Dostoyevsky understood through the character of Raskolnikov (chapter 5). The *overman* channels the energy of instinctual drives into higher, more creative, and less objectionable forms. Nietzsche called this the "sublimation" of energy, claiming that it was far more valuable than the suppression of the instincts urged by Christianity and other religions. In a distorted way, some serial killers are creative individuals, who sublimate their repressions through their horrific actions.

6.3.1 Ritual Killers

To see how ritual sublimation manifests itself in serial murder, consider the cases of a few famous serial killers, some of whom we have already discussed for other reasons. As we saw with Jeffrey Dahmer, the ritual may involve the mutilation of corpses. It may also implicate some kind of special positioning, which we saw with Glatman's positioning of his corpses as if they were in a photo shoot. Or it may inhere in the enactment of human sacrifice or some type of sadomasochistic ritual, as was the case with Dennis Rader, or in the decapitation of the victims, which is what Ted Bundy did.

These killers appear to use ritual for sublimation or cathartic purposes, cleansing themselves of their inner depravities and perversions by drawing on primitive symbolism and practices to justify their killings. The use of ritual weaves a sense of protection on the ritual maker, leading to a sense of self-empowerment, temporary healing, or transformation. Understanding the motivations for such ritualistic symbolism may lead to the solving and even prevention of these crimes. This train of thought may also explain cult-based murders such as the one in 1977, when a sixteen-year-old boy, named Luke Woodham, murdered his mother in Pearl, Mississippi, going on to kill two classmates and wound seven others. Woodham was part of a satanic cult, and as a requirement of his initiation ritual, he had to kill people sacrificially in order to show his allegiance and submission to the ideals of the cult. It was this insight that led police to the perpetrator and to the motive for the killing. The ritualistic aspects of the killings were seen as justification by Woodham for his actions.

In another case, a seventeen-year-old Welsh teenager, Mathew Hardman, broke into the house of a ninety-year-old woman, stabbing her to death and then positioning her body with the legs laid on a stool, two candlesticks placed on the corpse, and one on the mantelpiece. Hardman then carved her heart out and drained the blood from her leg, drinking it in a vampiristic ritual, believing all the time that these symbolic actions would render him immortal. When the police searched Hardman's bedroom, they discovered a large amount of books and Internet material on vampirism. Hardman came to be known as the "Vampire Boy Killer."

Criminal profilers have come to understand the power of ritual in serial murders. An early example was the one of Richard Trenton Chase, the so-called "Vampire of Sacramento," who murdered a woman in 1978, drinking her blood. The profilers observed the disorder that Chase left at the crime scene and concluded that the murderer was white, emaciated, in his mid-twenties, unemployed, and lived alone. They also surmised that he would kill again, which he did. Chase had a history of mental illness and admitted to the crimes, but did not think that he had done anything wrong. He told his interrogators that his own blood was turning to sand, which forced him to become a vampire. Killers like Chase have delusional thoughts, often thinking that they live in a fantasy world. They may hear "voices" that others cannot hear. They may believe that these "voices" carry messages from important people, or even from God. Like clinically-diagnosed schizophrenics, they seem to feel no emotions, or else display inappropriate emotions, such as laughing at sad situations. Some withdraw from their family and friends and talk mainly to themselves or to their "voices," as we saw with the Son of Sam.

Perhaps the most famous (or infamous) case of ritual serial killing is the one of Richard Ramirez, the "Night Stalker," who terrified the city of Los Angeles between 1984 and 1985 with his spree of thirteen murders (chapter 3). Ramirez would attempt to make his victims pledge their commitment to Satan. At his trial in 1989, he raised a hand with a pentagram design on it and proclaimed, "Hail Satan." Profilers believed that Ramirez used ritual as a cover or justification for his crimes. When sentenced to death, he shrugged it away revealing his mindset with the following words: "Big deal. Death always went with the territory. See you in Disneyland." A sensual man, he attracted a cult following from many females while in prison, even marrying one in October 1996. The criminal as an anti-hero reverberates with many mythic overtones.

Ritual killings, such as throat slitting, draining blood from a corpse, mutilation, carving symbols into flesh, and dismemberment, are not uncommon in serial murder cases. In 2002, the mutilated torso of a young boy was found floating in London's River Thames. It was found close to seven half-burned candles. The autopsy revealed all the hallmarks of a ritual killing consistent with a human sacrifice. A name on the sheet in which the candles had been wrapped suggested it was consistent with the kind of sacrifice sometimes carried out in Nigeria to bring good luck to the perpetrators. Orange shorts – orange being the color associated with the god of the Nigerian Yoruba peoples – were placed on the corpse. DNA analysis indicated that the boy came from West Africa. He was circumcised, which commonly occurs in that region as a passage rite to adulthood. Analysis of the boy's stomach contents and bone chemistry further indicated that he could not have been brought up in London. The cuts where the head and limbs had been severed from the body suggested the expert use of sharp knives. The flesh had first been peeled down to the bones, which were then slashed with a single blow from a weapon. The body was then held while the blood was drained from it. Investigators believe that those involved in this case included a magician or priest who would have carried out the ritual. It appears the boy may have been kidnapped and brought to London for the sole purpose of carrying out this ritual murder.

The use of ritual in serial killing is an obvious area of semiotic investigation. When rituals occur at a crime scene, the aid of a semiotician would add immeasurably to decoding the meanings of the crime, as certainly Edgar Allan Poe and Charles Peirce realized at the dawn of forensics as an investigative science. Ritual, mystery, and crime seem to go hand in hand. This became obvious as far back as the case of Jack the Ripper. Jack the Ripper terrorized London from August 31 to November 9, in 1888, when he killed five prostitutes. The murderer was called Jack the Ripper because he used a knife to cut the victims' throats and slash their bodies ritualistically. He was never caught despite the efforts of police, citizens, bloodhounds, and even fortunetellers. Scotland Yard identified three principal suspects, all known to be insane. However, the police failed to prove that any of them had committed the murders. Widespread charges of incompetence caused Sir Charles Warren, the commissioner of Scotland Yard, to resign on November 8, the day before the fifth murder. The police received hundreds of letters from individuals who confessed to being the murderer. Only one of the letters seemed to be authentic because part of a kidney of one of the victims was enclosed. The sender's address was "From Hell." The religious irony and perhaps distorted form of sublimation was transparent.

When caught and interviewed, ritual serial killers claim that they were compelled by inner urges to do so. For example, a serial killer from Medan, Indonesia, named Ahmad Suradji, murdered forty-two females over eleven years. Suradji buried his victims to their waists before strangling them with a cable wire, because he claimed that his father's ghost told him that by killing them in this way, and then drinking the victims' saliva, he would become a mystic healer. As suggested schematically in previous chapters, this can be called "monster theory," suggesting that certain criminal actions are attempts to either enact the monster within or to purge the monster from the psyche. A monster is any creature, found in legends or horror fiction, whose hideous appearance may produce fear. The word *monster* derives from Latin *monstrum*, meaning an "aberrant occurrence," usually physical (such as a birth defect) that was taken as a sign that something was wrong within the natural order or that the person with the defect was punished by the deities for some reason. Monsters are freaks of nature who do horrible things as a form of revenge or release from their inner turmoil. The root of *monstrum* is *monere* – which means to warn and instruct. So, the monster is a sign, as Saint Augustine (1912) claimed, who was not inherently evil, but a kind of natural error.

This conception of monster comes out clearly in the novel *Frankenstein* (1818) by Mary Shelley. It tells the story of Victor Frankenstein, a scientist who tries to create a living being for the good of humanity but instead produces a monster. He creates his monster by assembling parts of dead bodies and activating the creature with electricity. The monster is actually a gentle, intelligent creature. But everyone fears and mistreats him because of his hideous appearance. Frankenstein himself rejects his own creation and refuses to create a mate for him. The monster's terrible loneliness drives him to seek revenge by murdering his creator's wife, brother, and best friend. There are many implicit meanings for the study of serial crime in this story and in the whole concept of monster.

Some killers see ritual as a means of ascertaining their stake in the theater of fame (which has been called the Andy Warhol Effect here). Take Alexander Pichushkin, a Russian serial killer known as "The Chessboard Killer." His murder spree was a case of copycat crimes inspired by his fellow psychopath, Andrei Chikatilo, who murdered over fifty victims between 1978 and 1990. Alexander himself killed forty-eight confirmed victims, mostly older homeless males, simply for the thrill of it. He killed them by striking them from behind with a hammer and then tossing some of them into sewers. His goal was to kill sixty-four victims, so as to fill the squares on a chessboard, and more than Chikatilo, so as to beat him at his self-devised "chess game of murder." He was caught before achieving that heinous goal.

Chikatilo was known both as "The Red Ripper" and "The Rostov Ripper." He did not kill his victims in the same way each time, alternately stabbing, strangling, or beating them to death. But in all murders there was a ritualistic component, namely mutilation for sexual gratification. This was connected subsequently by investigators to the fact that Chikatilo was impotent due to a childhood illness, and to the fact that he himself claimed he could only become sexually aroused by committing violent acts. Chikatilo was certainly a monster in the psycho-semiotic sense used here. He apparently got his monstrosity from the unique horrors of a horrendous childhood, including the cannibalized death of his brother. This no doubt influenced his own cannibalism. As McNab (2010: 16) points out, "he would eat external and internal body parts, expressing a particular fondness for consuming the uterus of female victims." As McNab goes on accurately to say, "The attacks were crazed, monstrous affairs." During his trial, Chikatilo himself showed that he was aware of his monstrosity admitting that "I am a freak of nature, a mad beast."

Chikatilo felt inferior to others, so he compensated by committing serial murders to show that he was superior. Another example of a monster of this kind is ex-convict Charles Manson, who ordered the Tate-LaBianca murders in 1969. Screen actress Sharon Tate Polanski was murdered at her Bel-Air home in Benedict Canyon early in the morning of August 10 along with coffee heiress Abigail Folger, her common-law husband Wojiciech Frykowski, Hollywood hair stylist Jay Sebring, and delivery boy Steven Earl Parent. A day later in Los Angeles, supermarket chain president Leno LaBianca and his wife Rosemary were killed. The murders were planned and executed by members of a hippie cult family, led by Manson, who sought to carry out his twisted vendetta against society. He had brainwashed his followers with drugs, sex, and pseudo-religious notions, ordering them to commit the horrific murders.

Another relevant case is that of Richard Cottingham, who tortured and murdered four prostitutes between 1967 and 1980 in New York. He was nicknamed the "Torso Killer," because he dismembered his victims, leaving only a torso behind. In this case, the knife was eventually interpreted as being a phallic sexual weapon by investigators. Cottingham used it to gain sexual pleasure as a substitute for his genitalia. Freud believed the normal pattern of psychosexual development is interrupted in some people. These people become fixated at an earlier, immature stage. Such fixation could contribute to psychosis in adulthood and, in the case of a Richard Cottingham or an Andrei Chikatilo, who were impotent, to replacing sexual organs with phallic symbols of death. This may have also been the case with Jack the Ripper (Sugden 2002).

6.3.2 Zodiac Complex

Ritual serial killers who got away continue to intrigue us, as can be seen by the many fictitious and documentary revisitations of Jack the Ripper and the Zodiac Killer. This reveals that we, like them, are captivated by a neurotic form of ritual, fearing the monsters in them yet strangely attracted to them, as aberrant and perverse as it may seem. This complex of ambiguous emotions can be called the "Zodiac Complex," after the Zodiac Killer whose identity still escapes us and which we still continue to seek to unravel (Graysmith 1986). The Zodiac Killer used occult symbolism and cryptography, evoking memories of Edgar Allan Poe's gothic style of mystery writing. The Zodiac sent letters to newspapers announcing his crimes with letters that were filled with cryptic symbols such as "Me = 37, SFPD = 0," which was later decoded as the score of 37 (victims) for the killer and no points for the police.

As we saw in chapter 4, the Zodiac's writings are intriguing. They were typed out, but no identification of who he was by linguistic analysis was ever made. They showed a sense of control, superiority, and of self-importance (Gibson 2004). The Zodiac also provided a detailed description of his crimes as proof of his involvement so that he could show off his intelligence in the planning and execution of the crimes. In this way he taunted everyone, not just the police. Like many ritual killers of women he blamed women for the "brush offs" they gave him in previous years. The night he murdered Darlene Ferrin, on July 5, 1969, he crank-called her relatives. First, he called her home and her husband, Dean, answered only to hear heavy breathing. The Zodiac followed by calling other members of the Ferrin family, an hour and a half after her murder, and before they or the media knew of the crime. The Zodiac called Dean Ferrin in April 1970 (eight months after the murder), for the following reasons (Gibson 2004: 95): to brag about the murder to the victim's relatives, wanting to prolong their distraught emotions and confusion; to torture them; to implicate himself in all aspects of the victim's life; to confess while bragging at the same time; to self-congratulate himself and enjoy his handiwork in retrospect; and to express his philosophy of life.

As the movie *Se7en* (1995) suggests there is much more to serial killers than meets the eye. Religion plays a role in modern societies, as Durkheim (1912) noted, as a latent force that, when repressed, seeks expression in all kinds of ways, including aberrant ones. It would seem rather awkward today, scientifically speaking, to call serial killers evil sinners, but the movie and some of the facts of serial killing that we have discussed here suggest that this is still a valid explanatory framework for the crimes. The seven deadly sins may indeed be the motivations for many serial killings.

The connection between serial killers, mythology, and psychic themes is unmistakable. In the novel *Kiss the Girls* (2002) by James Patterson, a serial killer takes victims out to the woods where they are left to die. Being stranded in the darkness of the forest is one of the oldest mythic themes and images, from Dante's *Inferno* to the fairy tales of the Brothers Grimm. The forest is scary because it entails not knowing where you are, how to get out, and whether the captor is watching and waiting. In a copycat crime, serial killer Robert Hansen used the Alaskan wilderness for his hunting grounds, killing an estimated twenty-one women, kidnapping and raping them before releasing them into the grounds around his cabin. Then he hunted them down like animals (Ramsland 2006).

6.4 Thinking Like Sherlock Holmes

The modes of analysis that Sherlock Holmes uses to solve crimes are not much different from those used today in scientific CSI. Both inhere in decoding the signs of crime in a coherent logical way. In *The Hound of the Baskervilles* (1901), the terrified and distorted face of the victim, Sir Baskerville, is meant to signify the terror of confronting the ghost hound from his family legend. The lantern is used to observe the footprints and their meanings. Holmes infers that the man's footprints show that he was running in fear from a large dog, which also left footprints. This suggests a scene that seems to be consistent with the legend of a dog that would kill all of the Baskerville heirs. A letter turned out to be a contrived scheme to scare the next supposed victim of the ghost dog away. It is later revealed that the letter was, in fact, written by the main suspect's wife in such a way as to disguise that she was the one who wrote it. It is discovered that she did not want her husband to continue with his plan, and therefore tried to scare him through the letter. To Holmes, the scent of White

Jasmine emanating from the letter pointed to the wife who, despite her husband's insistence that she help him in his criminal plan, remained resistant to it, being too sensitive and caring to want another man to die. Finally, the dirt retrieved from the horse cab was tied to the suspect due to the fact that he carried out excavation digs on the moors. The cab-dirt, which appeared similar to the moor-dirt, was transferred from the moor to the suspect's boots and then to the horse cab.

The reasoning used by Holmes is truly impressive. The contorted facial features are first thought to be the physical response to a heart attack, but then, under his suggestion, the medical examiner concluded that it was in reaction to a monstrous hound that prompted the heart attack, hence the terrified facial expression. The lantern illuminated the signs, isolating them in the darkness from other kinds of visual information. The anonymous letter could only be written by a well-educated person, given that it was constructed with cutouts from a newspaper. The poor handwriting that appeared on the envelope as the address script, also, did not match the character of someone who would have a newspaper in his or her possession. Holmes stated that this was "obviously" the attempt of a well-educated individual to make it appear as if an uneducated man composed the letter. The note had a scent on it, which, as mentioned, turned out to be White Jasmine, the scent of the perfume that the suspect's wife wears.

The Holmes stories are essays in CSI as well as treatises on the nature of crime and why symbols and rituals often characterize crime scenes. Conan Doyle certainly understood that there is a moral subtext to crime and that through crimes we can penetrate the nature of morality more directly than we can with philosophical treatises.

6.4.1 Abduction

Holmes' solution to crimes puts on display the power of abduction. Incidentally, Holmes was introduced to the broader popular culture by the movie *The Adventures of Sherlock Holmes* (1939), directed by Alfred L. Werker. In the course of investigating a murder charge, Holmes prevented a second murder from happening by the hand of a scheming, villainous professor. The character of Holmes, as well as his famous epigrammatic line, "Elementary, my dear Watson," was popularized by this film. There have been numerous Sherlock Holmes films made ever since, but this one most defines how we perceive the Holmes character.

In two recent books (Konnikova 2013, O'Brien 2013), the importance of Sherlock Holmes to the development of modern forensic science is cogently emphasized, although there is no reference to Peirce or semiotics. It is relevant to note, that the stories of Sherlock Holmes have never dwindled from interest. They have becomes staples of a "popular crime fiction culture," with many roots in the stories being spun today featuring detectives and crime scene investigators. What really attracts us, as Peirce implied, was Holmes' powers of reasoning, which, as Konnikova also points out, involved observation, not just detection. Konnikova distinguishes between the "Watson system" of analysis, the natural tendency to believe what we hear and see, from the "Holmes system," the use of questions, observations, and presence of mind. It constitutes a kind of dialectic process that constantly generates hypotheses and inferences until these can be pared down to one conclusion – the only one that can be connected to a crime. This is exactly how abduction works.

Crime scene investigations are not only effective because they utilize a combination of scientific methods and procedures, but also, and especially, because they constitute a basic form of semiotic analysis à la Sherlock Holmes. Each sign present ay a crime scene has a plethora of possible meanings, which need to be examined in the context of the scene, in the light of relevant cultural and historical knowledge, and in terms of available scientific information, in order to be properly interpreted. Even if the first assumptions prove to be false, the placement of the signs in relation to the other signs present at the scene as a form of analysis may help guide the investigators to a logically connected system, which can be modified or even rejected. Like Holmes, forensic scientists solve baffling crimes through clever observation and logical abduction, using a broad knowledge of science and human nature to help them confirm, modify, or change initial hypotheses.

Abduction and semiotic analysis are especially applicable to the study of ritual serial murders, where symbolism and cultural themes such as monstrosity manifest themselves through the signs and signatures left at crime scenes. A basic argument presented here is that serial murders tell us much more about the human mind and its interaction with the body and the world than do scientific and philosophical treatises. As McNab (2010: 7) aptly observes: "Whatever our fascination with these people, however, the fact remains that we live in a world, society, and biology that still produces violent, predatory people."

Chapter 7
Criminality and Its Representations

We live in a world ruled by fictions of every kind – mass merchandising, advertising, politics conducted as a branch of advertising, the instant translation of science and technology into popular imagery, the increasing blurring and intermingling of identities within the realm of consumer goods, the preempting of any free or original imaginative response to experience by the television screen. We live inside an enormous novel. For the writer in particular it is less and less necessary for him to invent the fictional content of his novel. The fiction is already there. The writer's task is to invent the reality.

J. G. Ballard (1930–2009)

On police television reality shows, we see perpetrators go from "on-the-run" to "in-the-can" in sixty minutes or less. In documentaries of crime the police and forensic scientists take us behind the scenes to see how crimes are solved, allowing us to experience the CSI process itself. Combine this with 24-hour news channels, which showcase sensational crimes, and programs such as *Dateline NBC* and *48 Hours* that reconstruct a crime dramatically leading up to the trial verdict, and we have a recipe for a perfect cultural storm that has brought crime and criminals into the cultural limelight. Celebrities are now tried in the media, at the same time that they are in courtrooms. Often, the two become united, with the trials being televised and discussed by television pundits, who are modern-day priests sermonizing to us on the moral aspects of a celebrity's fall from grace. Martha Stewart's trial would have gone virtually unnoticed if not for the fact that she was a celebrity. The same can be repeated over and over – the O. J. Simpson trial, the Phil Specter trial, and so on and so forth. Crimes with a social and moral subtext – especially those involving beautiful young women such as Natalee Holloway – also garner media attention, which transforms them into morality plays putting modern society and its secular values on trial.

Why is crime so popular? Do representations of crime affect people? Do they spur some individuals to become criminals? Do documentaries on crimes and media trials affect the outcome? Crime is clearly of major interest in the contemporary world. And criminals have become a new type of dark celebrity, much like the outlaws and bandits of folklore. The question of the relation between the media, representations of crime (real and fictional), and criminals is, clearly, a significant one. And it falls perfectly within the domain of forensic semiotics of the second order (FS²). This chapter elaborates what some of the areas that FS² would deal with or at least telescope them for forensic science and criminology.

It is kept brief because many of its themes covered here have already been discussed intermittently in previous chapters – here the threads are tied together.

7.1 Fictional and Real Crime

The starting point for studying the modern obsession with crime is the fictional crime story, which, as mentioned a number of times, coincides with the rise of forensics as a contemporary scientific enterprise. The original storyline, as found in Poe and Conan Doyle, revolves around a detective who solves crimes using cleverness, ingenuity, and experience. The story, however, is not just about a particular crime, but what a crime tells us about the human species. Dupin and Holmes use their brains rather than weapons to make things right in the world. Later fictional detectives used both brains and brawn. An example of the "tough-guy detective" is Sam Spade, the protagonist of Dashiell Hammett's *The Maltese Falcon* (1930). The detective story brings us into the crime scene at the beginning, constituting the first example of interactive literature in history – a fact that may explain, in part, its appeal. We are confronted with a crime mystery, usually involving one or more murders. Like a puzzle, the crime cries out for a solution through the use of systematic reasoning along with some luck. We are given all the information needed to solve the crime, but we often cannot figure out who the killer is, because we are also given false leads or distracting information. So it is up to the detective, at the denouement, to reveal who the killer is. That is why these narratives are also called "whodunits." Once the detective explains the solution we can reconstruct the logical reasoning processes easily by becoming aware of the relevant signs that we missed or misinterpreted.

As mentioned, Edgar Allan Poe's story *The Murders in the Rue Morgue* (1841) was the first fictional detective story. Its appeal to a broad audience was immediate, perhaps given the rise of crime in burgeoning urban centers in the era, and thus providing a narrative channel to sublimate our fears of the unknown. Dupin was the first modern-day detective hero, whose superhuman qualities approached the Nietzschean ideal of the *overman*. He makes things right by using the brain, rather than brute force. The detective-as-hero became an instant figure in popular fiction, leading to the emergence of all kinds of such heroes in all media, from print to movies (James 2011). The distinction between real crime and fictional crime soon became a thin one, remaining so to this day, as real crime vied for public attention alongside fictional crime at the turn of the twentieth century and the advent of pulp fiction.

From this came a fascination with crime by tabloid journalism, which still garners a huge audience. Crime magazines and television programs carry out their own investigations on real crimes, using the same kinds of narrative techniques of fictional crime stories – suspense, a piecemeal interpretation of clues, connecting the dots among trace evidence, and so on, until we reach the denouement (if there is one). They pique our instinct for solving mystery puzzles while they actually carry out a veritable criminal investigation. By putting the pieces together little by little we can participate intellectually and narratively in solving the case and thus grasping the meanings of crimes at various levels of interpretation.

Crime mysteries, real and fictional, have become metaphors, begging such questions as: Has crime substituted the notion of sin and is it, therefore, a modern phenomenon? Is it a consequence of psychic expressive forces such as sublimation? Are criminals heroes or sinners?

The importance of crime as a metaphor of modern-day life can be seen in Michelangelo Antonioni's marvelous film *Blow-Up* (1966). A successful photographer in the city London, whose daily life revolves around fashion photography, pop music, marijuana, and easy sex, starts to realize that his life is boring and meaningless. He meets a beautiful young mysterious woman. He notices something frightfully suspicious in the background of one of the photographs he took of her in a park. After studying the blow-up of the photo, he uncovers details which suggest that a murder had taken place. He goes back to the crime scene, but the body has disappeared. Bewildered, he goes through the movie searching for the body or at least an explanation of why it is not there. Neither comes, so at the end he watches a tennis match (likely in a dream) with imaginary balls being used. The image of the match slowly fades leaving only the grass (where the body was photographed). The unsolved crime leaves the protagonist and the viewer in a state of suspension, emphasizing our inability to solve life's mysteries. When we end up not knowing the truth behind a crime we generalize this to our inability to understand the mystery of life and death.

Stories and legends have been written about criminals and villains throughout history. In American lore, outlaws such as Jesse James and Billy the Kid are as well known as heroes such as Davy Crockett and Jim Bowie. Their stories are metaphors of a specific kind – they bring out the fascination with criminals as challenging the status quo, urging society by implication to change and evolve towards an ideal state. Crime and criminals bring about a temporary dystopia within us that we seek to resolve by simply solving the crime and bringing the criminal to justice, thus allowing us to restore a psychic balance within us. This is perhaps why we are drawn to both heroes and villains, angels and monsters, and other oppositions that symbolize good and evil. Recall from chapter 2 that one of the poles in an opposition stands out, called the marked poll. Criminals are marked culturally and psychologically. As such they allow us to engage with the dark side of the psyche. Crime brings out truths about ourselves through opposition. The criminal, in effect, is a sign that represents Chaos; the detective is a sign function that destroys the Chaos brought about by crime, restoring Order.

By the 1920s crime novels and magazines (both fictional and factual) were being produced in bulk for mass consumption. Many social critics at the time pointed to this garish fascination with crime as a result of the rise of actual crime rates in large urban centers and the belief that crime agencies and police authorities were the unsung heroes of society. Fictional detectives and crime fighters such as Doc Savage, the Shadow, and the Phantom Detective thus became instant imaginary heroes – they could and did solve crimes. Crime had become an obsession and a growing cultural industry. Psychologists and sociologists also started arguing in the late 1930s that the increase in crime rates correlated with the fascination with crime fiction. Many individuals, they claimed, wanted to enact in real life what they read in stories or saw in movies. But, as just discussed, there may be another side to the modern-day obsession with crime. We no longer have sinners to help us understand the *good*-versus-*evil* dichotomy; we have criminals. Many of the early stories dealt with lurid crime plots and handsome heroes who solved them with a combination of wit, brawn, and sexual appeal. They were morality plays, with the heroes represent-ing Mankind, the criminals Vice. The morality play centered on an allegorical figure called Mankind. The figure represented common people and their souls. The antagonist of Mankind was Vice, who sometimes appeared as the Devil. Often Vice was a comic figure full of tricks and disguises, much like the Riddler and the Joker characters in the Batman comics. But despite his humorous side, Vice represented eternal damnation for the Mankind figure foolish enough to be deceived by him.

The original crime stories were made into radio and movie serials (the latter by Republic Pictures) in the 1930s and 1940s. Audiences loved them, in part, because they were designed to keep them in suspense as an episode ended with the hero or heroine, or his or her paramour, caught in a cliffhanger situa-tion. That situation was a metaphor for the suspense discussed above that remained unresolved in *Blow-Up*. The audience would come back or tune in the next week to find out how the situation would be resolved, resolving the suspense at the same time. The same cliffhanger formula is still evident in the James Bond movies, the Raiders of the Lost Ark films, with the situation being resolved within the same movie at various cliffhanger points. Some of the fictional characters of the serials, from Fu Manchu, Perry Mason, and Nick Carter to Secret Agent X and Dick Tracy, have become an enduring part of pop culture lore, representing Mankind. The archetypal villains, from Superman's nemesis Lex Luther to Batman's set of enemies (the Riddler, the Joker, and so on), have also become cultural figments, representing Vice.

The serial killer crime genre has become particularly popular, for reasons alluded to already in various parts of this book. It seems that serial killers are everywhere, in movies, in documentaries, and in real life – a fact that shows how much the line between fantasy and fact has become blurred. Channels such as the Identification Discovery one feature real serial killers as the dark stars. One of the key questions that this type of programming raises is whether or not the proliferation of real serial killers is a result of pop culture's fascination with them. Serial killers have become celebrities, with some even admitting in public to committing crimes in order to enjoy their celebrity status.

Media specialists have devoted considerable research to studying the crime genre. One relevant theory, called *cultivation theory*, developed by American theorists George Gerbner and Larry Gross (1976), provides a useful framework for understanding the popularity of crime stories and their effects on audiences. The theory asserts that individuals who spend a lot of time watching violent television programs, such as crime dramas, develop a belief that the world is a much more dangerous place than it really is. This causes them to be more anxious and mistrusting. This phenomenon has been termed the "mean world syndrome." At the same time, such programs cultivate existing norms. The reason for this is that they generally communicate the theme that crime does not pay, leading viewers to have a greater respect for law and order and thus to be more supportive of the police. In other words, crime shows are cathartic and socially-conservative, engendering support for the criminal justice system in place. They are morality plays which, as mentioned, dramatize moral events. They are essentially televised sermons. Their general theme is the struggle between good and evil, Order and Chaos.

7.1.1 Forensic Science and Crime Fiction

As pointed out several times, forensic science has itself become popular because of its use in solving crimes, real and fictional. Forensic science may be compared to a kind of exorcism tool that helps the hero detective root out evil. The crime scene is the setting of an intellectual contest between two opponents: the villain, the perpetrator of the crime, and the detective, the solver of the crime, who employs forensic science to carry out his craft. It is a battle of wits (and souls) between the delegates of lawfulness and those of unlawfulness, between the forces of Order and those of Chaos. Behind every crime hides an archetypal criminal and the crime scene is the riddle he leaves us. The detective must decipher the meanings of this riddle through the interpretation of the signs left at the scene. The crime scene is, so to speak, a moral text. The detective looks for the signifiers of this text. His or her response to them leads into an implicit (and sometimes even explicit) dialogue with the villain, similar to the dialogues between Mankind and Vice in the morality plays. The goal of crime solution, which is the moral denouement, is to restore Order in the world.

This level of interpretation can be applied to the whole array of crime story programs on television, such as *Hill Street Blues, Law & Order, NYPD Blue,* among many others. One of the more interesting ones was *The Singing Detective,* a six-episode miniseries that aired on the BBC in 1986. A mystery writer, bedridden by a skin illness, mentally composes his next novel; the latest in his series is based on a character called "the singing detective." This miniseries was a cornucopia of sign symbolism and forensic interpretation. One of the scenes featured the investigation of a murdered prostitute. Solving the crime in the story was critical to restoring the writer's physical and mental health.

In real and fictional crime investigations there are certain features that unite them ontologically. These constitute a disposition, as it may be called. The elements of this disposition are as follows:

- *The detective does not play by the rules*: The detective, like many heroes of folklore and myth, always follows his or her instinct, not the beaten path. This often leads him or her into conflict with superiors and leads to the use of unorthodox or atypical methods for investigating the crime, including entering the crime scene illegally (without a warrant or by force) or consorting with other criminals to further the investigation.
- *A dead end, then an epiphany*: In every investigation, there is an aporia that occurs at some point when the trail seems to go cold. A seemingly trivial detail, conversation or coincidence, however, triggers a thought process that inspires the key insight leading to the solution of the crime. This is a perfect depiction of how abduction occurs and, more generally, of how we make discoveries and come to understand the mysteries of life.
- *The detective revisits the crime scene*: The detective's initial visit to the crime scene is a moment of unexplained semiosis, in which the signs at the scene are open to various interpretations. There is an extensive period in which the detective takes his investigation away from the scene, so that he can reflect upon the meanings of the clues. Near the end, though, he or she is compelled to return and look for one last clue, which often proves to be critical.

– *Irony in the conclusion*: Nothing is what it seems to be in a crime scene. When a certain signifier of a crime scene reveals an unexpected signified, it is because that signifier was first dismissed as useless or insignificant. The irony is that insignificance is more powerful than significance in solving crimes and, by extension, the mysteries of life.

7.2 Crime on the Screen

Investigative crime programs are among the most popular on television, as mentioned above. A perfect example of what such programs are all about is the Italian Mediaset program *Quarto grado*. Two journalists discuss the facts of unsolved criminal cases that have captured the public's imagination, mainly through media emphasis itself – murdered women by their paramours, little children found murdered, and so on. Using images, interviews, unpublished documents, and other materials related to a crime, the case is displayed and argued on camera with experts in forensic science and criminology joining in the discussion. The idea is to present a case to the audience so that it can make up its own mind. Similar programs now exist throughout the world. In America, these include *America's Most Wanted, FBI Files, Unsolved Mysteries*, and so on. They too investigate crimes on television, often eclipsing and even guiding the actual investigations under way. Strangely, the police welcome this, since it can help them in their own investigations. As well, the police may often engage the media directly to help them identify victims or perpetrators. This interaction between the police and the media is now a veritable method of investigation itself.

7.2.1 Television

In many ways, television has become a tool of forensic investigations, but it is a selective tool, examining only those crimes that are deemed to be of interest to large audiences. An example of this is the Lacy Peterson case, a pregnant young woman who was murdered in 2002. The national attention she received because of media coverage was so emotionally compelling that some women were said to have faked their own kidnapping in order to garner interest in their loveless lives. The case showed, above all else, that the media pay attention only to victims who are themselves media-worthy. Thus, murdered attractive, young, white women usually receive the most attention; while many other victims who do not fit this media profile are ignored. Lacy's disappearance at Christmas was particularly captivating. She was pretty and pregnant; she was a typical sub-urban housewife who lived far from the squalor of inner city ghettos where a lot of crime occurs on a daily basis, but almost never makes it to the airwaves. The media mentioned the unborn child in every report, alluding in a subtextual way to the larger issue of abortion in the United States and the definition of "unborn child." Once it was discovered that Lacy's husband, Scott Peterson, had a girlfriend, the story became a veritable crime drama in the making. The case led to a made-for-TV movie and book, possessing all the elements of a Greek tragedy, revolving around the pathos of the situation.

To become a national media story the crime must have special properties. These are the same ones that are found in pulp fiction and tabloid stories of crime:

- If it revolves around the tantalizing mixture of sex and violence, especially if the characters involved are celebrities or famous people, it is a candidate for coverage.
- Cold and calculating murders that involve serial killings of young women are always bound to set the media coverage agenda.
- The hot-blooded and impulsive murders of spouses by men or women, especially rich and powerful ones, are more interesting than murders resulting in lower-class contexts (as can be seen in television programs such as *Dateline NBC*).
- If children are involved, then the cases will tend to garner media attention.
- Sensationalistic cases are always fodder for media coverage. Examples such as the abduction of three young women in Cleveland by sociopath Ariel Castro or the brutal murder by Jodi Arias of her boyfriend are cases-in-point.

American Justice, which ran for over a decade starting in the early 1990s, was a documentary television program which featured notable criminal investigations in the United States that had all of the above elements. The show was expository in nature, though each episode was narrated with creative commentary and featured dramatic reconstructions. Although it was based on reality, the program had all the characteristics of the detective thriller recounted through the narrator's voice. The use of forensics was highlighted throughout. Similarly, *Forensic Files* (which started in 1996) deals with the forensic science used in solving mainly crimes that have captured media attention, offering explicit insights into the use of various techniques in crime scene investigation. So too do *The FBI Files* and *Cold Case Files*. And Identification Discovery is an entire channel devoted to the investigations of real crimes, using thematic strategies that provide, by themselves, a typology of crime in terms of its moral implications – *Sins and Secrets, Evil I,* and so on.

7.2.2 Movies

Long before the advent of crime programs on television and even of entire channels devoted exclusively to real crime stories, crime fiction on the movie screen provided a powerful lens for understanding crime and its meaning to society. It is thus worthwhile to give a schematic survey of some movies that, in my view at least, have contributed to the constitution of this lens.

Directed by John Huston, the movie *The Maltese Falcon* (1941) introduced Sam Spade to a wide movie-going audience, establishing the character of the modern detective hero through the diffusion power of the Silver Screen. Spade finds himself a murder suspect following the death of his partner. He investigates the murder, and in so doing discovers a conspiracy to steal a valuable, golden statuette of a bird – the Maltese Falcon. The subtext here is rather transparent – there is much more going on in the world than meets the eye, and only someone with great investigative skills can uncover the truth. Although not related in plot structure and overall narrative intent, this theme is implicit in *L.A. Confidential* (1997), directed by Curtis Hanson. A deadly bar shooting in Los Angeles leads three police officers into a complex murder investigation, revealing a winding trail of evidence and the corruption of their own police force. Dead bodies are everywhere, as murders are committed in secret. Behind each crime scene, there is an elusive, unnamed perpetrator. Analogously, this movie suggests that there is much more to crime than meets the eye. It must be located somewhere in cultural space, not only in physical space, and must thus be interpreted as part of a larger struggle to find out where the truth really lies.

In the Heat of the Night (1967) brings racial relations into the spotlight, a very important topic in America, needless to say. Directed by Norman Jewison, the plot puts the spotlight on Virgil Tibbs, an African American homicide detective from Philadelphia, who is recruited by a police sheriff in a racist southern town to investigate a murder, because of his reputation as a skilled investigator. At the time, the movie was a powerful implicit indictment of endemic racism at the same time that it showed how senseless crime is, suggesting that racism itself is a crime. There is a critical scene near the beginning of the film when Tibbs inspects the victim's body for the first time. It recalls the abduction prowess of Dupin or Holmes, suggesting that African Americans are not only the equals of whites, but in some cases even superior to them. Near the end, Tibbs traces over the route taken by the initial investigating officer and infers the details of the crime based on the nature of the location, thus connecting himself emotionally to the white detective and, metaphorically, linking the races in the search for equal justice for everyone.

Physical difference, rather than race, is the theme of *The Bone Collector* (1999), directed by Phillip Noyce. A quadriplegic ex-police officer recruits a young cop to help him track the crimes of an elusive serial killer. The two develop a romantic partnership in the course of their forensic investigation. The movie tapped into the social debate about difference and alterity that is still going on in the U.S., using the serial killer crime genre as an entry point into that debate, thus capturing the popular imagination much more directly.

Blade Runner (1982), directed by Ridley Scott, revolves around the story of a future cop, Rick Deckard, who is charged with the task of terminating the lives of four replicants, humanoid clones that roam free in spite of the law that seeks to eliminate them. Deckard's investigation is unmistakably semiotic, as he is faced with finding the replicants through an interpretation of the signs they leave behind. One of the questions the movie raises is whether crime is a purely human phenomenon and whether or not it can be programmed into robots or if such a thing as crime is conceivable in artificial intelligence terms. Computers cannot sin; only humans can.

In *My Cousin Vinny* (1992), directed by Jonathan Lynn, two friends are mistakenly charged with the murder of a storeowner, calling upon a relative, Vince Gambini, to defend them in court. Vince's decoding of the evidence leads him into an investigation of the murder itself. Here, tire tracks and photographs are among the signs used to solve the murder and acquit the two young men. Metaphorically, the signs point to a deeper iniquity – secular society's inability to distinguish between good and evil, considering acts of evil as examples of mental dysfunction rather than in spiritual terms.

Perhaps the movie that is the most relevant to the discussion here is David Fincher's *Se7en* (1995), mentioned previously. Two detectives in New York follow a series of murders committed in the name of the seven deadly sins. They investigate each crime scene and attempt to catch the killer before he completes his murders and reveals the final meaning of his crimes. The detectives must decipher a series of messages left by the killer that indicate a comprehensive agenda to his crimes. The movie is a hermeneutic essay on crime in the modern age and its interpretations in secular (scientific) terms. Crime cannot be understood so easily, the movie argues; it is ensconced in morality or lack thereof, a fact that modern-day criminologists ignore or consider to be passé. The movie dramatizes the extent to which we have neglected the spiritual forces at work in evil actions. The concept of sin, rather than sociopathology or psychosis, cannot be so easily dismissed, claims the villain at the end.

7.3 The Simulacrum Effect

A former supervisory scientist with the FBI Laboratory, named Max Houck, has called the fact that juries have unrealistic expectations about forensic science the "CSI Effect," because they believe that criminal investigative science unfolds exactly like it does on television programs. This of course turns out to be untrue, but only partly so, because real CSI and fictional CSI share a common ground – the use of the same kinds of techniques to carry out investigations. Of course the difference is that television does not normally depict the often gruesome conditions present at a crime scene, even in the case of reality crime programs, such as *The First 48*, which masquerade the scene with camera work.

7.3.1 Baudrillard

The CSI Effect has another name in semiotics. It is called the *simulacrum effect*, a notion associated with the late French philosopher and semiotician Jean Baudrillard (1975, 1981, 1983, 1987). Baudrillard claimed that modern-day people, accustomed to seeing life unfold on screens that deliver everyday content (movies, television, computers) can no longer distinguish, or want to distinguish, between what is behind the screen and what occurs in real space. Consciousness of the differences between representation and reality, therefore, has utterly vanished or is neglected, collapsing into a *simulacrum*.

This term comes from Latin where it meant "likeness" or "similarity." It was used in the nineteenth century by painters to describe drawings that were copies of other paintings, rather than imitations of them. Aware of this designation, Baudrillard insisted that the simulacrum effect is not the result of a simple copying or imitation, but a form of consciousness, which he called *hyperreal*, that is felt in our age to be more real than real, being a perversion of reality. An example he used was that of Disney's Fantasyland and Magic Kingdom, which are copies of other fictional worlds. They are, in effect, copies of copies. But people experience them as more real than real. They are "simulation machines" which reproduce past images to create a new form of consciousness for them. Eventually, as people engage constantly with the hyperreal everything real, from politics to art, becomes shaped by simulacra. Only in such a world is it possible for advertising – the maximum manufacturer of simulacra – to become so powerful.

The simulacrum effect might explain a whole array of phenomena discussed in this book, from copycat crimes to the Andy Warhol Effect and the rise of the serial killer as a pop myth. Simulacra lead to the emergence of false notions that become believable after the fact, gaining credibility over time. Artificial notions seem real and are almost impossible to distinguish from events that actually occurred.

All this may be true, to an extent at least. But, as discussed here, there is much more going on in the human mind than simulation. In some ways, the media are projections of our inner eye, selecting reality according to its basic tendencies. The media do not create crime; crime has always been in the human species, even though it may have been named differently. Rather than impose its will on us, we impose our needs onto the media. The crime programs on television are popular because we want to understand crime, even if it has been filtered and manipulated by editors and narrators. And this is why we do not distinguish between real acts of crime and fictional representations. In both we seek to understand something about us.

7.3.2 Popular Crimes

The portrayal of crime in all media has led to the crystallization of what Bill James (2011) calls *popular crime*. From the case Lizzie Borden to the Lindbergh baby kidnapping and murder and the Black Dahlia case, James claims that showcasing how crimes have been committed, investigated, and prosecuted has profoundly influenced cultural groupthink about crime over the years, producing a simulacrum between real crime and its representation. Exploring such popular themes as serial murder, crime rates, the symbolic power of evidence, and the hidden ways in which fictional crimes have shaped our chronicling of real crime as well as our perception of it, James sees media sensationalism as creating a climate of popular criminality that is ultimately a self-fulfilling prophecy, leading to more and more real crimes. But James may have missed or ignored the fact that crimes that make it to the media platform are invariably those that have cultural value or that emphasize cultural biases, as discussed in this chapter. Crime has replaced sin in the modern world, but not its moral connotations, nor its social repercussions and implications. The cases of Lizzie Borden, the Lindbergh baby, and the Black Dahlia actually argue in favor of this hypothesis. In effect, they are not popular crimes; they simply reveal people's interest in crime as a metaphor.

Lizzie Borden (1860–1927) was the suspect in one of the most celebrated murder trials in American history, because of the fact that the crime was attributed to a woman and because it was gory and gruesome – a type of crime that women were not expected to commit in that era. Borden was accused of killing her father and stepmother with an ax. A jury found her not guilty. Borden's background was also a factor in popularizing her crime. She was the youngest daughter of Andrew J. Borden, a prominent banker, and Sarah Morse Borden. Sarah died when Lizzie was two years old. Two years later, her father married Abby Gray, whose father was a tin peddler. She scorned her stepmother, partly because of her family's inferior social position. After the bloody corpses of the two victims were found, suspicion fell on Lizzie, because she was in the house and had the best opportunity to commit the crime, and of course because of the background story. Lizzie had been active in charitable groups, and many wealthy townspeople, women's rights organizations, and other groups supported her. Many other people felt sure of her guilt. The case attracted national attention, and has since been the subject of books, a ballet, a ballad, and several plays. It became popular because it involved cultural definitions of womanhood and femininity which were starting to change at the time.

Charles Lindbergh, (1902–1974) made the first solo nonstop flight across the Atlantic Ocean in 1927. Other pilots had crossed the Atlantic before him, but Lindbergh was the first person to do it alone nonstop. This feat gained him international fame. Everyone idolized the shy, slim young man and showered him with honors. He was featured constantly in newspapers and movie clips. On March 1, 1932, his 20-month-old son, Charles Augustus, Jr., was kidnapped from the family home in New Jersey. The event became an immediate media sensation spurring on the entire nation to share the pain and suffering of a parent who had lost his child. Ten weeks later, the boy's body was found. The media went into a frenzy, as commentators interviewed police and the elements of the case were showcased constantly on radio, in newspapers, and in movie clips. In 1934, the police arrested a carpenter, Bruno Richard Hauptmann, and charged him with the murder. He was convicted of the crime (chapter 4). The press sensationalized the tragedy and the trial. Reporters, photographers, and curious onlookers pestered the Lindberghs constantly. In 1935, Lindbergh and his family moved to Europe in search of privacy and safety. Again, the case has led to books, films, television programs and countless websites. It too became popular because it was empathic – many parents could empathize with Lindbergh's loss. It brought out the fact that tragedy of this kind belongs to everyone – celebrities and common people alike.

The Black Dahlia was the nickname given to Elizabeth Short (1924–1947), a stunningly beautiful dark-haired woman found bludgeoned to death in Los Angeles in 1947. The initial mystery as to who the victim was, her sensual dark hair, her gorgeous looks, and the fact that it took place in Hollywood's backyard, led to the media popularization of this crime. Short's body was sliced in half at the waist. The murder has never been solved, but it has entered the domain of popular crime, where it has been etched permanently by books, movies, documentaries, and the like. More than 50 people confessed to the crime, obviously craving notoriety. Sex was the theme of this crime, and it remains so to this day. Sexual crimes, as discussed, engage us into an opposition of the *body*-versus-*the soul*, which goes on throughout our lives.

The Borden, Lindbergh, and Black Dahlia cases are metaphors tapping into some psychological or cultural theme. James has devised a scale by which a crime can be classified according to its potential for popular interest and, thus, media exposure. A celebrity such as O. J. Simpson has a high location on the scale. Sexual violence, along with victims who are children or considered to be beautiful (young, blonde, blue-eyed, and so on) are also placed high on he scale. Examples are the JonBenet Ramsey and Natalee Holloway cases, discussed several times in this book. But these become popular not simply because they are sensationalistic, but because they are perceived as morality plays. In other words, they reveal cultural emphases or problematics. Because of the popular dimension to crime, the justice system, James suggests, has evolved into an agency of the media, being constantly in collusion with the media, the two feeding off each other in front of the cameras. This aspect is, of course, true. The simulacrum between media show and reality is now an endemic part of American justice. Today, CNN, Identification Discovery, and other channels as well as websites is where justice unfolds – the courts can only confirm or disconfirm the conclusions reached in the media beforehand.

7.4 Objectives of Second-Order Forensic Semiotics

The relations between everyday real crime and its representations in fiction and in media is the subject matter of second-order semiotics. FS^2 would study how the representation of crime might double back on crime itself. It also looks at how crime and criminals are interpreted in different cultural contexts in order to assay how the phenomenon of crime has emerged in the human species and how it may evolve or mutate. It would, therefore, look at the interconnection among the body, the mind, and culture in the formation of the criminal mind. It also would look at the broader philosophical aspects of crime in order to bring it into a broader domain of inquiry.

Charles Peirce, as we have seen, referred to these three dimensions as firstness, secondness, and thirdness and Freud as the Id, the Ego, and the Superego. Crimes are interpretable by taking the interconnection among these three into account. Stealing because one is starving has a different interpretation than it does if the stealing occurred as part of an organized ring of robbers.

Crime is becoming a planetary phenomenon because of the global village, making the usefulness of semiotics to criminology even more compelling. The increasing interconnectedness of states is leading to a growing number of transborder activities of a criminal nature. FS^2 can be a source of insight, because it allows us to see how signs, texts, and codes are being reworked and adapted in cyberspace. The same technological innovations that facilitate economic and cultural interaction also provide fertile ground for international organized crime and terrorism. Global criminal activity ranges from worldwide trade in arms and drugs, complex money-laundering schemes, international financial fraud, trade in biological and chemical technology and human organs, to the smuggling of illegal immigrants and endangered species.

The international contextualization of crime is, in other words, part of a growing problem. Many citizens have been living in a state of radical uncertainty and insecurity since the early 1990s, when globalization brought about radical changes to national identities and to traditional political configurations. In some societies there continues to be greater commitment to the notion of the collective than is typical in many others. Unfortunately, this situation often involves the emergence of more and more dislocated groups and individuals, who seek to bring greater stability into their lives through the construction of identifiable boundaries. Some have sought to cope by engaging in crime. All this means that our definitions of crime may be changing again. Exploring these definitions is certainly well within the methodological purview of semiotics.

Conclusion

No punishment has ever possessed enough power of deterrence to prevent the commission of crimes. On the contrary, whatever the punishment, once a specific crime has appeared for the first time, its reappearance is more likely than its initial emergence could ever have been.

Hannah Arendt (1906–1975)

As a discipline applying scientific methods and techniques to the investigation of crime, forensic science shares a large territory with semiotics, as argued throughout this book, since sign-based phenomena such as body language, symbolism, ritual, metaphor, and the others discussed in the previous chapters are both at the core of crime detection and make up the overall study of the criminal mind in relation to the broader cultural and historical forces that shape human beings. With the incorporation of semiotic analysis into its paradigm forensic science can thus become an even more powerful tool for interpreting crime and criminals.

The signs of crime are just that, signs, which are interpretable in ways described and researched by semiotics. Today, many national forensic science laboratories are working together as efficient international networks of forensic scientists looking into expanding their scientific methodology, which includes studying the role of symbolism and ritual in various criminal activities. The European Network of Forensic Science Institutes, founded in 1995, holds regular meetings for its membership of forensic laboratories. The American Society of Crime Laboratories maintains an International Liaison so that the labs can collaborate across the globe. Within this movement lies the awareness that inter-disciplinarity is critical as an approach to crime and criminality. Needless to say, this awareness has a semiotic basis. Crime is essentially about meaning, or its absence, as we have seen throughout this book.

One insight regards the allure of criminality that comes from the media, even when, and especially when, the media actually attempt to condemn it. The moment that crime and the criminal are no longer glorified on the screen, on the printed page, and in other media, the allure of criminality will recede, by turning criminals back into mere sinners. As Nicaso and Danesi (2013) argue in their analysis of organized crime, the semiotic approach to crime consists, in the end, of demystifying it, or, more accurately, "desemiotizing" it. This occurs in two stages: first, becoming aware of the mystique that has brought crime into the semiosphere and then ignoring it. Significantly, and to the point, the heroic anti-Mafia Italian judge, Giovanni Falcone, who was murdered in the conduct of his crusade against the mob, observed that "the interpretations of signs, gestures, messages and silences is one of a man of honor's main activities" (cited in Dickie 2004: 6). Understanding and unmasking these activities will lead, as judge Falcone's statement implies, to an unmasking of the myth of crime that has taken a stranglehold on the popular imagination.

Forensic semiotics needs to exist and, hopefully, with this book a concrete case has been made for what it can do to help carry out crime research more effectively. This is just a starting point. There is much to do in order to establish forensic semiotics as a distinct subfield of forensic science. It is noteworthy, as a final word, that some juridical institutions are taking the semiotic approach seriously in explaining criminal behavior. A website maintained by the Edmonton police states that: "In determining whether an individual participates in or actively contributes to any activity of a criminal organization, the Court may look at the following: If they use a name, word, symbol, or other representation that identifies, or is associated with, that criminal organization."

As the great crime writer Agatha Christie put it, in her 1936 story *The ABC Murders*, crime reveals our very soul: "Try and vary your methods as you will, your tastes, your habits, your attitudes of mind, and your soul is revealed by your actions."

Glossary

A

abduction
a form of inferential, best-guess reasoning based on experience and associative blends of ideas

adaptor
a gesture, such as head scratching, that indicates some need or state of mind

affect display
a gesture or facial expression that communicates some emotional state

Andy Warhol Effect
the seemingly unconscious need to seek some sort of fame through media exposure of some kind

Autonomic Nervous System (ANS)
nervous system that controls the bodily functions not consciously managed, such as breathing, the heartbeat, and the digestive processes

B

Behavioral Analysis Interview (BAI)
interview technique consisting of fairly structured non-accusatory questions posed to the suspect or victim

behavioral cluster
a cluster of two or more behaviors occurring during the same question or response period exhibited by a suspect

behaviorism
school of psychology which claims that human behavior can be explained as a response system to stimuli, conditioned and unconditioned

Bertillon System
a system of body measurements for identifying criminals, which was widely used before the technique of fingerprinting

blood spatter analysis (BSA)
examination of blood spatter at a crime scene to determine characteristics of the scene through reconstruction

bloodstain pattern analysis (BPA)
collection and examination of bloodstains at a crime scene as part of evidence collection

brain fingerprinting
recording and analyzing a person's neurological response patterns (on a computer) to images and words flashed on a screen, so as to determine if the person is telling the truth.

C

code
system of signs and meanings that determine how we make messages and interpret them, as well as how we perceive reality

cognitive polygraphy
lie detection technique involving the activation of both brain hemispheres, in order to determine if the subject is telling the truth, which only activates blood flow in one hemisphere

cognitivism
school of psychology claiming that human thought and behavior can be understand as a result of the internal use of symbols and representations

computational forensics
branch of forensic science concerned with the development of algorithms and software to assist forensic examinations

conceptual metaphor
a general conceptual category that links two separate meaning domains, for example *people* and *animals*

condensation
Freud's term for parts of different sexual symbols that are combined into one that disguises the sexual content of a thought or dream

connotation
extended meanings of a sign, such as the fact that the word *cat* can also refer to a human being, as in *cool cat*

content analysis
connecting the content of some type of writing to a writer in order to determine who a suspect might be

Control Question Test (CQT)
use of questions with known answers in order to control the responses of the person being interrogated

conventional sign
any sign that is constructed and used by social convention

copycat effect
term referring to the fact that some crimes are modeled or inspired by a previous crime

coroner
medical doctor who investigates suspicious deaths

crime scene investigation (CSI)
process of collecting and analyzing evidence collected at a crime scene

criminal cant
type of language used by criminals for specific purposes

criminology
the scientific study of the causes of crime

CSI effect
the belief by people that criminal identification science unfolds exactly like it does on *CSI* television programs

Cusum (Cumulative Sum) Method
statistical analysis of texts in order to glean from them patterns that can be correlated to makers of the texts

D

denotation
the initial or intended meaning of a sign

digital forensics
the use of computer science techniques in order to recover data from electronic and digital media

discourse analysis
the analysis of how discourse unfolds

displacement
Freud's term for the substitution of one image for another which is associated with it but which is not explicitly sexual, thus avoiding the constraints that the Superego imposes

DNA fingerprinting
using DNA to identify a suspect or a victim

document analysis
the study of documents to determine authorship and message content or intent

E

Ego

Freud's term for the part of the mind that mediates between impulses (the Id) and conscience (Superego)

emblem

a gesture that corresponds to a word or expression, such as the Okay gesture

evidence

the clues, oral statements, and other information collected at crime scenes and admissible as testimony in a trial

eye movement

patterns in eye disposition in interactive settings

F

Facial Action Coding System (FACS)

procedures used to describe facial expression patterns

facial expression

motions of the face that reveal emotional states

Fight or Flight Response

response to a threatening situation

fingerprint

impression made by a fingertip that is unique to each human being

fingerprinting

the technique of collecting and analyzing fingerprints

footprint

impression made by a foot that is unique to each human being

forensic anthropology

the use of physical anthropology to identify corpses and the methods of death

forensic botany

the use of botanical methods to determine aspects of a crime involving plants present at a crime scene

forensic chemistry

the use of chemistry to analyze elements of a crime or crime scene (such as the chemical analysis of substances left at a crime scene)

forensic entomology

the analysis of insects connected to a crime scene that allows investigators to determine when a death occurred

forensic geology
the analysis of minerals and other natural substances connected to a crime scene that allows investigators to identify certain aspects of the crime

forensic linguistics
the study of language and discourse phenomena in order to identify criminals or to understand various texts created by criminals

forensic odontology
the analysis of the teeth of corpses in order to identify them

forensic podiatry
the use of podiatry to examine criminal elements at a crime scene connected with footprints, footwear and the like

forensic psychology
the psychological study of crime and criminals

forensic science
the science of crime detection

forensic semiotics
the semiotic study of crime and criminality

Functional Magnetic Resonance Imaging (fMRI)
equipment designed to measure changes in brain activity and blood flow

G
gesticulant
type of gesture that accompanies oral speech

gesture
sign made by the hands or other parts of the body

graphology
the study of handwriting

Guilty Knowledge Test (GKT)
a multiple-choice set of answers in which a correct answer is inserted and which a suspect reads, so as to record his or her physiological responses to determine if they are truthful or false

H
handwriting analysis
the analysis of handwriting in order to determine who the writer might be

haptics
the study of tactile communication

hermeneutics
the study of texts

I
I-sign
a sign (like a fingerprint or DNA) that can be used to identify someone

I-text
the reconstructed scene of a crime event considered to be a particular kind of text (= identification text)

icon
sign that stands for something by resemblance

Id
Freud's term for instinctive impulses

identisign
type of sign that can be used to identify a suspect (= I-sign)

index
type of sign that stands for something through relation or existence (location, tame, space)

K
kineme
minimal unit of bodily action

kinesics
the study of body language

L
L-sign
unwitting signs produced spontaneously by the body during deception

linguistics
the scientific study of language

Locard Exchange Principle
principle that every contact leaves a trace

Low Copy Number DNA
technologies that allow for a profile from samples containing only a few cells

M
markedness
the notion that in a binary opposition, such as *night-vs.-day*, one of the two is the default form (known as *unmarked*) and the other as the form that stands out or is a derivative (known as *marked*); so *night* is marked because it is perceived to be "absence of day," and not the other way around

metaphor
process whereby one concept is associated with another

modus operandi (MO)
patterns that identify the specific commission of crimes, helping to find a suspect

N
natural sign
a sign produced by nature

nonverbal semiotics
the study of nonverbal forms of semiosis

O
object
Peirce's term for the referent a sign encodes

Oedipus Complex
in Freudian theory, the unconscious desire for the parent of the opposite sex during childhood

opposition
in semiotics, the view that a sign takes on meaning in relation to another one through contrast, absence, and so on; so, the difference between *positive* and *negative* is identifiable because the two concepts form an opposition, one is understood in relation to the other

P
penology
the science of the punishment and treatment of offenders

polygraph
a device that detects and record changes in the physiological characteristics of an individual in response to questions

Polymerase Chain Reaction (PCR)
a technique for making multiple copies of a DNA sequence

Principle of Synchronization
the principle whereby the probability of detecting a lie increases in proportion to the similitude of outcomes that results from using various lie-detection techniques in combination

proxemics
the study of the zones people maintain while speaking

psychoanalysis
the study of the relation between conscious and unconscious states

pseudologia fantastica
the behavior of compulsive or pathological lying

psychological profiling
the making of a profile of a prototypical perpetrator on the basis of past crimes and psychological processes

Psychological Stress Evaluator (PSE)
a device that detects slight tremblings in the voice, so as to determine if a person is telling the truth

R

regulator
a gesture that regulates speech during a face-to-face interaction

representamen
Peirce's term for the sign itself, without consideration of its meaning

representation
the process of depicting something in a specific way

Restriction Fragment Length Polymorphism (RFLP)
the variation in the length of restriction fragments produced by a given enzyme in a sample of DNA

ritual killing
killing that involves the use of ritualistic elements

S

semiosis
the production and comprehension of signs and the interpretations they elicit

semiosphere
the adaptive use and creation of signs in a specific place and time that are as natural to species as is biological adaptation to environment

semiotics
the study of signs and their meanings

sign
anything that stands for something else in some determinable way

signal
a type of sign that is based on a specific meaning, being usually connected with the body

signature
the patterns and characteristics that specific criminals display in the commission of their crimes

signification
the process of connecting a sign to its meaning

signified
the concept, image, or meaning associated with a specific sign

signifier
the physical component of a sign

simulacrum
the inability to distinguish between fiction or representation and reality

structuralism
school of semiotics that sees signs as relational objects, whereby they take on meaning only in relation to other signs

stylometry
the statistical study of the styles of written texts in order to determine who the authors might be

sublimation
view that repressed urges are expressed through creativity

Superego
Freud's term for self-critical conscience acquired through upbringing

symbol
a sign that stands for something in a culture-specific or conventional way

symptom
a sign produced by bodily processes

T
text
a composition of sorts using specific kinds of signs and codes (such as a written letter or a mode of dress, and so on) that implies a certain set of interpretations

trace evidence
evidence such as fingerprints, gunshot residue, fibers, and so on that is collected at a crime scene

V

victimology

the study of the effects crimes have on victims

voice analysis

the analysis of speech sounds in order to determine the truthfulness of emotional state of a suspect

voiceprint

a visual record of speech in order to identify the speaker

References

Alexander, James. 2011. Blending in Mathematics. *Semiotica* 187: 1–48.

Andrews, Edna. 1990. *Markedness Theory*. Durham, NC: Duke University Press.

Andrews, Edna, and Tobin, Yishai (eds.). 1996. *Toward a Calculus of Meaning: Studies in Markedness, Distinctive Features and Deixis*. Amsterdam: John Benjamins.

Armstrong, David F., Stokoe, William C., and Wilcox, Sherman E. 1995. *Gesture and the Nature of Language*. Cambridge: Cambridge University Press.

Ashwell, Ken. 2012. *The Brain Book*. Buffalo: Firefly.

Augustine, Saint. 1912. *St. Augustine's Confessions*, trans. By W. Watts. Cambridge: Loeb Classical Library.

Bakhtin, Mikhail M. 1981. *The Dialogic Imagination: Four Essays*. Austin: University of Texas Press.

Barthes, Roland. 1957. *Mythologies*. Paris: Seuil.

Barthes, Roland. 1972. Sémiologie et medicine. In R. Bastide (ed.), *Les sciences de folie*, 37–46. Paris: Mouton.

Baudrillard, Jean. 1975. *The Mirror of Production*. St. Louis: Telos Press.

Baudrillard, Jean. 1981. *For a Critique of the Political Economy of the Sign*. St. Louis: Telos Press.

Baudrillard, Jean. 1983. *Simulations*. New York: Semiotexte.

Baudrillard, Jean. 1987. *The Ecstasy of Communication*. St. Louis: Telos Press.

Beavan, Colin. 2001. *Fingerprints: The Origins of Crime Detection and the Murder Case that Launched Forensic Science*. New York: Hyperion.

Binet, Alfred. 1888. *Etudes de psychologie expérimentale*. Paris: Doin.

Birdwhistell, Ray L. 1952. *Introduction to Kinesics*. Ann Arbor: University of Ann Arbor.

Birdwhistell, Ray L. 1970. *Kinesics and Context: Essays on Body Motion Communication*. Harmondsworth: Penguin.

Black, Max. 1962. *Models and Metaphors*. Ithaca, NY: Cornell University Press.

Bodziak, William J. 1995. *Footwear Impression Evidence*. Boca Raton, FL: CRC Press.

Boot, David. 1998. An Investigation into the Degree of Similarity in the Handwriting of Identical and Fraternal Twins in New Zealand. *Journal of the American Society of Questioned Document Examiners* 1 (2): 70–81.

Bourdieu, Pierre. 1977. *Outline of a Theory of Practice*. Cambridge: Cambridge University Press.

Bower, Gordon H. 1980. *Theories of Learning*, 5th ed. Boston: Pearson.

Bremer, Jan and Roodenburg, Herman (eds.). 1991. *A Cultural History of Gesture*. Ithaca: Cornell University Press.

Brenner, Charles. 1974. *An Elementary Textbook of Psychoanalysis*. Garden City, NY: Doubleday.

Buckland, William. 2007. Forensic Semiotics. *Semiotic Review of Books* 10 (3): 9–16.

Canter, David. 1994. *Criminal Shadows: Inside the Mind of the Serial Killer*. New York: Harper-Collins.

Carnap, Rudolf. 1937. *The Logical Syntax of Language*. New York: Harcourt Brace.

Chandler, Frank Wadleigh. 1907. *The Literature of Roguery*. Boston: Houghton Mifflin.

Chandler, Raymond. 1962. *Raymond Chandler Speaking*. Berkeley: University of California Press.

Coleman, Julie. 2008. *A History of Cant and Slang Dictionaries*. Oxford: Oxford Scholarship Online.

Coleman, Loren. 2004. *The Copycat Effect: How the Media and Popular Culture Trigger the Mayhem in Tomorrow's Headlines*. New York: Simon and Schuster.

Connelly, Michael. 2009. *In the Shadow of the Master: Classic Tales by Edgar Allan Poe*. New York: HarperCollins.

Cotterill, Janet. 2000. *Language and Power in Court: A Linguistic Analysis*. New York: Palgrave.

Coulthard, Malcolm and Johnson, Alison. 2007. *An Introduction to Forensic Linguistics*. London: Routledge.

Danesi, Marcel. 2004. *Poetic Logic: The Role of Metaphor in Thought, Language, and Culture*. Madison: Atwood.

Danesi, Marcel. 2007. *The Quest for Meaning: A Guide to Semiotic Theory and Practice*. Toronto: University of Toronto Press.

De Paulo, Bella M. et al. 1996. Lying in Everyday Life. *Journal of Personality and Social Psychology* 70: 979–995.

Deely, John. 2001. *Four Ages of Understanding: The First Postmodern Survey of Philosophy from Ancient Times to the Turn of the Twentieth Century*. Toronto: University of Toronto Press.

Deleuze, Gilles. 1968. *Difference and Repetition*. New York: Columbia University Press.

Deleuze. Gilles and Guattari, Felix. 1987. *A Thousand Plateaus*. Minneapolis: University of Minneapolis Press.

Dickie, John. 2004. *Cosa Nostra: A History of the Sicilian Mafia*. London: Hodder and Stoughton.

Douglas, John, Burgess, Anne, and Ressler, Robert. 1997. *Crime Classification Manual*. San Francisco: Jossey-Bass.

Douglas, John, Ressler, Robert, Burgess, Anne, and Hartman, Crol. 1986. Criminal Profiling from Crime Scene Analysis. *Behavioral Sciences and the Law* 4: 401–421.

Duncan, Starkey and Fiske, Donald W. 1977. *Face-to-Face Interaction*. Hillsdale, NJ: Erlbaum.

Durkheim, Emile. 1912. *The Elementary Forms of Religious Life*. New York: Collier.

Eco, Umberto. 1968. *Einführung in die Semiotik*. München: Fink.

Eco, Umberto. 1976. *A Theory of Semiotics*. Bloomington: Indiana University Press.

Eco, Umberto. 1983. *The Name of the Rose*. New York: Harcourt.

Eco, Umberto and Sebeok, Thomas A. (eds.). 1983. *Dupin, Holmes, Peirce: The Sign of Three*. Bloomington: Indiana University Press.

Ekman, Paul. 1973. *Darwin and Facial Expression: A Century of Research in Review*. New York: Academic.

Ekman, Paul. 1976. Movements with Precise Meanings. *Journal of Communication* 26: 14–26.

Ekman, Paul. 1980. The Classes of Nonverbal Behavior. In W. Raffler-Engel (ed.), *Aspects of Nonverbal Communication*, 89–102. Lisse: Swets and Zeitlinger.

Ekman, Paul. 1982. Methods for Measuring Facial Action. In K. R. Scherer and P. Ekman (eds.), *Handbook of Methods in Nonverbal Behavior*, 45–90. Cambridge: Cambridge University Press.

Ekman, Paul. 1985. *Telling Lies*. New York: Norton.

Ekman, Paul. 2003. *Emotions Revealed*. New York: Holt.

Ekman, Paul and Friesen, Wallace. 1975. *Unmasking the Face*. Englewood Cliffs: Prentice-Hall.

Farwell, Lawrence. 2001. *How Consciousness Commands Matter: The New Scientific Revolution and the Evidence that Anything Is Possible*. Cebu: Sunstar.

Fauconnier, Gilles and Turner, Mark. 2002. *The Way We Think: Conceptual Blending and the Mind's Hidden Complexities*. New York: Basic.

Faulds, Henry. 1905. *Guide to Fingerprint Identification*. Hanley: Wood, Mitchell & Company.

Fisette, Jean. 2007. Literary Practice on the Immediate Horizon of the Liberation of Semiotics: Peirce's Meetings with a Few Great Authors. *Semiotica.* 165: 67–89.

Frege, Gottlob. 1879. *Begiffsschrift eine der Aritmetischen nachgebildete Formelsprache des reinen Denkens.* Halle: Nebert.

Freud, Sigmund. 1901 [1965]. *The Interpretation of Dreams.* New York: Avon.

Freud, Sigmund. 1963. *Civilization and Its Discontents.* London: Hogarth.

Galton, Francis. 892. *Finger Prints.* London: Macmillan.

Gardner, Howard. 1985. *The Mind's New Science: A History of the Cognitive Revolution.* New York: Basic Books.

Genet, Jean. 1949. *The Thief's Journal.* London: Blond.

Gerbner, George and Gross, Larry. 1976. Living with Television: The Violence Profile. *Journal of Communication* 26: 76–89.

Gibson, Dirk C. 2004. *Clues From Killers.* New York: Praeger Publishers.

Graysmith, Robert. 1986. *Zodiac.* New York: Berkeley.

Greimas, Algirdas J. 1987. *On Meaning: Selected Essays in Semiotic Theory*, trans. by P. Perron and F. Collins. Minneapolis: University of Minnesota Press.

Grotjahn, Martin. 1966. *Beyond Laughter: Humor and the Subconscious.* New York: McGraw-Hill.

Hall, Edward T. 1959. *The Silent Language.* Greenwich: Fawcett.

Hall, Edward T. 1963a. Proxemics: The Study of Man's Spatial Relations. In I. Gal *Man's Image in Anthropology*, 442–445. New York: International University Press.

Hall, Edward T. 1963b. A System for the Notation of Proxemic Behavior. *American Anthropologist* 65: 1003–1026.

Hall, Edward T. 1964. Silent Assumptions in Social Communication. *Disorders of Communication* 42: 41–55.

Hall, Edward T. 1966. *The Hidden Dimension.* Garden City: Anchor.

Hall, Edward T. 1968. Proxemics. *Current Anthropology* 9: 83–108.

Hall, Edward T. 1974. *Handbook for Proxemic Research.* Washington, DC: Society for the Anthropology of Visual Communication.

Hall, Edward T. 1976. *Beyond Culture.* Garden City: Anchor.

Hall, Edward T. 1983. *The Dance of Life.* Garden City: Anchor.

Heisenberg, Werner. 2007. *Physics and Philosophy: The Revolution in Modern Science.* New York: Harper Perennial Modern Classics.

Herman, Edward S. and Chomsky, Noam. 1988. *Manufacturing Consent: The Political Economy of the Mass Media.* New York: Pantheon Books, 1988.

Heussen, Yana, Binkofski, Ferdinand, and Jolij, Jacob. 2011. The Semantics of the Lying Face. *International Journal of Psychophysiology* 77: 206–207.

Hilton, Ordway. 1982. *Scientific Examination of Questioned Documents.* New York: Elsevier.

Hinsie, Leland E. and Campbell, Robert Jean. 1970. *Psychiatric Dictionary.* New York: Oxford University Press.

Holmes, Ronald M. and Holmes, Stephen T. 2008. *Profiling Violent Crimes: An Investigative Tool.* London: Sage.

Honeck, Richard P. and Hoffman, Robert R. 1980. (eds.). *Cognition and Figurative Language.* Hillsdale, NJ: Lawrence Erlbaum Associates.

Horton, Richard A. 1996. A Study of the Occurrence of Certain Handwriting Characteristics in a Random Population. *International Journal of Forensic Document Examiners* 2: 95–102.

Hutton, Christopher. 2009. *Language, Meaning and the Law.* Glasgow: Edinburgh University Press.

Jakobson, Roman. 1978. *Six Lectures on Sound and Meaning*, trans. by John Mepham. Cambridge, Mass.: MIT Press.

James, Bill. 2011. *Popular Crime: Reflections on the Celebration of Violence*. New York: Scribner.

James, P. D. 2011. *Talking About Detective Fiction*. New York: Vintage.

Johnson, Mark. 1987. *The Body in the Mind: The Bodily Basis of Meaning, Imagination and Reason*. Chicago: University of Chicago Press.

Johnstone, John W. C. 1981. Youth Gangs and Black Suburbs. *The Pacific Sociological Review* 24: 355–375.

Jung, Carl. 1971. *The Portable Jung*. Harmondsworth: Penguin.

Kahn, David. 1967. *The Codebreakers*. London: Macmillan.

Kerr, Gordon. 2012. *Mapping the Trail of a Crime*. New York: reader's Digest.

Keppel, Robert D. and Birnes, William J. 2004. *Serial Violence: Analysis of Modus Operandi and Signature Characteristics of Killers*. CRC Online Press.

King, B. H. and Ford, C. V. 1988. Pseudologia fantastica. *Acta Scandinavica* 77: 1–6.

Knapp, Mark L. 1978. *Nonverbal Communication in Human Interaction*. New York: Holt.

Konnikova, Maria. 2013. *How to Think Like Sherlock Holmes*. New York: Viking.

Krippendorff, Klaus. 2004. *Content Analysis: An Introduction to Its Methodology*. Thousand Oaks, CA: Sage.

Lakoff, George. 1987. *Women, Fire, and Dangerous Things: What Categories Reveal About the Mind*. Chicago: University of Chicago Press, 1987.

Lakoff, George and Johnson, Mark. 1980. *Metaphors We Live By*. Chicago: Chicago University Press.

Lakoff, George and Johnson, Mark. 1999. *Philosophy in the Flesh: The Embodied Mind and Its Challenge to Western Thought*. New York: Basic.

Lakoff, George and Núñez, Rafael. 2000. *Where Mathematics Comes from*. New York: Basic.

Latiolais-Hargrave, J. 2008. St*rictly Business: Body Language: Using Nonverbal Communication For Power and Success*. Iowa: Kent Hunt Publishing.

Lesser, Simon O. 1957. *Fiction and the Unconscious*. Boston: Beacon.

Link, Frederick C., and Foster, D. Glenn. 1984. *The Kinesic Interview Technique*. Atlanta: Interrotec Associates.

Lombroso, Cesare. 1876. *L'Uomo Delinquente*. Milano: Hoepli.

Lotman, Yuri. 1991. *Universe of the Mind: A Semiotic Theory of Culture*. Bloomington: Indiana University Press.

Lunde, Paul. 2012. *The Secrets of Codes*. San Francisco: Weldonowen.

Luria, Alexander R. 1970. *Traumatic Aphasia: Its Syndromes, Psychology, and Treatment*. Berlin; Mouton de Gruyter.

Mallery, Garrick. 1972. *Sign Language among North American Indians Compared with That among Other Peoples and Deaf-Mutes*. The Hague: Mouton.

Marx, Karl. 1959. *Economic & Philosophic Manuscripts of 1844*. Moscow: Progress Publishers.

Mauss, Marcel. 1934. Les techniques du corp. *Journal de Psychologie* 32: 3–4.

McNab, Chris. 2010. *Serial Killer Timelines*. Berkeley: Ulysses Press.

McNeill, David. 1992. *Hand and Mind: What Gestures Reveal About Thought*. Chicago: University of Chicago Press.

McNeill, David. 2005. *Gesture & Thought*. Chicago: University of Chicago Press.

Mead, Margaret. 1964. *Continuities in Cultural Evolution*. New Haven: Yale University Press.

Meier-Faust, Thomas. 2002. The Importance of Non-Verbal Information in Diagnostic Assessment. Paper given at the *BDP=Kongreß für Verkerspsychologie 2002 (Regensburg)*.

Meyer, Pamela. 2010. *Liespotting: Proven Techniques to Detect Deception*. New York: St. Martin's.

Morris, Charles W. 1938. *Foundations of the Theory of Signs*. Chicago: Chicago University Press.

Morris, Charles W. 1946. *Writings on the General Theory of Signs*. The Hague: Mouton.

Morris, Desmond. 1969. *The Human Zoo*. London: Cape.

Morris, Desmond, et al. 1979. *Gestures: Their Origins and Distributions*. London: Cape.

Myerhoff, Howard L. and Myerhoff, Barbara G. 1964. Field Observations of Middle Class "Gangs." *Social Forces* 42: 328–336.

Neisser, Ulrich. 1967. *Cognitive Psychology*. Englewood Cliffs, NJ: Prentice–Hall.

Newman, Graeme R. (ed.). 2010. *Crime and Punishment around the World*. Santa Barbara: ABC-CLIO.

Newton, Michael. 1990. *Hunting Humans: An Encyclopedia of Modern Serial Killers*. New York: Breakout Productions.

Nicaso, Antonio and Danesi, Marcel. 2013. *Made Men: Mafia Culture and the Power of Symbols, Rituals, and Myth*. Lanham: Rowman & Littlefield.

Nietzsche, Friedrich. 2000. *Basic Writings*, trans, by Walter Kaufmann. New York: Modern Library.

Nuessel, Frank. 1992. *The Study of Names: A Guide to the Principles and Topics*. Westport: Greenwood.

O'Brien, James. 2013. *The Scientific Sherlock Holmes: Cracking the Case with Science and Forensics*. Oxford: Oxford University Press.

Oakley, Barbara A. 2008. *Evil Genes*. New York: Prometheus.

Ogden, Charles K. 1932. *Opposition: A Linguistic and Psychological Analysis*. London: Paul, Trench, and Trubner.

Olsson, John. 2008. *Forensic Linguistics*. London: Bloomsbury.

Olsson, John. 20120. *Word Crime*. London: Continuum.

Ortony, Anthony. 1979. (ed.). *Metaphor and Thought*. Cambridge: Cambridge University Press.

Pavlov, Ivan. 1902. *The Work of Digestive Glands*. London: Griffin.

Peck, Stephen R. 1987. *Atlas of Facial Expression*. Oxford: Oxford University Press.

Peirce, Charles S. 1931–1958. *Collected Papers of Charles Sanders Peirce*, Vols. 1–8, C. Hartshorne and P. Weiss (eds.). Cambridge, Mass.: Harvard University Press.

Pelc, Jerzy. 1992. The Methodological Status of Semiotics: Signs, Semiosis, Interpretation and the Limits of Semiotics. In M. Balat and J. Deledalle-Rhodes (eds.), *Signs of Humanity*, 247–259. Berlin: Mouton de Gruyter.

Pennebaker, James. 2011. *The Secret Life of Pronouns: What Our Words Say About Us*. New York: Bloomsbury.

Petrilli, Susan. 2009. *Signifying and Understanding: Reading the Works of Victoria Lady Welby and the Signific Movement*. Berlin: Mouton de Gruyter.

Pollio, Howard R., Barlow, Jack M., Fine, Harold J., and Pollio, Marilyn R. 1977. *The Poetics of Growth: Figurative Language in Psychology, Psychotherapy, and Education*. Hillsdale, NJ: Lawrence Erlbaum.

Potter Gary W. and Kappeler, Victor E. 2006. *Constructing Crime: Perspectives on Making News and Social Problems*. Prospect Heights: Waveland Press.

Quine, Willard. 1953. *From a Logical Point of View*. Cambridge: Harvard University Press.

Ramsland, Katharine. 2006. *Inside the Minds of Serial Killers: Why They Kill*. Westport: Praeger.

Reid, John E. 1991. *Interviewing and Interrogation: The Reid Technique*. Minneapolis: John E. Reid and Associates.

Ressler, Robert, Burgess, Anne, Douglas, John, Hartman, Crol, and D'Agostino, Ralph. 1986. Serial Killers and Their Victims: Identifying Patterns through Crime Scene Analysis. *Journal of Interpersonal Violence* 1: 22.

Reynolds, John Lawrence. 2006. *Shadow People: Inside History's Most Notorious Secret Societies.* Toronto: Key Porter Books.

Rosenheim, Shawn. 1989. The King of "Secret Readers"': Edgar Poe, Cryptography, and the Origins of the Detective Story. *English Literary History* 56: 375–400.

Ryan, Andrew et al. 2010. *Automated Facial Expression Recognition System.* http://humansensing. cs.cmu.edu/papers/Automated.pdf.

Saussure, Ferdinand de. 1916. *Cours de linguistique générale*, ed. by C. Bally and A. Sechehaye. Paris: Payot. [trans. by W. Baskin, Course in General Linguistics (New York: McGraw-Hill, 1958)].

Schane, Sanford A. 2006. *Language and the Law.* London: Continuum Press.

Sebeok, Thomas A. 1994. *Essays in Zoosemiotics.* Toronto: Toronto Semiotic Circle.

Sebeok, Thomas A. 2001. *Signs: An Introduction to Semiotics*, 2nd edition. Toronto: University of Toronto Press.

Sebeok, Thomas A. and Danesi, Marcel. 2000. *The Forms of Meaning: Modeling Systems Theory and Semiotics.* Berlin: Mouton de Gruyter.

Sebeok, Thomas A. and Umiker-Sebeok, Jean. 1980. *You Know My Method: A Juxtaposition of Charles S. Peirce and Sherlock Holmes.* Bloomington: Gaslight Publications.

Shon, Phillip C. and Milovanovic, Dragan (eds.). 2006. *Serial Killers: Understanding Lust Murder.* Durham: Carolina Academic Press.

Skinner. B. F. 1938. *The Behavior of Organisms: An Experimental Analysis.* New York: Appleton-Century-Crofts.

Sugden, Philip. 2002. *The Complete History of Jack the Ripper.* London: Robinson Publishing.

Synnott, Anthony. 1993. *The Body Social: Symbolism, Self and Society.* London: Routledge.

Tanner, Dennis C. and Tanner, Matthew E. 2004. *Forensic Aspects of Speech Patterns: Voice Prints, Speaker Profiling, Lie and Intoxication Detection.* Tucson: Lawyers & Judges Publication Company.

Thomas, Ronald R. 1999. *Detective Fiction and the Rise of Forensic Science.* Cambridge: Cambridge University Press.

Thrasher, Frederic. 1927. *The Gang: A Study of 1,313 Gangs in Chicago.* Chicago: University of Chicago Press.

Tiersma, Peter and Solan, Lawrence. 2002. The Linguist on the Witness Stand: Forensic Linguistics in American Courts. *Language* 78: 221–239.

Tomkins, Silvan and Izard, Carroll E. 1965. *Affect, Cognition, and Personality: Empirical Studies.* New York: Springer.

Uexküll, Jakob von. 1909. *Umwelt und Innenwelt der Tiere.* Berlin: Springer.

Van Dover, J. Kenneth. 1994. *You Know My Method: The Science of the Detective.* Bowling Green, OH: Bowling Green State University Popular Press.

Vronsky, Peter. 2004. *Serial Killers.* New York: Berkeley.

Wagner, Anne and Broekman, Jan M. (eds.). 2010. *Prospects of Legal Semiotics.* New York: Springer.

Wambaugh, Joseph. 1989. *The Blooding.* New York: Perigord.

Watson, John B. 1925. *Behaviorism.* New York: Norton.

Watson, John B. 1929. *Psychology from the Standpoint of a Behaviorist.* Philadelphia: Lippincott.

Watson, O. Michael. 1970. *Proxemic Behavior.* The Hague: Mouton.

Index

48 Hours 138
ABC Murders, The 154
abduction 1, 18, 26, 52, 68, 136, 137, 143, 146, 155
abrasion 122
adaptor 48, 155
Adventures of Sherlock Holmes, The 136
affect display 47
AFIS (Automated Fingerprint Identification System) 55, 66
After Innocence 56
Alexander's Weekly Messenger 87
alienation 106, 107, 108, 109, 128
ambivalence 116
American Justice 145
American Maniacs 101
American Polygraph Association 33
analepsis 97
Andrews, Tommy Lee 56
Andy Warhol Effect 133, 148, 155
anomie 106
anti-hero 110, 111, 131
Antonioni, Michelangelo 140
antonomasia 92
Aquinas, St. Thomas 2, 17
arch 9, 54, 55
archetype 111
Arias, Jodi 145
Aristotle 16
As You Like It 91
astrology 87
ATF (Bureau of Alcohol, Tobacco, Firearms, and Explosives) 61
audio 8, 35
Augustine, St. 16, 132
author identification 73
authorship 26, 73, 76
Autonomic Nervous System 32, 155
autopsy 8, 11, 12, 104, 131
avoidance 116

Bacon, Roger 17
Bakhtin, Mikhail 22
ballistics 61

Barthes, Roland 19
Basketball Diaries, The 109
Batman 141, 142
Baudrillard, Jean 148
Beccaria, Cesare 5
Behavioral Analysis Interview 51, 155
behaviorism 101, 102, 155
Bell, Allen 34
Bell, Joseph 52, 53
Bellman of London, The 90
Bénveniste, Emile 19
Berkowitz, David 71, 79, 80, 81, 82, 83, 84, 92, 96, 100, 116, 117
Bertillon, Alphonse 8, 9
Billy the Kid 140
binary model 23
binary opposition 37, 38, 160
Binet, Alfred 79
biology 44, 62, 137
biosemiotics 19
biosphere 22
Birdwhistell, Ray L. 39, 46, 49
bite mark 12, 65
Black Book, The 90
Black Dahlia 66, 149, 150, 151
Black, Max 94
Blade Runner 147
Blake, Edward 57
Bleak House 106
blood 6, 9, 10, 13, 57, 60, 62, 64, 67, 124, 130, 131
blood spatter 7, 12, 13, 14, 62, 63, 120, 123, 155
bloodstain 7, 62, 155
Blow-Up 140
body 7, 8, 11, 12, 15, 30, 31, 32, 37, 45, 46, 49, 50, 61, 62, 67, 108, 117, 118, 122, 123, 124, 137, 151, 155, 160
body language 1, 2, 14, 30, 39, 42, 43, 44, 48, 49, 50, 152
Body of Proof 27
Bond, Thomas 104
bone 10, 12, 57, 64, 122, 131
Bone Collector, The 147

Bones 27
Bonnie and Clyde 127
Borden, Lizzie 149, 150, 151
boredom 105, 106, 128
Borelli, Joseph 82
Bourdieu, Pierre 106
Bower, Gordon H. 40
Bowie, Jim 140
BPA (bloodstain pattern analysis) 62, 155
brain 5, 14, 21, 23, 36, 43, 45, 50, 68, 79,
    101, 103, 104, 112
brain fingerprinting 36, 101, 156
Breslin, Jimmy 96
Brothers Grimm 135
Brussel, James 104
BSS (Behavioral Sciences Services) 98
BSU (Behavioral Sciences Unit) 98
BTK killer 92, 114
Buckland, William,
bullet 7, 8, 61, 62, 65, 120
Bunderskriminalamt 78
Bundy, Ted 65, 71, 113, 114, 115, 117, 130

Callaghan, Dirty Harry 111
cant 73, 89, 90, 91, 92, 157
capitalism 106
Capone, Al 92
Capote, Truman 98
Carnap, Rudolf 22
Carpenter, Gloria 75
Carr, Sam 80
CART (Computer Analysis and Response
    team) 65
Castro, Ariel 145
Cavataio, Michele 92, 93
Caveat for Common Cursitors 90
celebrity 137, 142, 151
cellphone 77
Chandler, Raymond 5, 90
Chaos 84, 115, 141, 142, 143
Chase, Richard Trenton 130
Chessboard Killer 133
Chikatilo, Andrei 122, 133, 134
Christie, Agatha 154
chromatograph 64
civil law 28
Clockwork Orange, A 109

clue 1, 2, 5, 7, 14, 15, 26, 52, 53, 54, 58, 67,
    68, 120, 123, 140, 143, 158
CMT (Conceptual Metaphor Theory) 93, 94, 95
Cobra, The 92
CODIS (Combined DNA Index System) 10, 57
cognition 17, 103
Cognition and Figurative Language 94
cognitive polygraph 36, 156
cognitivism 103, 156
Cold Case 27
Cold Case Files 145
Collector, The 109
Columbine massacre 109
common law 28
computational forensics 11, 156
computer model 64, 104
Computer Voice Stress Analyzer (CVSA) 75
Conan Doyle, Sir Arthur 4, 26, 52, 66, 136,
    139
conceptual metaphor 94, 95, 96, 97, 105,
    116, 156
concussion 122
condensation 156
conditioning 102, 104
confession 6, 56, 84, 101
connotation 21, 22, 67, 86, 87, 125, 149, 156
content 73, 77, 78, 81, 82
Content Analysis (CA) 78, 81, 87, 99, 156
Control Question Test (CQT) 35, 156
contusion 122
Copycat 71, 109, 110
copycat crime 71, 102, 107, 109, 110, 133,
    135, 148
copycat effect 71, 109, 110, 157
coroner 6, 157
corpse 12, 13, 113, 129, 131, 158, 159
Cottingham, Richard 13, 134
Cours de linguistique générale 17, 73
court 5, 10, 27, 28, 33, 46, 58, 60, 61, 64,
    74, 76, 151
crime 1, 2, 3, 4, 5, 7, 11, 13, 14, 26, 27, 28,
    52, 53, 56, 64, 65, 67, 68, 71, 72, 100,
    102, 106, 109, 112, 117, 118, 134, 136,
    137, 138, 139, 140, 141, 142, 143, 148,
    149, 151, 154
Crime and Punishment 107, 108, 117
Crime Classification Manual 99

crime detection 6, 26, 52, 53, 68
crime laboratory 8, 10, 54, 61, 64, 65
crime mapping 65
crime multiplier effect 28
crime scene 1, 8, 9, 10, 53, 54, 55, 57, 58,
    59, 61, 62, 63, 65, 67, 101, 119, 121, 122,
    123, 124, 131, 137, 143, 155
crime scene investigation (CSI) 27, 121, 123,
    157
Crime, Media, Culture 27
criminal 1, 6, 7, 14, 29, 31, 56, 63, 67, 68,
    69, 70, 73, 77, 90, 92, 99, 103, 104, 107,
    108, 117, 125, 129, 131, 138, 140, 141,
    143, 150, 152, 153
Criminal Investigation 6
criminal investigation 6, 10, 11, 30, 32, 36,
    39, 40, 41, 45, 52, 53, 54, 73, 99, 140
criminal investigative analysis 98
criminal law 28
criminal mind 2, 4, 5, 26, 98, 100, 101, 103,
    105, 106, 108, 109, 113, 121, 151, 152
Criminal Minds 98
criminal organization 91, 123, 125, 153
criminal speech 2, 74, 89, 90, 93
criminal text 95, 97, 116
criminalist 64, 73
criminalistics 6
criminality 7, 11, 56, 77, 84, 102, 107, 112,
    119, 128, 138, 149, 152
criminologist 2, 5, 7, 13, 14, 26, 27, 28, 147
criminology 5, 7, 13, 14, 26, 27, 29, 68, 90,
    112, 119, 138, 144, 152, 157
Crockett, Davy 140
cryptogram 84
cryptography 85, 87, 134
cryptolectic language 91
cryptologist 77
CSI Miami 27
Culshaw, Edward,
cultivation theory 142
culture 27, 29, 35, 36, 39, 40, 41, 42, 43, 44,
    45, 46, 48, 51, 100, 104, 107, 109, 110,
    111, 112, 114, 123, 126, 128, 137, 140,
    141, 142, 149, 151
cyberspace 152

Dahmer, Jeffrey 71, 112, 113, 114, 118, 129
Daily News 96
Dante 135
Darrus, Bemjamin 109
Darwin, Charles 40
data-mining 77
Dateline NBC 138, 145
De doctrina christiana 16
De Salvo, Albert 71
deception 2, 26, 27, 30, 31, 32, 33, 35, 39,
    42, 50
Deckard, Rick 147
deduction 4, 52
Deely, John 19
definition 20, 21, 152
Defoe, Daniel 31
Dekker, Thomas 90
Demme, Jonathan 68
denial 116
denotation 21, 22, 157
Derrida, Jacques 19
detective 4, 35, 52, 53, 64, 65, 67, 68, 120,
    137, 139, 141, 142, 143, 146
detective story 1, 4, 5, 26, 27, 87, 120, 139
Dexter 27, 63
dialect 73, 74, 75
dialectology 73, 74, 75
Dick Tracy 27, 142
Dickens, Charles 106
Dictionnaire de Trévoux 18
différence 37
differential association 7
digital forensics 11, 157
Dirty Harry 111
discourse analysis 73, 74, 157
divine law 28
DNA (deoxyribonucleic acid) 9, 10, 11, 14, 53,
    56, 57, 58, 60, 64, 65, 68, 77, 79, 123,
    131
DNA fingerprinting 52, 56, 62, 157
DNABoost 58
document analysis 11, 157
Dostoyevsky, Fyodor 107, 109, 117, 129
Dover Road Gang 92
Duns Scotus, John 17

Dupin, C. Auguste 4, 7, 35, 52, 55, 68, 139, 16
Durkheim, Émile 106, 129, 135
dystopia 140

Eastern Promises 123, 125
Eastwood, Clint 111
Eco, Umberto 4, 19, 25, 26, 30
education 105
E-Fit (Electronic Facial Identification technique) 64
Ego 115, 116, 118, 151, 158
Ekman, Paul 34, 40, 42, 47
electroencephalogram (EEG) 31, 36, 101
electroencephalography (EEG) 31, 36, 101
Ellery Queen's Mystery Magazine 4
emblem 47, 85, 124, 158
ennui 106
ERT (Evidence Response Team) 65
Essay Concerning Human Understanding 17
ethnicity 105
evidence 2, 5, 6, 7, 8, 9, 10, 11, 12, 26, 27, 46, 52, 53, 54, 56, 57, 58, 59, 60, 61, 62, 63, 64, 65, 66, 68, 74, 77, 98, 119, 120, 121, 140, 158
Evidence Response Team (ERT) 65
Expression of the Emotions in Man and Animals 40
eye contact 30, 39, 41, 42, 43, 45

Facebook 77
facial expression 2, 7, 14, 27, 30, 31, 35, 39, 40, 41, 42, 43, 44, 51, 158
facial reconstruction 61, 63, 64
FACS (Facial Action Coding System) 34, 35, 36, 40, 42, 50, 158
Falcone, Giovanni 153, 154
Farwell, Lawrence A. 101
Faulds, Henry 54
FBI Files 144, 145
Federal Bureau of Investigation (FBI) 9, 51, 55, 61, 64, 65, 77, 98, 99
Ferrin, Darlene 134
Ferrin, Dean 134
fetishism 118
feudalism 28
fiber 7, 8, 61

fiction 1, 4, 5, 26, 27, 52, 55, 63, 67, 68, 110, 111, 117, 120, 121, 126, 138, 139, 140, 141, 142, 143, 145, 146, 148, 149, 151, 158
Fight or Flight Response 32
Fincher, David 111, 147
Finger Prints 54
firearm 8, 60, 61
firstness 24, 151
FISH (Forensic Information System for Handwriting) 78
fixation 105, 116, 134
flashlight 67
fMRI (Functional Magnetic Resonance Imaging) 36, 104, 159
Folger, Abigail 133
footprint 7, 12, 53, 58, 59, 60, 135, 158
forensic anthropology 11, 12, 158
forensic botany 11, 158
forensic chemistry 11, 158
forensic entomology 12, 158
Forensic Files 145
forensic geology 12, 159
forensic linguistics 11, 73, 74, 75, 77, 88, 89, 99, 159
forensic odontology 12, 159
forensic pathology 11, 12
forensic podiatry 12, 159
forensic psychology 12, 99, 101, 105, 159
forensic science 1, 2, 3, 5, 11, 13, 27, 30, 40, 52, 57, 65, 66, 68, 74, 136, 138, 142, 148, 159
forensic semiotics 1, 2, 3, 14, 25, 26, 27, 52, 53, 73, 97, 98, 105, 129, 138, 151, 153, 154, 159
forensic sketching 63
forensic toxicology 12
forensics 5, 7, 15, 26, 27, 66, 67, 119, 131, 139
Foster, Glenn 51
Foucault, Michel 19
fracture 122
Frankenstein 132
Frege, Gottlob 20, 22
Freud, Sigmund 107, 109, 115, 117, 134, 151
Friesen, Wallace V. 40
Frykowski, Wojiciech 133

FS¹ (first-order forensic semiotics) 27, 30, 31, 41, 43, 44, 45, 48, 49, 50, 58, 68, 89, 107, 123
FS² (second-order forensic semiotics) 27, 29, 68, 138, 151, 152

Galen of Pergamum 15
Galton, Sir Francis 9, 54
Gambini, Vince 141
gang 73, 89, 90, 91, 92, 125, 126, 127, 128
Gardner, Erle Stanley 27
gender 105
gene 9, 112, 113, 118
genetic 9, 56, 57, 100, 108
geographic profiling 69, 99, 105
gesticulant 47, 159
gesture 14, 27, 30, 35, 39, 43, 44, 45, 46, 47, 48, 91, 154 159
Glatman, Harvey 121, 129
Glenn, John Wayne 75
global village 152
Gold Bug, The 4, 87
Goldman, Ronald 28, 119
Gothic novel 4, 134
gradience 37
graphology 79, 159
Green River Killer 33
Greene, Robert 90
Greimas, Algirdas J. 19
Grinder, James 101
Gross Hans 6
gun 7
gunshot residue 61

habitus 116, 117
hair 7, 8, 9, 10, 50, 57, 61, 63, 67, 108
Hall, Edward T. 48
Hammett, Dashiell,
Hammurabi 28
handwriting 11, 78, 79, 80, 81, 83, 88, 89, 136, 159
Hansen, Richard 135
Hanson, Curtis 156
haptics 44, 159
Hardman, Mathew 130
Harman, Thomas 90
Harris, Eric 109

Harrison, Michael 4
Hauptmann, Bruno 78, 150
head movement 43, 44
Heirens, William 121, 122
Heisenberg, Werner 25
hermeneutics 14, 147, 159
Herschel, Sir William J. 9, 53
Hippocrates 15, 18
Hitchcock, Alfred 111
Hjelmslev, Louis 19
Holloway, Natalee 120, 138, 151
Holmes, Sherlock 4, 7, 26, 35, 52, 53, 55, 56, 67, 89, 99, 119, 135, 136, 137, 139, 146
homicide 6, 122
Hostel 111
Hound of the Baskervilles, The 26, 135
human law 28
Huston, John 146
hyperreal 148
hypoicon 24

icon 24, 58, 63, 120, 122, 123, 160
iconicity 24
Id 115, 116, 160
identification 7, 8, 9, 11, 55, 57, 58, 60, 62, 63, 65, 73, 74, 88, 125
Identification Discovery 27, 142, 145, 151
identifier index,
identity 1, 26, 53, 58, 59, 61, 63, 68, 75, 79, 124, 152
illustrator 47
image schema 104
Imperial Dictionary 18
In Cold Blood 98
In the Heat of the Night 146
indeterminacy principle 25
index 24, 55, 58, 59, 123, 160
indexicality 24, 56, 61, 101, 123
induction 4, 26, 52
Industrial Society and Its Future 81
Inferno 135
interdisciplinary 14, 25, 99, 129
Internet 86
interpersonal zone 48
interpretant 23

interpretation 14, 16, 22, 23, 26, 34, 36, 42, 44, 51, 63, 64, 65, 68, 77, 123, 140, 143, 147, 151, 153
interrogation 30, 35, 39, 41, 43, 48, 50, 51, 77, 99, 102, 114
investigation 3, 4, 5, 6, 11, 27, 30, 32, 36, 38, 39, 42, 43, 44, 52, 53, 54, 55, 56, 58, 67, 68, 73, 76, 77, 99, 119, 131, 137, 140, 143, 144, 145, 147, 153
irony 95
I-sign (identisign) 58, 63, 66, 69, 75, 77, 78, 82, 88, 160
I-text (identification text) 73, 160

Jack the Ripper 104, 110, 122, 131, 132, 134
Jakobson, Roman 19
Jeffreys, Alec 56
Jesse James 140
Jewison, Norman 146
Joker 151, 152
Jung, Carl 121

Kaczynski, Theodore 81
Kelly, Mary 104
Kinesic Interview Technique 51
kinesic sign 39
kinesics 39, 44, 46, 48, 50, 51, 160
Kiss the Girls 135
Klebold, Dylan 109
Krays 92
Kristeva, Julia 19
Kürten, Peter 71

L.A. Confidential 146
LaBianca, Leno 133
LaBianca, Rosemary 133
Lacan, Jacques 19
Lacassagne, Alexandre 64
laceration 122
Lacy, Mary 72, 144, 145
lantern 135, 136
Lantern and Candlelight 90
Larson, John A. 33
latent fingerprint 9, 54, 65
Law & Order 27
Lecter, Hannibal 68, 111

legal semiotics 74
Lévi-Strauss, Claude 19
Levy, Chandra 66
lie detection 31, 32, 33, 34, 35, 38, 41, 47, 50, 51, 101
Lie to Me 42
Life on the Mississippi 65
Lindbergh, Charles 78, 79, 149, 150, 151
linguistic proficiency analysis 73
linguistics 19, 25, 73, 74, 93, 160
Link, Frederik 51
Lipstick Killer 121
Literature of Roguery 90
Locard Exchange Principle 64, 160
Locard, Edmond 64, 65
Locke, John 17, 18
Lodger, The 111
Lombroso, Cesare 6, 7, 108
Lonely Hearts Killer 121
loop 9, 54, 55
Lotman, Yuri 19, 22
Low Copy Number DNA 58, 160
L-sign (lie-sign) 31, 32, 33, 35, 37, 38, 39, 41, 46, 48, 49, 50, 51, 160
Lucania, Salvatore 92
Lucky Luciano 92
Lynn, Jonathan 147

MacKenzie, Sir James 31
Mafia 91, 124, 125, 126
Mafioso 92, 93
Maltese Falcon, The 139, 146
Manhunter 111
Mankind 141, 142, 143
Manson, Charles 133
Mark of Cain 125
marked 37, 38, 39, 44, 45, 50, 141
markedness 37, 38, 51, 160
Marlowe, Christopher 90
Marmeladov, Sonya 107
Marston, William Moulton 33
Marx, Karl 106
Matrix, The 109
Mead, Margaret 40
meaning 3, 16, 18, 19, 20, 21, 22, 23, 25, 37, 39, 40, 43

media 1, 2, 27, 28, 71, 77, 88, 101, 102, 109, 110, 111, 119, 138, 142, 144, 145, 149, 151, 153
medical examiner 6, 8, 11
Melias, Robert 56
Men in Black 56
Merleau-Ponty, Maurice 19
MERMER (Memory and Encoding Related Multifaceted Electroencephalograhic Response) 101
Merrell, Floyd 19
metaphor 93, 94, 95, 96, 97, 153, 161
metaphor analysis (MA) 73, 93, 94, 95, 96, 97, 105
Metesky, George 105
metonymy 95
microexpression 40, 41, 43
micro-tremor 75
Middleton, Thomas 90
Milosevic, Slobodan 112
mimesis 107, 109, 110, 128
missionary killer 99, 100
mitochondrial DNA 58
MLU (Mean Length of Utterance) 87, 88
modus operandi (MO) 69, 104, 161
Money Train 109
monster 116, 132, 133
Morris, Charles 18
Mortensen, Viggo 123
Moses 28
Mosso, Antonio 31
movies 1, 109, 110, 111, 141, 146, 148, 150
Mr. Frost 2
Murders in the Rue Morgue, The 4, 68, 139
My Cousin Vinny 147
mystery 4, 119, 131, 139, 140
mystery play 120
Mythbusters 36

Name of the Rose, The 26
narratology 19
National Crime Prevention Council 128
natural born killer 98, 100, 112, 114
Natural Born Killers 100, 109
nature 7, 16, 22, 41, 108, 112
NCIC (National Crime Information Center) 65
NDIS (National DNA Index System) 10, 57, 65

neuroscience 38, 43, 103
New York Times,
NIBIN (National Integrated Ballistics Information Network) 61
nickname 91, 92, 93
Nietzsche, Friedrich 129, 139
Night Stalker 66, 131
nominalist 17
nonverbal 30, 31, 39, 43, 49, 161
Norteños 126
Norwood Builder, The 56
Notes from the Underground 118
Noyce, Phillip 147
nuclear DNA 58

O'Sullivan Maureen 40
object (of a sign) 23
Oedipus Complex 117, 161
Office of the Coroner 6
onomastics 92
opposition 37, 38, 101, 140, 141, 151, 160, 161
Order 141, 142, 143
outlaw 126, 127, 138, 140
overman 129, 139

parasympathetic system 32
Parent, Steven Earl 133
Patterson, James 135
Pavlov, Ivan 102
Peirce, Charles S. 4, 5, 14, 18, 19, 22, 23, 24, 25, 26, 52, 67, 123, 131, 136, 137, 151
penology 5, 14, 102, 161
perpetrator 1, 2, 5, 6, 7, 27, 52, 53, 55, 58, 59, 61, 62, 65, 68, 69, 70, 71, 73, 76, 78, 82, 87, 102, 103, 104, 105, 119, 120, 122, 123, 138, 142, 144
Perry Mason 27, 141
Peterson, Lacy 144, 145
Peterson, Scott 145
photograph 8, 27, 54, 59, 62, 65, 121, 147
Pichushkin, Alexander 133
picquerism 122
pizzini 90
Plains people 30
Plato 16
plethysmograph 31

Poe, Edgar Allan 4, 5, 66, 67, 68, 87, 111, 117, 120, 131, 134, 139
Poinsot, John 17
polygraph 31, 32, 33, 34, 35, 36, 50, 51, 101, 156, 161
Polymerase Chain Reaction (PCR) 10, 56, 57, 161
popular crime 137, 149
Porfiry 107, 108
posture 30, 39, 44, 50
pragmatics 18
Prague Linguistic Circle 37, 38
Principle of Synchronization 34, 36, 50, 60, 75, 161
profiling 7, 68, 69, 70, 71, 98, 99, 100, 101, 102, 103, 104, 105, 108, 110, 116,
projection 116, 149
proxemics 48, 49, 162
pseudologia fantastica 50, 162
psyche 67, 107, 115, 122, 132
psychoanalysis 114, 115, 117, 162
Psychological Stress Evaluator (PSE) 75, 162
psychology 25, 31, 38, 81, 99, 101, 103
Psychology and the Poetics of Growth 94
Pudd'nhead Wilson 56
pupil dilation 32, 39, 50
Purkinje, Jan 54
Purloined Letter, The 4

Quarto grado 144
Quincy, M.E. 27
Quine, Willard O. 20

racial profiling 119
racism 146
Rader, Dennis 114, 115, 116, 130
Ramirez, Richard 76, 131
Ramsey, JonBenet 72, 73, 88, 89, 151
Ramsey, Patsy 89
ransom note 72, 73, 74, 79, 88, 89
Raskolnikov, Rodion Romanovich 107, 109, 109, 129
rationalization 116
reaction formation 116
realism 17
reconstruction 14, 61, 63, 64, 76, 120, 145, 155

Red Ripper 133
reference 20, 21
referent 14, 15, 20, 21, 22, 23, 24, 55, 82, 95, 96, 113
regression 116
regulator 48, 162
Reid Technique 51
Reid, John Edward 33
religion 135
representamen 24, 162
repression 116, 117, 118
Restriction Fragment Length Polymorphism (RFLP) 10, 57, 162
Richardsons 92
Ricoeur, Paul 19
Riddler 141, 142
Ridgway, Gary 33, 56, 101, 117
ritual 1, 118, 119, 122, 123, 129, 130, 131, 133, 134, 136, 153
ritual killer 129, 131, 132, 134, 162
Robin Hood 126
Rostov Ripper 133

Sabini Brothers 92
sacrifice 130, 131
sadomasochism 114, 130
Sam Spade 139, 146
San Francisco Chronicle 84
San Francisco Examiner 84
Saussure, Ferdinand de 17, 18, 22, 23, 24, 25, 37, 38, 73
Saw 111
Scarface 92
Scholasticism 16, 17
Scotland Yard 6, 132
Scott, Ridley 147
Se7en 11, 111, 135, 147
Sebeok, Thomas A. 4, 19. 25
Sebring, Jay 133
secondness 24, 151
semantics 18
semeion 15, 18
semen 10, 56, 57
semiology 17, 18, 25
semiosis 19, 22, 23, 24, 25, 31, 44, 67, 110, 123, 143, 162
semiosphere 22, 153, 162

semiotics 1, 2, 3, 4, 5, 14, 15, 17, 18, 19, 20, 21, 25, 26, 27, 30, 31, 37, 38, 48, 53, 62, 66, 67, 68, 73, 116, 124, 148, 152, 153, 162
sense 20, 21, 22
serial killer 2, 26, 61, 68, 69, 70, 71, 81, 84, 98, 99, 100, 101, 104, 109, 110, 111, 112, 113, 114, 115, 116, 117, 118, 122, 123, 124, 129, 132, 133, 135, 142, 147, 148
serologic testing 62
seven deadly sins 2, 135, 147
sex 12, 104, 116, 117, 120, 133, 145, 151
Shadow archetype 111, 112
Shakespeare, William 101
Shelley, Mary 132
shoeprint 53, 58, 59, 60
Short, Elizabeth 66, 90, 150
sign 4, 7, 14, 15, 16, 17, 18, 19, 20, 21, 22, 23, 24, 26, 30, 31, 37, 38, 39, 41, 44, 45, 46, 47, 48, 49, 50, 51, 53, 55, 58, 59, 66, 68, 69, 91, 98, 119, 120, 121, 123, 132, 137, 139, 141, 143, 147, 152, 153, 154, 162
sign function 30, 141
signa data 16
signa naturalia 16
signature 67, 69, 78, 104, 105, 118, 121, 122, 123, 124, 137, 163
significs 18
signified 23, 43, 66, 144, 163
signifier 23, 43, 44, 66, 78, 143, 144, 163
Silence of the Lambs 68, 98, 111
Simpson, Nicole 28, 119
Simpson, O. J. 28, 29, 119, 138, 151
simulacrum 148, 149, 151, 163
Skinner, B. F. 102
slang 74, 90, 91
social disorganization theory 14
social learning theory 14
soil 7, 12, 59
Son of Sam 79, 80, 82. 96, 114, 131
source domain 94
Specter, Phil 138
spectrograph 60, 76, 77
spectrophotometer 64
splinter 7, 8, 61
statistics 71

Starling, Clarice 68
Stewart, Martha 138
Stoics 16
Stone, Oliver 100, 107
Study in Scarlet, A 4, 52
style 74, 78, 79, 81
stylometry 78
sublimation 114, 116, 129, 130, 132, 140, 163
Superego 115, 116, 151, 157, 158, 163
suppression 116, 129
Suradji, Ahmad 132
Sureños 126
Sutherland, Edwin H. 7
sweat 32, 46
symbol 1, 24, 85, 86, 105, 117, 119, 121, 123, 124, 125, 126, 134, 136, 154, 163
symbolism 117, 123, 124, 126, 128, 129, 130, 134, 137, 143, 153
sympathetic system 32
symptom 15, 16 163
syntactics 28

target domain 94
Tate Polanski, Sharon 133
Tate-LaBianca murders 133
tattoo 124, 125, 126, 128
Taxi Driver 109
teeth 10, 57, 76, 159
television 42, 79, 110, 120, 138, 140, 142, 144, 145, 146, 148, 149
Ten Commandments 38
testimony 6, 35, 50
text 14, 62, 63, 81, 88, 123, 163
thirdness 24, 151
Thrasher, Frederic 127
Tibbs, Virgil 146
tire track (print) 53, 59, 60, 147
Toddlers and Tiaras 72
Tomkins, Silvan 40
Toms, John 61
tooth imprint 12
Torso Killer 134
touch 44, 45
trace evidence 8, 11, 12, 15, 61, 66, 121, 140, 163
trauma 67, 122
Treatise on Signs 17

triadic model 23
Triads 91
Twain, Mark 56
Twitter 77

Uexküll, Jakob von 22
Unabomber 81
unmarked 38, 44, 45, 50
unsub (unknown subject) 98, 103, 121
upbringing 2, 5, 7, 14, 41, 100, 102, 108, 112, 123, 127
Ur-Nammu 28

Vallejo Times-Herald 84
Vampire of Sacramento 130
vampirism 83, 130
Vaux, James Hardy 90
Vice 141, 142, 143
victimology 104, 164
video 8, 14, 35
violence 71, 100, 102, 114, 122, 145, 151
visionary killer 99, 100
vocabulary 26, 88, 105
voice analysis 36, 164
voice identification 73, 74

voiceprint 53, 60, 75, 76, 77, 164
Vucetich, Juan 54

Warren, Charles 132
Washington Post 81
Watson, Doctor 4, 52
Watson, James B. 102
Weaver, Sigourney 71
Wedding Crashers 109
Welby, Lady Victoria 18
Werker, Alfred L. 136
whorl 9, 54, 55
William of Ockham 17
Williams, Wayne 61, 70
Winter's Tale, The 91
witness 6, 27, 63, 64
Woodham, Luke 130

Yakuza 91, 125
Yardies 92

Zodiac 111
Zodiac Complex 134
Zodiac Killer 84, 85, 86, 87, 92, 107, 111, 114, 120, 134